Playing to Learn with Reacting to the Past

C. Edward Watson • Thomas Chase Hagood
Editors

# Playing to Learn with Reacting to the Past

Research on High Impact, Active
Learning Practices

*Editors*
C. Edward Watson
Association of American Colleges
   and Universities
Washington, DC
USA

Thomas Chase Hagood
University of Georgia
Athens, Georgia
USA

ISBN 978-3-319-87152-3     ISBN 978-3-319-61747-3   (eBook)
DOI 10.1007/978-3-319-61747-3

Cover image © milos luzanin / Alamy Stock Photo

Printed on acid-free paper

This Palgrave Macmillan imprint is published by Springer Nature
The registered company is Springer International Publishing AG
The registered company address is: Gewerbestrasse 11, 6330 Cham, Switzerland

# Foreword

## Being There

Mark C. Carnes, Barnard College, Columbia University

Students come to class. Nearly every student. Nearly every class. Some instructors report perfect attendance—for an entire semester. Many tell astounding tales of students' insistence on coming to class:

- When a freak snowstorm shut down the University of Texas at Austin, Julie Casey's students were dismayed: "Seriously, this is the one time I'm upset about a snow day," a junior posted on the class's Facebook page. Within an hour students arranged to hold class at an off-campus conference center.
- When Dordt College's Historian Paul Fessler announced that the semester would end before his class had completed all phases of the French revolution game, his students begged him to schedule additional classes. He agreed, but his students couldn't find a mutually acceptable time. When they finally came up with a free-time slot, Fessler blanched. For the final 2 weeks of class, every student showed up for the additional sessions at 7:30 am!
- Pat Coby, then chair of political science at Smith College, learned that one of his students had been hospitalized that morning for a collapsed lung. He was boggled when she showed up that afternoon to give a speech for *Henry VIII and the Reformation Parliament* game. (When I related this story at a faculty workshop, a provost declared that he did

not believe it. I reported his skepticism to Coby, who forwarded a video of that class. See https://www.youtube.com/watch?v=lUqSn PHQoUQ.) The student with the collapsed lung—identified as the Bishop of Colchester—can be heard coughing.

- In December 2016, Joe Sramek, a historian at Southern Illinois University, reported that when his class was playing *Defining a Nation: The Indian Subcontinent on the Eve of Independence, 1945,* the student "leading" the Communist Party of India was on the verge of pulling off a Maoist-style takeover of several provinces. He asked Sramek if he could "attend" class via Skype: His wife was about to go into labor. Sramek said no. The following day, the "Maoist" was absent, but one of his allies was texting feverishly. "What are you doing?" Sramek asked. "I'm communicating with my leader," she said. Sramek relented, and within minutes, the "Maoist" was delivering a speech to the class—from the delivery room.

These stories are among many told by college instructors who use Reacting to the Past, where students play complex in-class games, set in the past, their roles informed by classic texts. Students run the games; the instructor, after a two-session "setup" phase, serves as the game master, providing behind-the-scenes advice and encouragement and grading papers and oral presentations. Reacting games are taught in general education courses as well as courses ranging from classics, history, and political science to philosophy, religion, science, communications, and first-year English. During the past decade, Reacting has spread to over 350 colleges and universities, and nearly everywhere, Reacting instructors compile a cache of strange stories about students who will do nearly anything to come to class.

Sceptics dismiss such accounts as anecdotal. Others discount the importance of attendance: The fact that students are sitting in a classroom does not mean they are learning. This generalized skepticism about attendance, widely shared by faculty and students, is supported by considerable research: Many studies show a weak link between classroom attendance and learning.

Much of this research has focused on mandatory attendance policies. Multiple studies have shown that students who attend under duress do not learn much (Hyde and Flournoy 1986; St. Clair 1999). But what about the contrary case—students who brave a blizzard to come to class or who fight to make it to class while struggling to draw a breath of air? No one has researched this phenomenon because few researchers, until recently, could imagine such a scenario. For that matter, course surveys seldom make any attempt to ascertain the strength of student motivation. Has any standard evaluation ever posed questions such as:

- Do you look forward to coming to class?
- How valuable is the classroom experience?
- Which do you prefer: (a) going to parties, (b) talking with friends, (c) playing video games or sports, or (d) coming to class?

Many students would snicker at such questions, and many professors would be outraged by the suggestion that instructors were in some way responsible for motivating students. Instructors are supposed to teach the material; students are supposed to come to class and be prepared to learn. If students lack the motivation to do so, they don't belong in college, or so many educators insist.

Most assessment instruments therefore focus on whether instructors "teach the material." To this end, the most common means of assessment is the multiple-choice test, administered at the end of a chapter or the course itself. Nowadays, many such tests are offered online and graded instantly. Instructors—teaching to the test—rely on the lecture, which is well-adapted to conveying masses of information quickly. Mindful that fact-filled lectures benumb the minds of students, instructors hope that students will remember the material long enough to pass the test. Few instructors imagine that students will long retain what they have "learned" in this way.

Even sophisticated assessment tends to reinforce traditional pedagogy. Recently, researchers with the Wabash National Study, after examining thousands of surveys, found that students who experienced academic gains gave their instructors high marks for using class time effectively, for being well-organized, and for explaining concepts clearly; conversely, students who experienced no such gains were more likely to report that their instructors had been disorganized, unclear, and ineffective in management of class time. The authors concluded that the "mundane practice of clear and organized instruction" had a greater impact on student learning than ostensibly "high-impact" practices such as learning communities, internships, and active learning. The authors advised instructors to "hone" their craft: begin class on time, organize lectures carefully, and emphasize clarity and comprehension (Blaich et al. 2016, p. 8).

This advice is good. Lecturers would do well to take these principles to heart. And yet, this conclusion is fundamentally flawed. Consider the experience of anthropologist Rebekah Nathan, who spent a year pretending to be a first-year student at a large state university. Nathan faithfully attended an "excellent" lecture class in which "the professor presented what I considered to be interesting, beautifully organized, and up-to-date lecture material" (Nathan 2005, p. 119). But Nathan counted heads and compared them to the official roster. Half the students were absent from every class.

According to the standards of the Wabash Study, Nathan's instructor had been exemplary; yet, half of her students derived no benefit from that skill and diligence. This dilemma encapsulates the central paradox of higher education during the past half century. On the one hand, the learning platform for undergraduate education has been significantly broadened and strengthened. Libraries, laboratories, and teaching centers have been designed and staffed in accordance with the highest standards of professionals in those fields. Instructors have undergone exhaustive training and hiring committees have plucked the best from among vast pools of qualified applicants. Curricula and syllabi have been endlessly scrutinized, reviewed, and revised. Nearly all aspects of undergraduate education have undergone continuous assessment and improvement.

But if the learning platform has improved, it has largely failed to stimulate learning. For decades, nearly half of those admitted to college fail to earn a degree.[1] Dozens of major studies have reported high levels of disengagement, poor levels of effort, and paltry gains in learning. Probably the fairest assessment was offered by Derek Bok, former president of Harvard and one of the staunchest defenders of higher education. After surveying hundreds of studies in scores of disciplines, he insisted that critics were wrong to say that students don't learn anything in college—the problem is that students just don't learn very much. He put it delicately. Today's colleges "underachieve" (Bok 2006).

Bok explained that instructors and administrators persisted in relying on pedagogical modes—lectures and unstructured seminars—that research has proven to be inadequate. "What are the prospects for turning colleges into effective learning organizations?" he asked, and then offered a blunt reply: "Not good, unfortunately" (p. 323). Instructors were wedded to woefully

---

[1] In 2010, President Barack Obama, while noting that much had been done to improve access to college, bemoaned the fact that one-third of the nation's college students failed to earn a degree. (The actual figure was closer to one-half.)

deficient teaching traditions and administrators were powerless to induce change (p. 323).

During the past decade, many critics of higher education have nevertheless called for "pedagogical innovation." Usually, they equate this with online learning, which has promised to revolutionize higher education and has attracted hundreds of millions of dollars of investment capital. But results have fallen far short of expectations. If traditional pedagogies have been deficient, online alternatives have so far proven little better. There is no reason to believe that new pedagogical modes are necessarily better ones.

\*    \*    \*

Reacting students come to class; often they exhibit astonishing levels of engagement. Instructors don't need sophisticated assessment metrics to make this determination: They've stood in the front of half-empty classrooms and watched helplessly as students' eyes glaze over and then close, one by one, as if a fog had descended upon a cityscape at nighttime. Instructors know when students are "there" and when they've tuned out. And instructors have observed Reacting classes where students aren't in their seats—not due to absence, but because they're standing up and shouting.

Such observations prove little if anything. Serious assessment requires research. When Steven Stroessner, a Columbia psychologist, received a contract from the Fund for the Improvement of Post-Secondary Education (FIPSE) to assess the impact of Reacting at four separate colleges, he recognized that a radically new pedagogy required a different type of assessment. After running focus groups at each school, he was struck by the Reacting students' strong emotional response to the pedagogy. He designed a long questionnaire to be administered at both the beginning and end of the semester, whose questions were drawn from a cluster of standard psychological assessment tools. In addition to the questionnaire, he included special tests of students' speaking and writing skills. He then trained researchers at each college to administer the tests to students in Reacting and in traditional first-year seminars.[2]

---

[2] To test speaking skills, test subjects met individually with a researcher, who gave them a list of talking points about a familiar issue, such as gun control, and asked them to prepare a brief speech on the issue. After a few minutes of preparation, students then delivered the speech, which was tape-recorded. The tape-recorded speeches were then blindly scoured according to a standard speaking rubric.

It took several years to compile enough data to generate statistically significant results and to ensure that the groups were similar enough to justify comparison. Eventually, he learned that Reacting students, who spent nearly all of class time speaking and debating, improved far more in rhetorical skills than students in traditional classes. (With respect to writing, Reacting students improved as much as [but no better than] students in standard seminars.)

The results to the psychology questionnaires were more complicated. Most of the clusters showed no change during the semester among any of the students. This was to be expected: A single course rarely leaves an imprint on a student's psyche.

But then came the shocker. As the number of completed tests increased to the point where they generated statistical significance, some puzzling results emerged. At the end of the semester, Reacting students were more likely to indicate that closing scenes of movies moved them and they liked to watch people open presents. No such shift appeared in the surveys of students in the traditional classes. By inhabiting various roles during the semester, the Reacting students had become more empathetic (Stroessner et al. 2009, p. 611).[3]

Stroessner and colleagues noticed a similar shift in several other psychological categories. From an educational perspective, the most important concerned the extent to which students agreed with standard statements on the malleability of the self, such as "You can't teach an old dog new tricks." Reacting students, having assumed multiple roles and identities during the semester, were more likely to agree that people could change in fundamental ways; the opinions on such matters of students in the traditional seminars underwent no change. Psychologists have found this belief in the malleability of the self to be one of the strongest psychological elements conducive to educational growth (see Dweck 2000).

As Stroessner and colleagues' study was making its way through the multiple reviews of the *Journal of Educational Psychology*, James Sloat, director of assessment of Washington and Jefferson College, embarked on a major research project comparing his institution's seven Reacting First-Year Forum classes with its twenty-one traditional (thematic) First-Year

---

[3] The questions relating to empathy were drawn from psychologist Albert Mehrabian's Balanced Emotional Empathy Scale, a standard measure for determining the empathy of potential nurses, social workers, and foster parents.

Forums. His team analyzed writing, critical thinking, and other reasoning skills of students in both types of classes based on a sampling of papers and essays at multiple points in the semester. At the end of the semester, Sloat's team also asked students and instructors to assess the courses. His study concluded that:

- Students gave Reacting sections a higher evaluation—even though they reported working harder in those sections.
- Faculty reported an increase in student learning and engagement in Reacting sections following the midterm—as compared to a slight decline in Thematic sections.
- Student test performance improved in the Reacting curriculum for both their best and worst students. Middling students also did a better job of integrating course materials when they were in the Reacting curriculum. Middling students, though, did fare generally better in the Thematic curriculum (Sloat 2007).

This last point is significant. It suggests that different students may respond to pedagogical innovation in different ways. Like the Stroessner study, the Washington and Jefferson study shifted emphasis from *what* teachers do to *how* students respond. This shift in frame of reference is crucial. Educators must do more to determine *what* motivates students to come to class, to take charge of their own learning, and to embrace the life of the mind.

As more institutions of higher education pursue pedagogical innovation and widen its definition to encompass active learning strategies within the classroom, they must also embrace innovation in assessment. The essays in this volume do much to advance this new perspective. They perform two related functions. They deepen our understanding of Reacting, arguably the most radical of the "high-impact" pedagogies; and they provide new approaches to the process of assessment itself.

To be sure, serious assessment is often expensive. The Stroessner, Beckerman, and Whittaker study (2009) and the Sloat study (2007) required researchers to tape-record and grade student speeches or essays, to administer long questionnaires, and to code and analyze masses of data. When asked to replicate such procedures, administrators may well balk at the expense and/or time commitment. Existing assessment tools endure partly because they are inexpensive and easy to implement.

The strategies outlined in this volume represent ingenious, and often inexpensive, approaches to innovative assessment. Many illuminate various facets of subtle issues of student motivation. Educators at even the most cash-strapped institutions will find it easy to apply these or similar modes of assessment at their own institutions, often at very little cost. But even if these strategies are beyond the reach of some college educators, they can instantly and almost effortlessly employ an even simpler mode of assessment. They can count heads in classrooms.

Because if students aren't in class, they aren't learning much. In higher education—and in life—being there matters.

## References

Blaich, C., Wise, K., Pascarella, E. T., & Roksa, J. (2016). Instructional clarity and organization: It's not new or fancy, but it matters. *Change: The Magazine of Higher Learning, 48*(4), 6–13.

Bok, D. (2006). *Our underachieving colleges: A candid look at how much students learn and why they should be learning more.* Princeton: Princeton University Press.

Dweck, C. S. (2000). *Self-theories: Their role in motivation, personality, and development.* Philadelphia: Psychology Press.

Hyde, R. M., & Flournoy, D. J. (1986). A case against mandatory lecture attendance *Journal of Medical Education, 61,* 175–176.

Nathan, R. (2005). *My freshman year: What a professor learned by becoming a student.* Ithaca: Cornell University Press.

Sloat, J. M. (2007). *Freshman forum: Thematic v. reacting—A multi-stage assessment.* Unpublished manuscript.

St. Clair, K. L. (1999). A case against compulsory class attendance policies in higher education. *Innovative Higher Education, 23,* 171–180.

Stroessner, S. J., Beckerman, L. S., & Whittaker, A. (2009). All the world's stage? Consequences of a role-playing pedagogy on psychological factors and writing and rhetorical skill in college undergraduates. *Journal of Educational Psychology, 101*(3), 605–620.

# Acknowledgments

During the summer of 2015, we issued a call for chapter proposals seeking faculty wishing to further examine the impact of their applications of the Reacting to the Past pedagogy. In our call, we also encouraged multi-author approaches that coupled the expertise of faculty teaching with Reacting with that of educational researchers or assessment professionals. As a result, this book represents a collaborative effort of faculty and researchers from many different institutions and institution types. Most of the proposals we received were from faculty hopeful of beginning a research project they had been considering for some time. Faculty were notified in early fall to allow time for planning for a research study that most likely would occur during the spring semester 2016. Drafts of chapters were then delivered in July of that same year. We are grateful to this wonderful group of colleagues who spent nearly a year thinking about and studying their pedagogical practice and how it influences the learning and perceptions of their students.

We would also like to thank Sarah Nathan at Palgrave Macmillan who initially reached out to us concerning the possibility of a project regarding active learning pedagogies. We were then guided further through the prospectus submission process by Mara Berkoff, also at Palgrave Macmillan, but most of our collaboration with our publisher has been with Milana Vernikova and her editorial colleagues. We are deeply grateful to Milana for her patience and her quick responses to our inquiries and e-mails. We are very fortunate to have worked with such a great editorial team, and this book benefited greatly from this collaboration.

Ultimately, this project would not exist if it were not for Mark Carnes and Naomi Norman. Barnard College professor Mark Carnes' pioneering work with Reacting began in the 1990s and continues to this day. What began as his brainchild now involves faculty from hundreds of colleges and universities throughout the United States as well as internationally, and we are indebted to his vision and to his commitment to his students' learning throughout his career. We are also indebted to Naomi Norman, classics professor extraordinaire and associate vice president for instruction at the University of Georgia (UGA). Her own pedagogical practice and campus-wide leadership regarding Reacting set the stage for us to become enculturated into Reacting practices and the associated communities that exist at UGA and beyond. Her passion for Reacting and her conversations with us over the years provided the foundation on which this book was conceived. Thanks Mark and Naomi for your foresight, commitment, and leadership.

We would also like to acknowledge the Reacting community—from the Facebook Faculty Lounge to the annual Summer Institute and, now, multiplying regional workshops and events. Leaders among the community like John Burney, Gretchen McKay, Nick Proctor, Jennifer Worth, and many others continue to move the pedagogy forward in welcoming newcomers, from any discipline, to explore the world of Reacting by offering them any resources the community, and consortium, can muster. The energy, innovation, and passion that propel the Reacting movement were early indicators that a book like this could be produced. The almost indescribable breadth and depth of Reacting faculty's commitment to the pedagogy, and more so, to our students, is impressive and deeply appreciated.

From C.E.W.: I first want to first thank my co-editor and co-author, Dr. Thomas Chase Hagood. You have been a wonderful collaborator and friend over the years, and I'm grateful for the opportunity to work more closely with you on this project. I also want to thank my two sons, Liam and Carter, who are always very encouraging of my writing projects and provide me with my most compelling stories about teaching and learning. Keep sharing those with me! I extend my deepest gratitude to my wife, Joan. She's the most creative and effective teacher I have ever known and inspires me to better understand how learning works and how to apply that knowledge in my own classrooms. This book would not exist without her encouragement.

From T.C.H.: Immeasurable thanks to my co-editor and co-author, Dr. C. Edward Watson. Eddie, you are truly an innovator in higher education, and I trust this will not be our last project together. I must also thank my colleague, co-director, and co-author, Dr. Naomi J. Norman. Naomi, your leadership is deeply admired and your friendship cherished. We've spent many hours on our "RTTP roadshows" and, together, have built a sustainable program at UGA. Looking back, it's been a lot of work and I've enjoyed every moment of it. All my professional and personal accomplishments (including this volume) have been possible because of my partner, Lori Prince Hagood. Lori, your intellect, patience, grit, kindness, fierceness, and grace impress me every day. My ideas are sharper, my will stronger, my hope deeper because of you.

# Contents

# List of Contributors

## Editors

**Thomas Chase Hagood** University of Georgia, Athens, GA, USA

**C. Edward Watson** Association of American Colleges and Universities, Washington, DC, USA

## Authors

**Christine L. Albright** University of Georgia, Athens, GA, USA

**Jeffrey L. Bernstein** Eastern Michigan University, Ypsilanti, MI, USA

**Robert S. Bledsoe** Augusta University, Augusta, GA, USA

**Mark C. Carnes** Barnard College, Columbia University, New York, NY, USA

**David M. Dees** Kent State University, Kent, OH, USA

**Elizabeth E. Dunn** Indiana University South Bend, South Bend, IN, USA

**Marie Gasper-Hulvat** Kent State University, Kent, OH, USA

**Thomas Chase Hagood** University of Georgia, Athens, GA, USA

**Mark D. Higbee** Eastern Michigan University, Ypsilanti, MI, USA

**Colleen M. Kuusinen** University of Georgia, Athens, GA, USA

**April Lidinsky** Indiana University South Bend, South Bend, IN, USA

**Lee Anna Maynard** Augusta University, Augusta, GA, USA

**Dawn McCormack** Middle Tennessee State University, Murfreesboro, TN, USA

**Patsy D. Moskal** University of Central Florida, Orlando, FL, USA

**Naomi J. Norman** University of Georgia, Athens, GA, USA

**Russ Olwell** Merrimack College, North Andover, MA, USA

**Hyeri Park** University of Georgia, Athens, GA, USA

**Karen K. Petersen** Middle Tennessee State University, Murfreesboro, TN, USA

**Deborah South Richardson** Augusta University, Augusta, GA, USA

**Carolyn A. Schult** Indiana University South Bend, South Bend, IN, USA

**Anthony V. Shreffler** Kent State University, Kent, OH, USA

**Mary Grace Strasma** Eastern Michigan University, Ypsilanti, MI, USA

**C. Edward Watson** Association of American Colleges and Universities, Washington, DC, USA

**Keri Watson** University of Central Florida, Orlando, FL, USA

**Brittany M. Williams** University of Georgia, Athens, GA, USA

**Lisa Fetheringill Zwicker** Indiana University South Bend, South Bend, IN, USA

# LIST OF FIGURES

# LIST OF TABLES

# CHAPTER 1

# Reacting to the Past: An Introduction to Its Scholarly Foundation

*Thomas Chase Hagood, C. Edward Watson, and Brittany M. Williams*

Since being introduced in first-year seminars at Barnard College, Reacting to the Past (RTTP) has offered instructors in the United States, Canada, Australia, and Europe a high-engagement, active learning alternative to traditional instruction in higher education. RTTP is a student-centered pedagogy that provides college students and faculty unique learning and teaching opportunities. At its core, RTTP is a game-based pedagogy examining some of the most conflicted moments in human history: from the fight to restore democracy in ancient Greece to the trial of Galileo, the struggles of the American and French revolutions, more modern concerns on the nature of Art in Paris circa 1890, the American social security act, the rise of a democratic South Africa, and the science of global climate change. Most of the games are currently with W.W. Norton press; others are published by the Reacting Consortium Press, an imprint of the University of North Carolina Press. Set in a liminal space of authentic historical struggle, students are given roles, read primary texts, conduct research, craft arguments, and engage their peers and the instructor in considering the big issues of

T.C. Hagood (✉) • B.M. Williams
University of Georgia, Athens, GA, USA

C.E. Watson
Association of American Colleges and Universities, Washington, DC, USA

© The Author(s) 2018

C.E. Watson, T.C. Hagood (eds.), *Playing to Learn with Reacting to the Past*, DOI 10.1007/978-3-319-61747-3_1

a conflicted historical moment through argumentation, plots, and counter-plots as students (alone or within factions) strive to win the game (Carnes 2004).

Pioneered by historian and Barnard College professor, Mark C. Carnes, RTTP has currently been adopted by faculty at over 350 colleges and universities (see http://reacting.barnard.edu). RTTP offers faculty elegantly designed games complete with primary evidence and supporting materials to engage students in one-day to, more typically, multi-week experiences to inspire deep explorations of assigned characters' worldviews and perspectives. The pedagogy leverages students' innate desires to win, as well as research, composition, debate, and collaborative work among peers, to compel them to grapple with the contingencies of the past and the complexities of human agency. Reacting to the Past is not "re-enacting"; games can depart from the historical record as students' actions—papers, speeches, strategies—determine game outcomes. RTTP's purposeful and creative design assists faculty as they seek to promote student participation, critical reflection, and meaningful engagement with course content.

The unique structure of the Reacting Consortium and the level of faculty and administrative support throughout the United States, as well as the enthusiasm among the RTTP community, are worthy of brief note. Since initial dissemination of the pedagogy in 2001, a thriving community of faculty game authors and implementers gather annually at a Summer Faculty Institute at Barnard College in June followed by a Game Development Conference in July (hosts have included small colleges and research universities). Winter of 2017 saw the first ever national RTTP conference at the University of Georgia where grant-funded faculty teams representing universities and colleges from across the United States gathered to explore curricular revisions through implementation of RTTP at their home institutions.

From regional weekend conferences throughout the United States to campus faculty development workshops, teaching presentations at national organizations including the Organization of American Historians, the American Historical Association, and the Association of American Colleges and Universities, recent sessions at South by Southwest (SXSW.edu), online resources at http://reacting.barnard.edu, a YouTube channel (http://youtube.com/user/RTTPOfficialVideos), a lively but controlled-access Faculty Lounge on Facebook, and an informative Twitter account @ReactingTTPast, the RTTP national community is well connected and growing. With historic and ongoing support from entities like the Carnegie

Corporation of New York, Christian A. Johnson Endeavor Foundation, Spencer Foundation, National Science Foundation, Teagle Foundation, and Fund for the Improvement of Postsecondary Education of the US Department of Education, RTTP has evolved from Carnes' nascent idea that this teaching method could set "minds on fire" to a national movement of faculty embracing an active learning pedagogy with results they can see and hear well beyond their grade books or teaching evaluations (Carnes 2014a).

The excitement and growing national interest in RTTP are at least partially facilitated by anecdotal narratives of successful faculty practice shared via conferences and communities; however, the RTTP concept is built upon an exemplary theoretical and scholarly foundation, and RTTP's efficacy in practice is being examined and confirmed through emerging empirical inquiry. This book represents a significant leap forward regarding the latter. In truth, RTTP is a pedagogy of deep engagement designed to maximize student learning and leverage what we know, broadly, about how people learn. A phrase that is most often applied to RTTP is *active learning*.

## ACTIVE LEARNING

Active learning, as a general collection of pedagogical approaches, by its very name, suggests there are alternative strategies that might be termed passive or traditional learning. The key differentiator is one of cognitive processing. You can often "spot" active learning strategies in classrooms if students "are forced to think about, reflect on, grapple with, explain, synthesize, support, and/or defend aspects of the content of the course" (Bowen and Watson 2017, p. 121). In other words, active learning means that students are required to engage in cognitive processing, and the best active learning strategies are structured in a way so that all the students in a class are compelled to be a part of the learning process. Therefore, a key trait of impactful active learning strategies is that it is difficult for students to opt out of participation. Alternatively, passive or traditional instruction provides numerous avenues and opportunities for students to disengage. It is easy to imagine how students might disconnect from class during lectures, demonstrations, or videos. In those settings, there are no social requirements or overt expectations that students pay attention, work with the course content, or do little more than not be disruptive. The goal in passive settings is often for a student to simply catch the content via note-taking. While note-taking can be useful to help students pay attention in class, students often see the act of note-taking as data gathering in advance of the real learning that might then take place when they study their notes at a later date. We have known for decades that verbatim note-taking requires little, if any, cognitive processing and results in minimal learning in class (Hartley and Davies 1978), and now that most students have laptops and can type faster than they can write, verbatim note-taking is easier for more students to perform than ever before. Within our new technological note-taking context, recent research has again confirmed that this approach is ineffective for learning (Mueller and Oppenheimer 2014). If we agree that the key purpose of our pedagogy is to increase the probability that students will learn from our efforts, there is compelling evidence that suggests higher education should be in a continual process of moving away from passive strategies.

While new, active learning studies are being published every day, it is important to note that the research question regarding the effectiveness of active versus passive learning has been clearly and definitively answered over time. The first meta-analysis examining active learning research was published in 1987 (McKeachie et al. 1987), and it indicated that "the amount of active thinking by students may be more important as a mediating variable than the teaching method" (p. 77). For many who teach, that single notion re-orients how they might approach each class, which traditionally may have focused on content delivery. Now that we know the core question is no longer about active versus passive learning, as this has been confirmed via numerous meta-analysis and large-scale studies across a full range of disciplines (see Freeman et al. 2014; Hake 1998; Light 2001), we are concerned with how we maximize active, meaningful learning and thinking in our classroom settings, and which active learning strategies are the most effective at achieving specific student learning outcomes. Progress has been made in these areas as well.

## High-Impact Practices

Kuh et al. (2005) examined the full range of instructional practices used across higher education and reviewed the empirical evidence for each in search of those strategies that have a disproportionately positive impact on student learning and other student success metrics (see Table 1.1). Given the compelling nature of the findings of their work, the Association of American Colleges and Universities (AAC&U) made the resulting list of strategies a cornerstone element of their national Liberal Education and

**Table 1.1** AAC&U's ten high-impact practices

| *High-impact practices* | |
| --- | --- |
| First-year seminars and experiences | Service/community-based learning |
| Undergraduate research | Writing-intensive courses |
| Common intellectual experiences | Internships |
| Diversity/global learning | Collaborative assignments and projects |
| Learning communities | Capstone courses and projects |

America's Promise (LEAP) Initiative, where they collectively describe these strategies as "high impact educational practices" (Kuh 2008). Upon review of the ten strategies identified as high-impact practices (see Table 1.1), some common elements emerge. They are deeply active from a cognitive standpoint. They often involve social learning. Many take place over time and might take weeks or months to complete. They often have a broad structure or scaffold; however, the activity within that structure is not clearly defined and requires significant, ongoing critical thinking and decision-making. These are all traits that describe RTTP as well. In 2016, AAC&U elected to include ePortfolios and associated pedagogical practices as an eleventh high-impact practice due to the evidence base that has emerged in support of them through research over the past decade (Watson et al. 2016). Given the common traits between RTTP and other high-impact practices, it is conceivable that a similar recognition for RTTP could develop if the triangulation of research findings confirms what the theoretical foundations for RTTP suggest.

## Gaming

While exceptionally compelling, it is important to note that the theoretical foundations for RTTP are not limited to notions of active learning and commonalities with AAC&U's high-impact practices. There are additional notions at "play" as well, and one of those is the topic of gaming. Over the last two decades, a great deal has been written about notions of gaming (often video games, see Gee 2007) for the purposes of learning; however, a specific type of gaming, role-playing or role-immersion, has been found to be highly effective in more traditional course settings (Van Ments 1999) and is a defining attribute of RTTP (Carnes 2014a). When done well, with established objectives, defined constraints, and an active role for the instructor, the course context can recede into the background because of students' high engagement in the game itself. Csikszentmihalyi, a psychologist who researches highly focused mental states, refers to such deep engagement as "flow" (1990) and specifically cites gaming contexts as being capable of inducing this state. Flow is theorized to result in deep learning and to connect a student's satisfaction with the learning process.

## FLOW AND EMOTIONS

The domain of affective neuroscience, which is currently emerging, is now exploring the role that emotion plays in learning. Immordino-Yang (2015) argues and her research confirms that emotions are deeply connected to learning, memory, and retention. It is theorized that this is due to the role that emotion historically played in our survival, and it is true that we only think deeply about things about which we care deeply (Immordino-Yang 2015). A fully realized understanding of how flow and emotions impact learning is only beginning to emerge, but within the game-based, role-immersion model of RTTP, both concepts relate and resonate with our general understanding of what motivates students to engage, participate, and learn.

While the connections between RTTP pedagogical practice and active learning, social learning, high-impact practices, game-based learning, flow, emotions, and other learning theories and associated research are logically apparent, and while we recognize a need for ongoing research into RTTP's impact on learning and other student outcomes, this is not to suggest that no research has been performed specifically within the RTTP context. There have indeed been a number of studies that have provided relevant insights, and this book builds upon this empirical foundation as well as the theoretical pedigree described above.

## PRIOR RTTP RESEARCH

Research studies specifically into RTTP's efficacy have been undertaken that provide initial confirmation of its impact in multiple contexts. Generally, RTTP offers incredible promise as an active pedagogical approach, especially for engaging the first-year undergraduate student (Lazrus and McKay 2013; Olwell and Stevens 2015). Beyond the first year, RTTP serves as an open environment to explore threshold concepts across the undergraduate experience—with its inherent transdisciplinary character (Westhoff 2015).

However, the most formative, holistic research conducted on the impact of RTTP pedagogy to date has come from Burney et al. (2010). Burney et al., in their lengthy white paper report for the Teagle Foundation, drew on the ways in which RTTP sits at the crux of active learning and transformative pedagogy for not only students but their faculty as well. The authors explained the pedagogy in layman's terms and contextualized the uses of RTTP in a demographically and socially rich environment like twenty-first-century higher education. Moreover, they illuminated the role of RTTP in creating space for active learning, facilitating specific learning and content acquisition, and the ways in which the practice can enhance and inform not only liberal arts and humanities but the hard sciences and liberal education in general (Burney et al. 2010).

Beyond the 2010 Teagle report, the remaining literature does include individual site studies that are foundational for new arguments on the efficacy of RTTP. The seminal work to date focused on the psychosocial impacts of RTTP and sought an empirical foundation for claims regarding the wide-ranging benefits of role-playing for students' motivation, interaction, exploration of divergent perspectives, moral reasoning, as well as critical and creative thinking skills development (Stroessner et al. 2009). The authors examined the collaborative nature of play in history survey classrooms via three phases of student focus groups: within one institution in the first-year experience environment, at a home institution and affiliated campuses to replicability of results from phase one, and at a third affiliate institution, where all students were required to complete a course employing RTTP. This last group was interviewed to find differences in predicting the success of the pedagogy. Their findings suggest the following: RTTP was more popular than traditional pedagogies and that across phases one and two, RTTP showed "elevated self-esteem, greater empathy with the needs and feelings of others, greater agreement with the belief that human characteristics are amenable to change across time and contexts, and improved rhetorical ability" (p. 612) as well as an "endorsement of the view that [human] characteristics are malleable" over the course of a semester of game play (p. 614). Additional findings included improved rhetorical skills, but unaffected writing skills. Phase three findings suggest that the enjoyment of the pedagogy did not align with students' grades. Stroessner et al. concluded that RTTP "appears to increase motivation and engagement in course materials" and "also produces several benefits that typically have been associated with academic success" (p. 617). And yet, the authors cautioned:

Effects have not yet been documented at institutions with students who have substantially different backgrounds [highly qualified, highly motivated, and generally upper-middle-class students] and characteristics. The findings obtained in those different contexts will ultimately be the basis for judging the degree and nature of the consequences associated with this role-playing pedagogy. (p. 618)

Adding to Stroessner et al., Kelly (2009) examined RTTP experiences within the context of a yearlong game. Kelly explored a classroom space where two RTTP games were employed and suggested that students, faculty, and program members alike felt accomplished with the pedagogy. Students felt strongly that they could gain a close reading of the texts and analyze them in ways that allowed them to remain closely in character and to act upon the knowledge that they had learned rather than filing it away for later use. Many students also indicated how much they enjoyed the yearlong length of the course, and many expressed an increased interest in history and learning more broadly.

Gorton and Havercroft (2012) examined the role of RTTP in political theory as a model for improving classroom dialogue, commitment, and engagement. Their findings suggest that students drew connections across content areas and time periods, in addition to demonstrating an increased ability to interpret political history and action. The authors maintained a commitment to traditional lecture and discussion-based learning, but do acknowledge RTTP and similar pedagogies as promising enhancements to the learning environment, though they did not recommend the practices as the sole models for student engagement. Similar studies by Lightcap (2009) and Weidenfeld and Fernandez (2016) in the field of political science support Gorton's and Havercroft's (2012) contention of increased engagement. Lightcap (2009) looked specifically at RTTP within first-year seminars by conducting student surveys to measure engagement through their play of two RTTP games set in political contexts: *Rousseau, Burke, and the Revolution in France, 1791* (Carnes and Kates 2005) and *Defining a Nation: India on the Eve of Independence, 1945* (Embree and Carnes 2005). Lightcap found that using RTTP games was a success:

It provided students with a learning experience quite unlike what they had been exposed to before and, if their testimony and evaluation survey results are to be credited, achieved the pedagogical goals set for the course...[and] it stimulated their interest in political science as a result of the course. (p. 179)

Weidenfeld and Fernandez (2016) added to this vein of research on RTTP by querying RTTP as an effective tool for greater student engagement in teaching political theory by integrating pre-simulation and post-simulation surveys as well as focus groups in their study. Weidenfeld and Fernandez (2016) structured the timing of their surveys to gauge in and out of class engagement and found that students' levels of engagement increased during the simulation in their political science course—and that this increased engagement resulted from the liminal nature of RTTP games.

Similar studies and reflections have also been authored on the teaching of classics (Anderson and Dix 2008), history (Carnes 2005; Greenbaum 2016; Higbee 2008; Karabin 2015), music history (Burke 2014), chemistry (Henderson and Henderson 2013), evolutionary biology (Grossman and Fleet 2016), methodological secularism (Henderson 2008), religion (Porter 2008), English for non-native speakers (Davison and Goldhaber 2007), theater (Hughes et al. 2006), non-violence and empathy (Lee 2005; Slater 2005), textual translations (McDonough 2015), French (Schaller 2012), and art history (Watson 2015; Watson and Salter 2016). Many studies have been authored, as well, on the gaming dynamics of RTTP (Carnes 2014b, c, d; Lang 2014a, b), on classroom community (Webb and Engar 2016), on course design (Ed Policy Group 2014), and on the impact of RTTP on revitalizing the classroom for instructors (Bowen 2016; Flaherty 2016; Houle 2006; Lang 2014c; Weston 2015).

## This Book

Given the theoretical foundation and evidence-based research on teaching and learning with RTTP, this volume offers a collective set of studies designed to further explore if, through what nuanced applications and in what specific contexts, RTTP serves as a high-impact practice for student learning and engagement. The chapters focus mainly on research conducted within RTTP classrooms with the express purpose of building an evidence base across multiple disciplines and institution types regarding the efficacy of RTTP in higher education classroom settings. Such action research is often referred to as the Scholarship of Teaching and Learning. Multi-author proposals were sought and strongly encouraged as one overarching goal of this volume was to have experienced RTTP instructors join with educational research and/or assessment specialists to devise highly rigorous and well-designed research studies. Additionally, while student perceptions of the RTTP experience are valuable and insightful, chapter proposers were encouraged to develop research designs that examine various student learning outcomes as well as provide rich narratives regarding their applications of RTTP. The following chapters contribute significantly to a broader understanding of the RTTP pedagogy throughout higher education in the United States and abroad as a wide range of institution types, sizes, academic disciplines, and game selections are represented in the pages that follow.

In Chap. 2, "Impact and Perception: Reacting to the Past at Middle Tennessee State University," Dawn McCormack and Karen Petersen investigated two questions: what is the impact of RTTP on retention and persistence rates at Middle Tennessee State University and what kind of impact does participating in RTTP courses have on students' attitudes toward the liberal arts?

For Chap. 3, "The Crowded Streets of Paris: Using RTTP in Less than Ideal Situations," Robert S. Bledsoe, Lee Anna Maynard, and Deborah Richardson assess the RTTP game *Modernism* vs. *Traditionalism: Art in Paris* and the issues of class sizes and scale within the RTTP pedagogy. The *Art in Paris* game was originally designed for 11–28 student players; however, the authors' enrollments for their Humanities 2002 course are capped at 40 students. So, how might running this game (or any RTTP game) with "too many" participants affect student learning and engagement?

Carolyn A. Schult, April Lidinsky, Lisa Fetheringill Zwicker, and Elizabeth E. Dunn supplied Chap. 4, "Strengthening Students' Self-Efficacy through Reacting to the Past." This contribution assesses the impact of the RTTP pedagogy on student engagement and self-concept by adapting Barry's and Finney's (2009) College Self-Efficacy Survey and asking open-ended questions about how the course changed the students and who was responsible for the students' learning. Five professors using Reacting games in their courses administered the survey during the first and last week of the semester.

In Chap. 5, "Scaling a Reacting Game For Use At a Large Public University," Keri Watson and Patsy Moskal analyze and evaluate student learning outcomes associated with RTTP learning activities and correlate those outcomes with final exam and overall course grades. The faculty perspective is also evaluated for valuable information for others interested in scaling an RTTP game for larger classes.

For Chap. 6, "Eliciting Meaningful Engagement in an Art History Survey Course: Reacting to the Past and Active Learning," Marie Gasper-Hulvat and David M. Dees examine whether an RTTP experience increases students' ability to engage in art historical thinking more effectively than other active learning strategies.

Christine L. Albright offers "Reconvening the Senate: Learning Outcomes after Using the Reacting to the Past Pedagogy in the Intermediate Latin Class" as Chap. 7. Therein, Albright presents student survey research about students' RTTP experiences, but, more importantly, the voluntary and anonymous survey asked students to score their learning using a numerical scale. Their responses were then compared to students in other Latin 2001 classes.

In Chap. 8, "What Happens After Reacting? A Follow Up Study of Past RTTP Participants at a Public Regional University," Jeffrey L. Bernstein, Mary G. Strasma, Russell B. Olwell, and Mark Higbee explore long-term impacts on student outcomes from RTTP use, such as engagement, career choice, and college retention, and which specific strategies or aspects of RTTP experience, if any, can be connected to these outcomes.

For Chap. 9, "Playing with Learning and Teaching in Higher Education: How Does Reacting to the Past Empower Students and Faculty?" Thomas Chase Hagood, Naomi J. Norman, Hyeri Park, and Brittany M. Williams take a research-based approach to assess both sides of the RTTP classroom by presenting the results of two national surveys that illuminate students' and faculty's perceptions of both the pedagogy and its high-impact elements. The surveys permit Hagood et al. to evaluate how students view the impact of RTTP on their learning within RTTP course(s), as well as how the pedagogy influenced their study habits, appreciation of the discipline, and their greater sense of autonomy as learners. Additionally, the faculty survey provides key insights into how RTTP implementation influenced faculty members' approaches to teaching and instruction in RTTP-based classes and non-RTTP classes.

In Chap. 10, "How to Perform Educational Research in Reacting to the Past Settings: A Primer for the Scholarship of Teaching and Learning," Colleen Kuusinen and C. Edward Watson present a brief manual regarding how to perform Scholarship of Teaching and Learning research within course settings with a specific emphasis on studying RTTP. Intended as a primer rather than a comprehensive educational research manual, this chapter selectively reviews protocols and strategies that are relatively easy to employ while also resulting in meaningful research findings. Topics include guidelines for conducting educational research (connecting to relevant literature/theory, IRB, ethical considerations, and resources and tools), identifying and clarifying an area to study, selecting appropriate research designs, collecting and analyzing data, and guidelines and recommendations for disseminating findings.

## CONCLUSION

A single study rarely, if ever, answers broad educational research questions alone, and the scope of possibility associated with RTTP is certainly extensive. Social science research studies, like those found here, build upon one another and begin to fit together, much like the bricks within a cobblestone road. Collectively, over time, through the combined work of many practitioners, scholars, and researchers, the path to successful teaching and learning becomes smoother, and best practices emerge that provide clear guidance regarding how best to move the pedagogy forward. While this volume is certainly not the first step of inquiry along the Reacting to the Past thoroughfare, its editors, authors, and peer reviewers are hopeful that it serves to deepen higher education's understanding of effective RTTP pedagogical practices and accelerates the rate of investigation into the impacts of RTTP on students, faculty, and the student success agenda.

## REFERENCES

Anderson, C. A., & Dix, T. K. (2008). "Reacting to the past" and the classics curriculum: Rome in 44 BCE. *The Classical Journal, 103*(4), 449–455.

Barry, C. L., & Finney, S. J. (2009). Does it matter how data are collected? A comparison of testing conditions and the implications for validity. *Research & Practice in Assessment, 4*, 17–26.

Bowen, J. A. (2016, July 15). Reacting to the past will revive your teaching. *Teaching Naked Blog.* Retrieved from http://teachingnaked.com/reacting-to-the-past-with-revive-your-teaching/

Bowen, J. A., & Watson, C. E. (2017). *Teaching naked techniques: A practical guide to designing better classes.* Hoboken: Jossey-Bass.

Burke, K. R. (2014). Roleplaying music history: Honing general education skills via "reacting to the past". *Journal of Music History Pedagogy, 5*(1), 1–21.

Burney, J., Powers, R. G., & Carnes, M. (2010). *Reacting to the past: A new approach to student engagement and to enhancing general education.* New York: Teagle Foundation.

Carnes, M. C. (2004). The liminal classroom. *The Chronicle of Higher Education, 51*, B7.

Carnes, M. C. (2005). Inciting speech. *Change: The Magazine of Higher Learning, 37*(2), 6–11.

Carnes, M. C., & Kates, G. (2005). *Rousseau, burke and revolution in France, 1791*. New York: W.W. Norton and Company.

Carnes, M. C. (2014a). *Minds on fire: How role-immersion games transform college*. Cambridge, MA: Harvard University Press.

Carnes, M. C. (2014b). From Plato to Erikson: How the war on 'bad play' has impoverished higher education. *Arts and Humanities in Higher Education, 14* (4), 383–397.

Carnes, M. C. (2014c, October 30). Role immersion games in the higher ed classroom [Audio podcast]. *Teaching in Higher Ed*. Retrieved from http://teachinginhighered.com/podcast/021-role-immersion-games-higher-ed-classroom-podcast/

Carnes, M. C. (2014d). Plato's war on play. *Chronicle of Higher Education, 61*, B4. Retrieved from http://www.chronicle.com/article/Platos-War-on-Play/148987/

Csikszentmihalyi, M. (1990). *Flow: The psychology of optimal experience*. New York: Harper and Row.

Davison, A., & Goldhaber, S. (2007). Integration, socialization, collaboration: Inviting native and non-native English speakers into the academy through "reacting to the past". In J. Summerfield & C. Benedicks (Eds.), *Reclaiming the public university: Conversations on general and liberal education* (pp. 143–161). New York: Peter Lang.

Ed Policy Group. (2014). *Five points on change in the college classroom*. Retrieved from http://www.edpolicygroup.com/five-points-change-college-classroom/

Embree, A. T., & Carnes, M. C. (2005). *Defining a nation: India on the eve of independence, 1945*. New York: W.W. Norton and Company.

Flaherty, C. (2016, September 28). Scaling up high-impact instruction. *Inside Higher Ed*. Retrieved from https://www.insidehighered.com/news/2016/09/28/new-grants-help-institutions-embed-reacting-past-other-high-impact-teaching.

Freeman, S., Eddy, S. L., McDonough, M., Smith, M. K., Okoroafor, N., Jordt, H., & Wenderoth, M. P. (2014). Active learning increases student performance in science, engineering, and mathematics. *Proceedings of the National Academy of Sciences, 111*(23), 8410–8415.

Gee, J. P. (2007). *What video games have to teach us about learning and literacy* (2nd ed.). New York: Palgrave Macmillan.

Gorton, W., & Havercroft, J. (2012). Using historical simulations to teach political theory. *Journal of Political Science Education, 8*(1), 50–68.

Greenbaum, D. J. (2016, June 23). How to think about the past. *Commentary*. Retrieved from https://www.commentarymagazine.com/american-society/college-campus-thinking-past/

Grossman, W. E., & Fleet, C. M. (2016). Changes in acceptance of evolution in a college-level general education course. *Journal of Biological Education*. Retrieved from http://www.tandfonline.com/doi/full/10.1080/00219266.2016.1233128

Hake, R. R. (1998). Interactive-engagement vs. traditional methods: A six-thousand-student survey of mechanics test data for introductory physics courses. *American Journal of Physics, 66*, 64–74.

Hartley, J., & Davies, K. (1978). Notetaking: A critical review. *Programmed Learning and Educational Technology, 15*, 207–255.

Henderson, D. E. (2008). Implementing methodological secularism: The teaching and practice of science in contentious times. In A. Keysar & B. A. Kosmin (Eds.), *Secularism & science in the 21st century* (pp. 105–116). Hartford: Institute for the Study of Secularism in Society and Culture, Trinity College.

Henderson, S. K., & Henderson, D. E. (2013). Challenging the food pyramid – A reacting to the past simulation game for chemistry and nutrition courses. In K. Symcox (Ed.), *Using food to stimulate interest in the chemistry classroom* (pp. 141–151). Washington, DC: American Chemical Society.

Higbee, M. D. (2008). How reacting to the past games "made me want to come to class and learn": An assessment of the Reacting pedagogy at EMU, 2007–2008. *The Scholarship of Teaching and Learning at EMU, 2*(4). Retrieved from http://commons.emich.edu/sotl/vol2/iss1/4/

Houle, A. (2006). Reacting to "reacting". *Change: The Magazine of Higher Learning, 38*(4), 52–53.

Hughes, A., Stevenson, J., & Gershovich, M. (2006). Community through discourse: Reconceptualizing introduction to theatre. *Theatre Topics, 16*(1), 85–101.

Immordino-Yang, M. H. (2015). *Emotions, learning, and the brain: Embodied brains, social minds, and the art of learning.* New York: Norton.

Karabin, S. (2015, Fall). Reenacting the past: Student role-playing make major historical events come alive in the classroom. *Barnard Magazine*, pp. 24–27.

Kelly, K. A. (2009). A yearlong general education course using "reacting to the past" pedagogy to explore democratic practice. *International Journal of Learning, 16*(11), 147–156.

Kuh, G. (2008). *High-impact educational practices: What they are, who has access to them, and why they matter.* Washington, DC: Association of American Colleges and Universities.

Kuh, G. D., Kinzie, J., Schuh, J. H., & Whitt, J. H. (2005). *Assessing conditions to enhance educational effectiveness: The inventory for student engagement and success.* San Francisco: Jossey-Bass.

Lang, J. (2014a). Being Nehru for 2 days. *Chronicle of Higher Education.* Retrieved from http://www.chronicle.com/article/Being-Nehru-for-2-Days/147813/

Lang, J. (2014b). Stop blaming students for your listless classroom. *Chronicle of Higher Education.* Retrieved from http://www.chronicle.com/article/Stop-Blaming-Students-for-Your/149067/

Lang, J. (2014c). How students learn from games. *Chronicle of Higher Education*. Retrieved from http://www.chronicle.com/article/How-Students-Learn-From-Games/148445/?cid=inline-promo

Lazrus, P. K., & McKay, G. K. (2013). The reacting to the past pedagogy and engaging the first-year student. In J. E. Groccia & L. Cruz (Eds.), *To improve the academy: Resources for faculty, instructional, and organizational development, volume 31* (pp. 351–363). San Francisco: Jossey-Bass.

Lee, J. T. H. (2005). Teaching nonviolence in times of war. *Academic Exchange Quarterly, 9*(2), 240–246.

Light, R. J. (2001). *Making the most of college: Students speak their minds*. Cambridge, MA: Harvard University Press.

Lightcap, T. (2009). Creating political order: Maintaining student engagement through reacting to the past. *PS: Political Science and Politics, 42*, 175–179.

McDonough, D. J. (2015). Reacting to translations past: A game-based approach to teaching translation studies. *Translation and Interpreting Studies, 10*(1), 133–152.

McKeachie, W. J., Pintrich, P. R., Lin, Y. G., & Smith, D. A. F. (1987). *Teaching and learning in the college classroom: A review of the research literature*. Ann Arbor: National Center for Research to Improve Post-Secondary Teaching and Learning.

Mueller, P. A., & Oppenheimer, D. M. (2014). The pen is mightier than the keyboard: Advantages of longhand over laptop note taking. *Psychological Science, 25*(6), 1159–1168.

Olwell, R., & Stevens, A. (2015). "I had to double check my thoughts": How the reacting to the past methodology impacts first-year college student engagement, retention, and historical thinking. *The History Teacher, 48*(3), 561–572.

Porter, A. L. (2008). Role-playing and religion: Using games to educate millennials. *Teaching Theology & Religion, 11*(4), 230–235.

Schaller, P. (2012). Can (role-) playing the French revolution en Français also teach the eighteenth century? *Digital Defoe: Studies in Defoe & His Contemporaries, 4*, 41–60.

Slater, N. W. (2005). Re-inventing the Trivium: Debate, dialogue—And empathy. *LiberalArtsOnline, 5*(5). Retrieved from http://www.liberalarts.wabash.edu/lao-5-5-debate-dialogue-empath/

Stroessner, S. J., Beckerman, L. S., & Whittaker, A. (2009). All the world's stage? Consequences of a role-playing pedagogy on psychological factors and writing and rhetorical skill in college undergraduates. *Journal of Educational Psychology, 101*(3), 605–620.

Van Ments, M. (1999). *The effective use of role-play: Practical techniques for improving learning*. London: Kogan Page Publishers.

Watson, C. E., Kuh, G. D., Rhodes, T., Light, T. P., & Chen, H. L. (2016). Editorial: ePortfolios – The eleventh high impact practice. *International Journal of ePortfolio, 6*(2), 65–69.

Watson, K. (2015). *There's a game for that: Teaching art history with "reacting to the past".* Retrieved from http://arthistoryteachingresources.org/2015/04/there s-a-game-for-that-teaching-art-history-with-reacting-to-the-past/

Watson, K., & Salter, A. (2016). Playing art historian: Teaching 20th century art through alternate reality gaming. *International Journal for Scholarship of Technology Enhanced Learning, 1*(1). Retrieved from http://ejournals.library.gatech.edu/ijsotel/index.php/ijsotel/article/view/8

Webb, J., & Engar, A. (2016). Exploring classroom community: A social network study of reacting to the past. *Teaching & Learning Inquiry, 4*(1), 1–17.

Weidenfeld, M. C., & Fernandez, K. E. (2016). Does reacting to the past increase student engagement? An empirical evaluation of the use of historical simulations in teaching political theory. *Journal of Political Science Education, 13*, 46–61.

Westhoff, L. M. (2015). Reacting to the past in the gilded age and progressive era classroom. *The Journal of the Gilded Age and Progressive Era, 14*(4), 580–582.

Weston, A. (2015). From guide on the side to impresario with a scenario. *College Teaching, 63*(3), 99–104.

# CHAPTER 2

# Impact and Perception: Reacting to the Past at Middle Tennessee State University

*Dawn McCormack and Karen K. Petersen*

## INTRODUCTION

In the last few years, the state of Tennessee has changed the funding formula for public institutions, moving away from numbers of enrolled students toward student success markers, including graduation and retention rates. Also, in the fall of 2015, Tennessee initiated a program, the Tennessee Promise, which allows students to attend a community college at no cost rather than matriculating at a four-year college beginning in the freshman year. These factors forced Middle Tennessee State University (MTSU), a regional institution with more than 20,000 undergraduate students (Office of Institutional Effectiveness, Research, and Planning, n.d.), to closely monitor graduation and retention rates and to seek creative solutions for recruiting and retaining students in an effort to maintain enrollment numbers.[1]

Like most liberal arts programs in the country, the College of Liberal Arts at MTSU has experienced a substantial drop in enrollment over the past six

---

[1] We would like to acknowledge Benjamin Simpkins, former Director of Data Management and Institutional Research at Middle Tennessee State University, who aided in survey design, administration, and data entry and compiled student data for our study. See also: http://tennesseepromise.gov/

D. McCormack (✉) • K.K. Petersen
Middle Tennessee State University, Murfreesboro, TN, USA

C.E. Watson, T.C. Hagood (eds.), *Playing to Learn with Reacting to the Past*, DOI 10.1007/978-3-319-61747-3_2

years. Declining enrollments, the state mandate to improve retention and persistence and a national climate that undervalues the liberal arts have created a need to ensure that students recognize the importance and value of their liberal arts experiences. At MTSU, most of the general education courses are housed in the College of Liberal Arts (with the next greatest number in the College of Basic and Applied Sciences). Typically, whether students are enrolled in Liberal Arts majors or not, they pass through these classes on the way to obtaining a degree.

As part of the university's *Quest for Student Success* initiative (Middle Tennessee State University, n.d.), a comprehensive plan designed to improve academic and non-academic elements that contribute to retention and completion, MTSU faculty have been involved in voluntary course redesign, especially in general education courses. Some of the faculty in the College of Liberal Arts have adopted *Reacting to the Past* (RTTP) as part of the course redesign program. By the end of the spring 2016 semester, 1318 students had participated in RTTP courses (courses in which at least one RTTP game is included).[2] Many of these games occurred in history general education courses, some of the most predictive[3] on campus for student success (all students are required to take two out of three history courses—US Survey I or II or Tennessee History).

A political science professor, Karen Petersen, began using RTTP in her classes in 2006 and continued to do so intermittently. In 2013, Dawn McCormack discovered RTTP at the Archaeological Institute of America conference in Seattle, Washington. She was immediately attracted to this pedagogy as a possible solution for increasing student engagement in her history classes. That summer, she attended the RTTP Summer Institute; she began using the games in her classes that fall. Before beginning her first game in the classroom, McCormack worked with the provost, Brad Bartel, to sponsor a university-wide RTTP workshop in the spring of 2014. The workshop exposed other faculty members to the pedagogy, and its use has grown in the two years since with additional professors adding RTTP games

---

[2] Note that this number, which is based on course enrollments at the beginning of the relevant semesters, includes some students who have taken multiple courses with Reacting to the Past experiences as well as some students who may have withdrawn early in the semester.

[3] Predictive courses are those in which a student's performance is a strong determinant of whether or not he or she will persist to graduation in a particular major. History general education courses are predictive across majors in part, we suspect, because of the emphasis on effective (written) communication and critical thinking skills necessary for success in college.

each semester. Support for these efforts was also encouraged through a Faculty Learning Community in the 2014–2015 Academic Year. As of the spring semester of 2016, 13 professors had offered 53 sections of courses including RTTP. Games offered included published ones as well as those in development (some being created by MTSU faculty members) in three departments (Art, History, and Political Science). The bulk of the sections (40) have been offered by history faculty.

For the most part, studies relating to the assessment of RTTP at universities have been anecdotal or have concentrated on a small number of students or a narrow focus (based often on the results of one course section).[4] This study is based on analysis using a larger sample size across multiple course sections and a corollary online survey to capture student participants from previous semesters in order to provide a next step in understanding the impact of RTTP at a regional university.

As an institution with a diverse population, including a large number of first-generation students, finding effective methods of engaging our students is a priority. RTTP has been cited as a high-impact practice (HIP) in the context of freshman seminar experiences (Burke 2014; Lazrus and McKay 2013; Lidinsky 2014), but it should be considered a HIP at any point in an undergraduate education.[5] Studies suggest that participating in multiple high-impact practices throughout an undergraduate education positively impacts student success, especially in certain traditionally underrepresented populations (Brownell and Swaner 2010; Huber 2010; Kuh and Schneider 2008). The Association of American Colleges and Universities (AAC&U) defines HIPs as "techniques and designs for teaching and learning that have proven to be beneficial for student engagement and successful learning among students from many backgrounds" (AAC&U, n.d.). At our university, RTTP can engage students from diverse backgrounds without the often-prohibitive costs associated with some types of HIPs, such as study abroad and internship programs. The demographics of the MTSU student population range widely from traditional to non-traditional with significant minority (about 35% non-white) and Pell-eligible (50%) populations (Office of Institutional Effectiveness, Research, and Planning, n.d). Since we do not have a freshman seminar experience at

---

[4] For example, see Carnes 2014; Higbee 2008; Kelly 2009; Lightcap 2009; Olwell and Stevens 2015.

[5] For the definition and characteristics of high-impact practices, see Kuh and Schneider 2008.

our university,[6] our study involves both general education and upper-division courses. It concentrates largely on the effect RTTP has on student attitudes toward learning and on habits that predict success in college, something HIPs appear to affect in a positive manner.

## METHOD

In this study, we assess whether RTTP experiences impact student awareness of and appreciation for what they learn in liberal arts or general education classes and whether students perceive an increase in their confidence that they are acquiring the skills associated with those courses. We also wanted to see how much being in an RTTP course affected habits commonly associated with HIPs such as time spent studying, working with others, developing friendships, and civic engagement. In order to measure these types of items, we developed a series of surveys. While administering the surveys, we collected student identification numbers (which we later removed from the datasets) so that we could collect further statistical information on the students and compare pre-test and post-test results.

### *Survey Design*

We constructed three surveys to administer during the spring 2016 semester (See Appendix). The first was an online survey which we used to obtain data from students who had taken RTTP courses through the fall of 2015. We administered this questionnaire through *Survey Monkey* in the middle of the semester. The other two surveys were administered in person at the beginning and end of the spring 2016 semester in classes with and without RTTP games in order to establish a pre-test/post-test dataset.

---

[6] Note that freshman seminars are considered to be HIPs whether or not they include RTTP. Thus, analyzing RTTP within other contexts is something that is necessary to understand the impact of this pedagogy itself.

**Table 2.1** Demographics of the survey samples

| Variable | In-class surveys | | Web surveys | MTSU population[a] (fall 2015, undergraduate only) |
| --- | --- | --- | --- | --- |
| | RTTP | Non-RTTP | | |
| # of responses | 104 | 247 | 207 | 20,140 |
| % female | 52 | 46 | 72 | 54 |
| % non-white | 16 | 28 | 22 | 35 |
| % Pell-recipient | 43 | 41 | 40 | 49.8 |
| % first generation | 23 | 25 | 27 | – |
| % part-time | 10 | 6 | 7 | 20 |
| ACT composite (mean) | 24 | 22 | 25 | 22 (incoming freshmen) |
| HS GPA (mean) | 3.4 | 3.4 | 3.5 | – |
| Earned hours (mean) | 84 | 62 | 52 | – |
| Cumulative GPA (mean) | 3.1 | 3.0 | 3.3 | – |
| Credit hour load in spring 2016 (mean) | 13 | 14 | 14 | 12 (fall 2015) |
| % Liberal Arts majors | 66 | 24 | 43 | 12 |

[a]Office of Institutional Effectiveness, Research, and Planning, n.d.

## RESULTS

We collected 207 web surveys (21% response rate) and in-class data from 351 individuals who completed both the pre-test and post-test surveys. Table 2.1 contains the demographic data from the two groups and for the MTSU population.

Our RTTP in-class sample has a lower rate of minority students than the non-RTTP in-class sample and the population in general and more female students than the non-RTTP in-class sample, and the RTTP students have a higher mean ACT composite score. Our web survey overrepresents female students, while all of our sample underrepresents part-time students. Liberal arts majors are overrepresented in the sample due to the use of games in upper-division courses, which tend to be populated primarily by majors and minors in the respective disciplines.

The first hypothesis we examine is that participation in a course with an RTTP game will increase student engagement as defined by participation in class and on campus (Kuh et al. 2008). Using the National Survey of Student Engagement (NSSE) as a framework,[7] we developed a series of questions

[7] http://nsse.indiana.edu

**Table 2.2**    Student engagement and RTTP: respondents agree or strongly agree

| Statement | Post-test value (% change from pre-test) | | Online RTTP |
|---|---|---|---|
| | In-class RTTP | In-class Non-RTTP | |
| Never ask a question or discuss in class | 0.0% (−1.9%) | 4.8% (+2.4%) | 3.7% |
| Uncomfortable speaking in public | 25.0% (−4.8%) | 23.0% (−5.2%) | 21.8% |
| Very/often form lasting friendships | 61.2% (+6.4%) | 45.0% (+1.1%) | 44.3% |
| Very/often spend time on campus outside of class | 64.7% (+4.1%) | 61.3% (+2.9%) | 66.0% |

to measure a student's perception of how frequently he or she demonstrated specific behaviors that are indicators of engagement. Using unique student identification numbers, we were able to match the pre-test and post-test responses for students surveyed in class in order to analyze the change in student perception over the semester. In Table 2.2, we show the post-test response to each item and the mean percent change from the pre-test to the post-test. For online respondents, Table 2.2 shows the response only as pre-test data are not available.

We compared the pre-test and post-test responses for all respondents in RTTP courses to all respondents in non-RTTP courses. By the end of the semester, none of the RTTP students report that they never ask questions or participate in discussion despite having reported this behavior at the beginning of the semester. Students in non-RTTP sections appear to have been discouraged from participating over the course of a semester in that they start out with a greater willingness to ask questions at the beginning of the semester and end up more likely to say that they never ask questions in class by the end of the semester (+2.4%).

Asking questions can be a forced behavior, particularly in an RTTP class. So, we also examined the level of comfort with a critical skill—public speaking. While RTTP does force public speaking, it does not follow automatically that student comfort with such behavior will increase as a result. That is, students need to see value in the behavior and practice the behavior in order to increase comfort (Palmer 2000). RTTP provides both value and practice, whereas a typical public-speaking assignment, if it exists at all, may feel like an exercise for its own sake with no greater value attached.

All student groups report lower levels of anxiety about public speaking at the end of the semester, with the reduction in discomfort slightly higher for non-RTTP students (−5.2%).[8] Those students who had experience with RTTP in a previous course and started the semester uncomfortable with public speaking did not change their level of discomfort, which is interesting given that they knew the choice to enroll in an RTTP course would entail public speaking. Experienced students whose responses to the public-speaking question were neutral in the pre-test did report levels of comfort by the end of the RTTP course (not shown). Online respondents, for whom pre-test data are not available, reported the lowest level of discomfort with public speaking at 21.8%.

Students in RTTP courses are required to engage in public speaking, some of it planned and some of it impromptu. The use of both techniques, particularly for first-time participants, does appear to decrease discomfort with public speaking. In the open-ended responses in the survey, students often noted that they improved their public-speaking skills. One respondent noted:

> I also felt less anxiety about speaking on-the-fly in the game because sometimes your speech may not be polished but when the relevant issues get brought up, you have to step up and speak to support or counter what's just been said.

Another engagement question dealt with the likelihood students would form lasting friendships with classmates. All students report a higher likelihood of forming lasting friendships, but that effect is significantly higher for RTTP students (+6.4%). One student stated, "I didn't want anything to do with people, now I have friendships that'll last a lifetime." The forced interaction in and out of class for RTTP participants appears to pay off in that it helps create bonds between students that are predictive of success (Pascarella and Terenzini 1991; Reason 2009). Interestingly, the online

---

[8] 24% of students in an RTTP course who completed the pre-test and the post-test knew the course contained an RTTP game, so some self-selection into RTTP classes is likely to have occurred. Because there may be differences between those students who participated in RTTP previously and first-time participants, we examined the responses for students in RTTP classes for the first time and found that they report a substantially larger decline in discomfort with public speaking on the post-test (−7.9%) and are less likely to report never asking questions in class than the other groups (−3.2%).

**Table 2.3**  Civic engagement and RTTP: respondents agree or strongly agree

| Statement | Post-test value (% change from pre-test) | | Online RTTP |
|---|---|---|---|
| | In-class RTTP | In-class Non-RTTP | |
| Participating in politics is critical to the health of our democracy | 77.0% (−4%) | 71.0% (+1%) | 88.0% |
| Citizens need to understand how decisions are made | 81.0% (−8%) | 83.0% (−3%) | 94.0% |

respondents reported the lowest level of friendship formation (44.3%). It may be that the friendship effect is most discernible immediately, and the source of the friendship is forgotten eventually. Or, students think the friendships will be long-lasting and discover later that they are not.

Based on our experiences with RTTP, we expected students in courses with these games to show higher levels of civic engagement by the end of the semester than students in non-RTTP courses. Table 2.3 shows the post-test agreement with two key civic engagement questions and the percent change from the pre-test.

Contrary to our expectations, in-class RTTP participants agreed less with civic engagement statements at the end of the semester than they did at the beginning (although they agreed with the statement at a higher rate than non-RTTP participants). It is possible that the civic engagement lessons we hoped to see do not appear until students have had time to reflect on their experience. Therefore, we turned to our online survey of previous participants, those who had participated in an RTTP game at least one semester prior to completing the survey. In that sample, 88% of respondents agree with the statement that participation in politics is critical to the health of democracy, and 94% agree that citizens need to understand how political decisions are made, both substantially higher than the response of RTTP participants at the end of the semester in which they participated in RTTP. Given that these post-test values are much higher than those collected during the semester, it is reasonable to assume that some lessons take more time to manifest and that RTTP participation does improve the civic engagement, or at least an awareness of the importance of civic engagement.

The awareness of civic engagement issues and their importance also shows in student comments in the open-ended responses. One student wrote:

> It has been about 2 years so my memory is not exact. We did ours on civil rights. Since it was a game constructed of teams it really helped highlight the motives and objectives of different groups of people. While the issues and people change, the real world application of identifying groups and objectives is priceless. It is the difference between misguided frustration and people finding a solution.

In the open-ended responses, another student credits an RTTP experience with providing the motivation to work on a political campaign and run for mayor in the future.

Finally, we hypothesize that RTTP participants will have a more favorable perception of the value of both general education courses and courses in the liberal arts.[9] Based on the finding that the perception of the value of civic engagement was higher for those surveyed at least one semester after participating in RTTP, we compared the in-class and online survey results for these questions as well. As with civic engagement, RTTP students report higher levels of agreement with statements about the value of general education in the web survey than in the in-class results (even the in-class post-test results) as shown in Table 2.4.

While RTTP students surveyed in class held more positive perceptions of general education as a whole, the results demonstrate a decline in positive perceptions of general education from the beginning to the end of the semester for students surveyed in class, suggesting we need to be more intentional about articulating the value of general education in those courses and beyond. The results for perceptions of the value of Liberal Arts classes were much better overall and improved across the semester in some cases.

Comparing the in-class, post-test results to the online results, only 38% of RTTP students surveyed at the end of the course agree with the statement that general education courses challenged them to think critically; but 57% of RTTP students surveyed at least one semester after RTTP agree with that statement. A total of 48% of RTTP students report that they perceive general education courses as valuable when asked at the end of their

---

[9] Specifically, Communication, English, Foreign Languages, History, Fine & Performing Arts, Philosophy, Political Science, & Sociology.

**Table 2.4**  The value of general education and the liberal arts and RTTP: respondents agree or strongly agree

| Statement | Post-test value (% change from pre-test) | | Online RTTP |
|---|---|---|---|
| | In-class RTTP | In-class Non-RTTP | |
| General education is a valuable part of the academic experience | 48% (−5%) | 45% (−14%) | 62% |
| I learned a lot in my general education courses | 39% (−9%) | 44% (−3%) | 44% |
| My general education courses challenged me to think critically | 38% (−2%) | 36% (−7%) | 57% |
| Courses in the Liberal Arts provide students with skills essential for success in college | 74% (+2%) | 60% (−4%) | 85% |
| Courses in the Liberal Arts provide students with skills essential for success in their careers | 74% (−2%) | 55% (−2%) | 81% |
| Courses in the Liberal Arts provide students with skills essential to good citizenship | 71% (+6%) | 53% (+1) | 80% |
| I understand the complicated factors that shape historical and political decisions | 75% (+9%) | 55% (+7%) | 86% |

RTTP semester compared to 62% at least one semester later. Students are more likely to agree with the statement that they understand the complicated factors that shape historical and political decisions when asked later (86%) as opposed to at the end of the semester (75%). Notably, only 55% of students in non-RTTP classes agree with this statement at the end of the semester.

We also asked students whether courses in the liberal arts provide the skills necessary for success in college and in their career. In all cases, non-RTTP students were significantly less likely to respond positively, and RTTP students asked at least one semester after completing their RTTP class report the highest level of agreement, over 80% in both cases. It appears that the RTTP experience does create an appreciation for general education and the Liberal Arts as well as an understanding of the complex nature of historical and political events, but it might take time for students to realize the gains.

One online survey respondent states:

The Reacting to the Past courses I participated in allowed me to immerse myself in a different worldview and consider oftentimes radically different perspectives than my own. In the workplace the ability to consider alternate points of view is imperative and treat varying opinions with respect is imperative, and the Reacting courses gave me a great opportunity to develop those skills. In addition, the classes allowed me to formulate an effective and persuasive argument by utilizing key sources and facts, not just my own opinion. I know going forward that being able to defend my position or argument with rational data and sources will be invaluable. Additionally, the courses gave me the opportunity to coordinate effectively with a group of my peers, all working together towards a common goal.

What these results tell us is that students continue to process the lessons learned in their RTTP classes after the semester ends and that subtler lessons take time to process. While not surprising, it is important to note the lag effect of some of what we anticipate RTTP will do for students, particularly when analyzing pre-test and post-test survey data. Had we neglected to survey previous participants, our results would indicate no effect on civic engagement or the appreciation of the value of key components of one's higher education experience.

## DISCUSSION

I absolutely loved this! It made me step out of my comfort zone and talk in front of the class every day. I actually enjoyed learning about history which is not usual. Making students get into the history really helped me better understand what was going on and the importance of the issues that these people went through.

There is no doubt that Reacting to the Past has had a positive impact upon many students who have participated in courses using this pedagogy at MTSU. With our university's emphasis on student success, the results of this survey indicate that RTTP is an effective pedagogical tool for student engagement and, thus, can contribute to the retention of students.[10] It is also clear that students gain important skills and content from these experiences which might help them to have a greater appreciation for the role of

---

[10] Note, however, Olwell and Stevens in their cautions against having a single solution for retention issues (2015, pp. 570–571).

the liberal arts in preparing them for their future while helping them to become engaged in society as well.

When formulating this study, we did not anticipate or plan for the lag effect and recommend further research designed specifically to test the hypothesis that RTTP participation increases a student's perception of the value of general education, the liberal arts, and civic engagement, among other things. Such a study would need to include a control group, the lack of which leads us to be tentative in our conclusions above. Additionally, while not looking specifically for differences, we did find that perceptions of public-speaking comfort and willingness to participate in class discussion improve more for first-time participants. Future research that explores how and why the benefits of RTTP differ depending on previous experience would be a useful contribution to our understanding of RTTP and, perhaps, other high-impact practices as well.

# APPENDIX

Impact and Perception: Reacting to the Past at Middle Tennessee State University
Online Survey Content

Name:_____     M#:_____

1)   How much do you agree/disagree with the following statements? (circle the number corresponding to your response)

1. Strongly Agree 2. Agree 3. Neutral 4. Disagree 5. Strongly Disagree 6. Don't know/Not applicable

|   |   |   |
|---|---|---|
| a. | I am comfortable speaking in front of groups. | 1 2 3 4 5 6 |
| b. | I can write a persuasive essay competently. | 1 2 3 4 5 6 |
| c. | I work well as part of a team. | 1 2 3 4 5 6 |
| d. | I know how to learn independently. | 1 2 3 4 5 6 |
| e. | I can identify reliable sources of information. | 1 2 3 4 5 6 |
| f. | I enjoy learning about history/political science/art. | 1 2 3 4 5 6 |
| g. | Reading about history/political science/art is exciting. | 1 2 3 4 5 6 |
| h. | I understand the complicated factors that shape historical and political decisions. | 1 2 3 4 5 6 |
| i. | I enjoy(ed) my general education classes. | 1 2 3 4 5 6 |
| j. | I learn(ed) a lot in my general education classes. | 1 2 3 4 5 6 |
| k. | My general education courses challenge (d) me to think critically. | 1 2 3 4 5 6 |
| l. | General education is a valuable part of the academic experience. | 1 2 3 4 5 6 |
| m. | Courses in the liberal arts (Communication, English, History, Fine & Performing Arts, Political Science, Philosophy, Sociology) provide students with skills essential for success in college. | 1 2 3 4 5 6 |
| n. | Courses in the liberal arts (Communication, English, History, Fine & Performing Arts, Political Science, Philosophy, Sociology) provide students with skills essential for success in their careers. | 1 2 3 4 5 6 |

1. Strongly Agree 2. Agree 3. Neutral 4. Disagree 5. Strongly Disagree 6. Don't know/Not applicable

o.   Courses in the liberal arts(Communication,         1 2 3 4 5 6
     English, History, Fine & Performing Arts,
     Political Science, Philosophy, Sociology)
     provide students with skills essential for good
     citizenship.

p.   Participating in politics (voting, campaigning,     1 2 3 4 5 6
     advocating, etc.) is critical to the health of our
     democracy.

q.   Citizens need to understand how political           1 2 3 4 5 6
     decisions are made.

2) During a semester in which you participated in a Reacting to the Past game, how often did you: (circle one option for each)

a.   Ask a question or contribute to class discussion

                              More than 3 times   1-3 times   never

b.   Prepare two or more drafts of a paper

                              More than 3 times   1-3 times   never

c.   Work with other students on a class project

                              More than 3 times   1-3 times   never

d.   Give an oral presentation

                              More than 3 times   1-3 times   never

e.   Work with primary source materials

                              More than 3 times   1-3 times   never

f.   Connect your learning to societal problems

                              More than 3 times   1-3 times   never

g.   Try to understand someone else's views by imagining how an issue looks from his or her perspective

More than 3 times    1-3 times   never

h.  Learn something that changed the way you understand an important issue or concept

More than 3 times    1-3 times   never

i.  Attend a lecture or event on campus

More than 3 times    1-3 times   never

j.  Miss a class session

More than 3 times    1-3 times   never

3)  In semester(s) when you did Reacting to the Past in a course, how many hours per week did you spend: (fill in the blank)

    a.  Working with groups on class projects outside of class _____

    b.  Working on independent research outside of class _____

    c.  Doing homework _____

    d.  Watching/reading news about current events _____

4)  During the semester(s) when you did Reacting to the Past in one or more courses, how often did you: (circle one option for each)

    a.  Form lasting friendships with classmates  Not Often Often Very Often

    b.  Spend time on campus outside of classes  Not Often Often Very Often

5)  Please list or describe the knowledge, skills, or experiences from Reacting to the Past courses that you believe will be most relevant for you in the future.

Impact and Perception: Reacting to the Past at Middle Tennessee State University
In-Class Survey—Beginning of the Semester

Name:_____    M#:_____

1) Why did you enroll in this course? (circle all that apply)?

        a.    General Education requirement
        b.    Major requirement
        c.    Minor requirement
        d.    Elective
        e.    I don't know

2) When you enrolled in this course, did you know the course included a simulation experience? (select one)

        a.    Yes
        b.    No
        c.    I don't know

3) Have you participated in other Reacting to the Past simulations in other classes? (select one)

        a.    Yes
        b.    No
        c.    I don't know

3) How much do you agree/disagree with the following statements? (circle the number corresponding to your response)

1. Strongly Agree 2. Agree 3. Neutral 4. Disagree 5. Strongly Disagree 6. Don't know/Not applicable

        a.    I am comfortable speaking in front of groups.    1 2 3 4 5 6

        b.    I can write a persuasive essay competently.    1 2 3 4 5 6

        c.    I work well as part of a team.    1 2 3 4 5 6

        d.    I know how to learn independently.    1 2 3 4 5 6

        e.    I can identify reliable sources of information.    1 2 3 4 5 6

        f.    I enjoy learning about history/political science/art.    1 2 3 4 5 6

        g.    Reading about history/political science/art is exciting.    1 2 3 4 5 6

        h.    I understand the complicated factors that shape historical and political decisions.    1 2 3 4 5 6

| | | |
|---|---|---|
| i. | I enjoy my general education classes. | 1 2 3 4 5 6 |
| j. | I learn a lot in my general education classes. | 1 2 3 4 5 6 |
| k. | My general education courses challenge me to think critically. | 1 2 3 4 5 6 |

1. Strongly Agree 2. Agree 3. Neutral 4. Disagree 5. Strongly Disagree 6. Don't know/Not applicable

| | | |
|---|---|---|
| l. | General education is a valuable part of the academic experience. | 1 2 3 4 5 6 |
| m. | Courses in the liberal arts (Communication, English, History, Fine & Performing Arts, Political Science, Philosophy, Sociology) provide students with skills essential for success in college. | 1 2 3 4 5 6 |
| n. | Courses in the liberal arts (Communication, English, History, Fine & Performing Arts, Political Science, Philosophy, Sociology) provide students with skills essential for success in their careers. | 1 2 3 4 5 6 |
| o. | Courses in the liberal arts (Communication, English, History, Fine & Performing Arts, Political Science, Philosophy, Sociology) provide students with skills essential for good citizenship. | 1 2 3 4 5 6 |
| p. | Participating in politics (voting, campaigning, advocating, etc.) is critical to the health of our democracy. | 1 2 3 4 5 6 |
| q. | Citizens need to understand how political decisions are made. | 1 2 3 4 5 6 |

4)   In a typical semester, how often do you: (circle one option for each)

a.   Ask a question or contribute to class discussion

More than 3 times   1-3 times   never

b.   Prepare two or more drafts of a paper

|  |  |  | More than 3 times | 1-3 times | never |

c.    Work with other students on a class project

|  |  |  | More than 3 times | 1-3 times | never |

d.    Give an oral presentation

|  |  |  | More than 3 times | 1-3 times | never |

e.    Work with primary source materials

|  |  |  | More than 3 times | 1-3 times | never |

f.    Connect your learning to societal problems

|  |  |  | More than 3 times | 1-3 times | never |

g.    Try to understand someone else's views by imagining how an issue looks from his or her perspective

|  |  |  | More than 3 times | 1-3 times | never |

h.    Learn something that changed the way you understand an important issue or concept

|  |  |  | More than 3 times | 1-3 times | never |

i.    Attend a lecture or event on campus

|  |  |  | More than 3 times | 1-3 times | never |

j.    Miss a class session

|  |  |  | More than 3 times | 1-3 times | never |

5)    In a typical semester, how many hours per week do you spend: (fill in the blank)

   a.    Working with groups on class projects outside of class _____

   b.    Working on independent research outside of class _____

   c.    Doing homework _____

   d.    Watching/reading news about current events _____

6)    In a typical semester, how often do you: (circle one option for each)

   a.    Form lasting friendships with classmates    Not Often  Often  Very Often

   b.    Spend time on campus outside of classes    Not Often  Often  Very Often

Impact and Perception: Reacting to the Past at Middle Tennessee State University
In-Class Survey—End of the Semester

Name:_____     M#:_____

1)    How much do you agree/disagree with the following statements? (circle the number
      corresponding to your response)

1. Strongly Agree 2. Agree 3. Neutral 4. Disagree 5. Strongly Disagree 6. Don't know/Not
applicable

| | | |
|---|---|---|
| a. | I am comfortable speaking in front of groups. | 1 2 3 4 5 6 |
| b. | I can write a persuasive essay competently. | 1 2 3 4 5 6 |
| c. | I work well as part of a team. | 1 2 3 4 5 6 |
| d. | I know how to learn independently. | 1 2 3 4 5 6 |
| e. | I can identify reliable sources of information. | 1 2 3 4 5 6 |
| f. | I enjoy learning about history/political science/art. | 1 2 3 4 5 6 |
| g. | Reading about history/political science/art is exciting. | 1 2 3 4 5 6 |
| h. | I understand the complicated factors that shape historical and political decisions. | 1 2 3 4 5 6 |
| i. | I enjoy my general education classes. | 1 2 3 4 5 6 |
| j. | I learn a lot in my general education classes. | 1 2 3 4 5 6 |
| k. | My general education courses challenge me to think critically. | 1 2 3 4 5 6 |
| l. | General education is a valuable part of the academic experience. | 1 2 3 4 5 6 |
| m. | Courses in the liberal arts (Communication, English, History, Fine & Performing Arts, Political Science, Philosophy, Sociology) provide students with skills essential for success in college. | 1 2 3 4 5 6 |
| n. | Courses in the liberal arts (Communication, English, History, Fine & Performing Arts, Political Science, Philosophy, Sociology) provide students with skills essential for success in their careers. | 1 2 3 4 5 6 |

1. Strongly Agree 2. Agree 3. Neutral 4. Disagree 5. Strongly Disagree 6. Don't know/Not applicable

    o.   Courses in the liberal arts (Communication,    1 2 3 4 5 6
English, History, Fine & Performing Arts,
Political Science, Philosophy, Sociology)
provide students with skills essential for good
citizenship.

    p.   Participating in politics (voting, campaigning,    1 2 3 4 5 6
advocating, etc.) is critical to the health of our
democracy.

    q.   Citizens need to understand how political    1 2 3 4 5 6
decisions are made.

2)    In a typical semester, how often do you: (circle one option for each)

    a.   Ask a question or contribute to class discussion

        More than 3 times   1-3 times  never

    b.   Prepare two or more drafts of a paper

        More than 3 times   1-3 times  never

    c.   Work with other students on a class project

        More than 3 times   1-3 times  never

    d.   Give an oral presentation

        More than 3 times   1-3 times  never

    e.   Work with primary source materials

        More than 3 times   1-3 times  never

    f.   Connect your learning to societal problems

        More than 3 times   1-3 times  never

g.  Try to understand someone else's views by imagining how an issue looks from his or her perspective

More than 3 times    1-3 times   never

h.  Learn something that changed the way you understand an important issue or concept

More than 3 times    1-3 times   never

i.  Attend a lecture or event on campus

More than 3 times    1-3 times   never

j.  Miss a class session

More than 3 times    1-3 times   never

3)  In this semester, how many hours *per week* did you spend: (fill in the blank)

a.  Working with groups on class projects outside of class _____

b.  Working on independent research outside of class _____

c.  Doing homework _____

d.  Watching/reading news about current events _____

4)  In this semester, how often did you: (circle one option for each)

a.  Form lasting friendships with classmates    Not Often Often Very Often

b.  Spend time on campus outside of classes    Not Often Often Very Often

5)  Please list or describe the knowledge, skills, or experiences from ***this course*** that you believe will be most relevant for you in the future.

6)  Please list or describe the knowledge, skills, or experiences you did not get from ***this course*** that you ***expected*** to get.

7)  Please list or describe the knowledge, skills, or experiences you did not get from a Reacting to the Past course that you ***expected*** to get.

## REFERENCES

AAC&U. (n.d.). *LEAP campus toolkit: Resources and models for innovation.* Retrieved from http://leap.aacu.org/toolkit/high-impact-practices

Brownell, J. E., & Swaner, L. E. (2010). *Five high-impact practices: Research on learning outcomes, completion, and quality.* Washington, DC: Association of American Colleges and Universities.

Burke, K. R. (2014). Roleplaying music history: Honing general education skills via "reacting to the past". *Journal of Music History Pedagogy, 5*(1), 1–21.

Carnes, M. C. (2014). *Minds on fire: How role-immersion games transform college.* Cambridge, MA: Harvard University Press.

Higbee, M. D. (2008). How reacting to the past games "made me want to come to class and learn": An assessment of the reacting pedagogy at EMU, 2007–2008. *The Scholarship of Teaching and Learning at EMU, 2*(4). Retrieved from http://commons.emich.edu/sotl/vol2/iss1/4/

Huber, B. J. (2010). *Does participation in multiple high impact practices affect student success at Cal State Northridge? Some preliminary insights.* Northridge: Office of Institutional Research, California State University Northridge. Retrieved from http://www.csun.edu/sites/default/files/MultHIPOvervie wFinal.pdf

Kelly, K. A. (2009). A yearlong general education course using "reacting to the past" pedagogy to explore democratic practice. *International Journal of Learning, 16* (11), 147–155.

Kuh, G. D., Cruce, T. M., Shoup, R., Kinzie, J., & Gonyea, R. M. (2008). Unmasking the effects of student engagement on first-year college grades and persistence. *Journal of Higher Education, 79*(5), 540–563.

Kuh, G. D., & Schneider, C. G. (2008). *High-impact educational practices: What they are, who accesses them, and why they matter.* Washington, DC: Association of American Colleges and Universities.

Lazrus, P. K., & McKay, G. K. (2013). The reacting to the past pedagogy and engaging the first-year student. In J. E. Groccia & L. Cruz (Eds.), *To improve the academy: Resources for faculty, instructional, and organizational development* (Vol. 31, pp. 351–363). San Francisco: Jossey-Bass.

Lightcap, T. (2009). Creating political order: Maintaining student engagement through reacting to the past. *PS: Political Science and Politics, 42,* 175–179.

Lidinsky, A. (2014). "Reacting to the past" to be proactive in the present: Feminist roots of high-impact practices. *Feminist Teacher, 24*(3), 208–212.

Middle Tennessee State University. (n.d.). *Quest for student success 2013–2016: A comprehensive, strategic initiative designed to improve retention and completion rates.* Retrieved from http://www.mtsu.edu/docs/QuestforStudentSuccess.pdf

Office of Institutional Effectiveness, Planning, and Research, Middle Tennessee State University. (n.d.). *2015 fact book: Middle Tennessee State University.* Retrieved from http://www.mtsu.edu/iepr/factbook/factbook_2015.pdf

Olwell, R., & Stevens, A. (2015). "I had to double check my thoughts": How the reacting to the past methodology impacts first-year college student engagement, retention, and historical thinking. *The History Teacher, 48*(3), 561–571.

Palmer, S. R. (2000). Student responses to activities designed to develop generic professional skills. *Journal of Professional Issues in Engineering Education and Practice, 126*(4), 180–185.

Pascarella, E. T., & Terenzini, P. T. (1991). *How college affects students: Findings and insights from twenty years of research.* San Francisco: Jossey-Bass.

Reason, R. D. (2009). An examination of persistence research through the lens of a comprehensive conceptual framework. *Journal of College Student Development, 50*(6), 659–682.

# CHAPTER 3

# The Crowded Streets of Paris: Using RTTP in Less-Than-Ideal Situations

*Robert S. Bledsoe, Lee Anna Maynard,*
*and Deborah South Richardson*

## INTRODUCTION

Mark Carnes developed the concept of Reacting to the Past out of his desire to revitalize his small, core-text, discussion-based freshman seminars (Carnes 2014). As more instructors embraced Carnes' approach and developed new materials, they introduced Reacting to the Past (RTTP) games into more varied educational environments, including traditional lecture-based courses. Despite this expansion, a survey of the games currently available from Norton and those listed on the "Big List of Reacting Games" maintained by Nicolas Proctor indicates that games are generally designed for a maximum of 25–30 participants. That is to say, the games still reflect the particular classroom context from which they emerged. Some games accommodate more participants; for instance, *Rousseau, Burke, and Revolution in France, 1791* has 41 roles (Popiel et al. 2015). In efforts to expand their use in larger classes, some instructors generate new roles. Alternatively, Offutt (2015) has suggested that instructors using *Patriots, Loyalists, and Revolution in New York City, 1775–1776* double characters. We take him to mean that students are given the same role sheet—perhaps with a different name—but that each operates independently. This led us to

R.S. Bledsoe (✉) • L.A. Maynard • D.S. Richardson
Augusta University, Augusta, GA, USA

© The Author(s) 2018
C.E. Watson, T.C. Hagood (eds.), *Playing to Learn with Reacting to the Past*, DOI 10.1007/978-3-319-61747-3_3

consider using RTTP in our classes and to study the effects of scaling up an RTTP game for use in a course with more students than the game is written to accommodate.

The game *Modernism* vs. *Traditionalism: Art in Paris, 1888–89* is designed for 11–27 players; however, enrollment in our Humanities courses is typically at or near 40 students. To meet this logistical challenge, we needed to reconsider the game's original parameters while preserving the student-engagement benefits of the Reacting game. This study considers two different configurations for implementing the game in larger courses: the first configuration pairs students so that a single role is played by two students working together, while in the second configuration, students who did not receive a specific historical role in the game act as journalists and produce a bulletin that reports on game-day events.

Although our primary interest was the effect of the different approaches to the game on measurable student learning, we consider their perception of the experience, which we determined via their self-reported assessments of engagement and learning. Since our modified implementation of the game altered the nature of that engagement for some students, it seemed especially valuable to gather this student-reported data. We looked for measureable differences between the engagement of the students who took more active roles in the game, portraying figures such as artists and art dealers, and those who participated as quasi-bystander journalists.

### Description of Game

*Modernism* vs. *Traditionalism: Art in Paris, 1888–89* offers "students a chance to view, describe, and debate the full range of artistic styles and movements in 1888 and 1889. The discussions and views about art all culminate in the 1889 World Exposition held in Paris....[S]tudents...recreate the World Exposition as the culminating finale to the game" (McKay et al. 2014, p. 9). During the game, students take on the roles of artists, art critics, or dealers (a list of the roles is included in the Appendix A of this chapter). As with all RTTP games, *Modernism* vs. *Traditionalism* emphasizes the development of written and oral communication skills. With its focus on the visual arts at the end of the nineteenth century, the game has three key goals specific to its cultural moment: (1) students should develop skills in visual analysis and emerge from the game with the ability to read a painting using formal analysis, (2) students should understand that this period marks the emergence of the avant-garde as a challenge to traditional painting and to the conservative ethos of the Academy, and (3) students should understand that art in this period is a commodity as well as an aesthetic object.

To meet these goals, students complete four primary assignments in the game, as it is originally conceived. As a warm-up and lead-in to active role-playing, they provide brief character introductions during the last class meeting before the first Reacting to the Past game session. Over the course of the game (at various times, depending on their roles), each student gives a longer presentation and writes an argumentative paper advocating for his or her character's vision of the nature of art and its role in culture. Finally, as part of the sustained role-playing, students work in teams to organize exhibitions of artwork from characters in the game. The exhibitions take place on the last game day, when visitors come to the class' recreation of the World Exposition of 1889 to view, discuss, and potentially "purchase" work from exhibitions.

### Game in Context of Course

We use *Modernism* vs. *Traditionalism* in HUMN 2002, the second semester of a required, two-course sequence in World Humanities. The course situates the arts—specifically, music, art, and literature— in their cultural and historical contexts. The balance among the three disciplines varies by instructor or instructional team as some sections are team-taught, while others have a single instructor, and as instructors' educational backgrounds encompass a range of disciplines. HUMN 2002 covers Romanticism in Northern Europe, Song China, European Modernism, and Post-Colonial Nigeria. Our choice of games was limited by the common learning goals, course design, and content our program has adopted across all sections of the course. The RTTP game fits fairly seamlessly into the course because its emphasis "on the development of speaking, writing, reasoning and the deep understanding of a specific historic moment" (McKay et al. 2014, p. 32) aligns well with the learning outcomes (LOs) for the course, which indicate that students should be able to (1) understand formal elements of various media and apply these elements to analyze specific works of art, literature, and music; (2) articulate a culture's perspectives on common human themes, as expressed in works of art, music and literature; (3) organize and communicate ideas effectively, both orally and in writing; (4) compare representative works from at least two different media (art/literature/music) within a given culture; (5) compare values or perspectives of at least two different cultures, citing evidence from representative works of art, literature, or music; and (6) understand how the past and other cultures illuminate life today.

During the game, students are assessed on their ability to apply formal terms from the visual arts to analyze specific works of art (LO 1) in the argumentative essay and oral presentations. We also assess their ability to organize and communicate ideas effectively, both orally and in writing (LO 3) through the argumentative essay and the oral presentations, as well as in oral interpersonal exchange during class debate and with the guests during the last game day. Although we do not ask them to compare representative works from two different media within a given culture (LO 4), the argumentative essay instructs them to compare two representative works from two different artistic movements within a given culture.

Furthermore, by immersing themselves in the struggle to define "art" at the historical moment of 1888–1889, the students also satisfy learning outcome two (LO 2), which is concerned with identifying and articulating a culture's perspectives on prevalent human themes via analysis of cultural artifacts. As in-character students debate appropriate subject matter for paintings and form coalitions to promote and sell art that represents "their" visions of humanity, civilization, and social issues, they learn about competing and changing cultural values and are able to connect these views to practical and economic outcomes.

### Study Design

For the purposes of the study, we implemented the game in four different sections of the course. One section (section H) was identified as the Standard Configuration group, because the class was divided into two groups, and each group ran the game independently. Thus, there were two simultaneous implementations of the game as originally conceived, with 17 students playing assigned historical roles in each game. In the Paired Configuration section (section E), students were placed in pairs that collaboratively assumed one role in the game. For this configuration, then, the game was still implemented with the same roles originally written but with the variation that two students would be representing each artist, art dealer, or critic, so that 38 students were assigned to 19 characters. In the two Journalist Configuration sections (sections A and G), some students were assigned to act as journalists and produce a bulletin that reported on the

**Table 3.1**   Game configurations

| HUMN 2002 section | Game configuration employed | Section enrollment | Role distribution |
| --- | --- | --- | --- |
| A: Journalist Configuration | Individual role-players and journalists | 38 | 24 characters 14 journalists |
| E: Paired Configuration | Students work in pairs to play assigned roles | 38 | 19 characters |
| G: Journalist Configuration | Individual role-players and journalists | 36 | 24 characters 12 journalists |
| H: Standard Configuration | Two independently-running games with traditional role assignments | 34 | 34 characters |

events of the game, while other students held the roles designated by the original iteration of the game (see Table 3.1).

In sum, across the four sections, 82 students participated as individual historical characters (active role-players), 38 participated as members of a pair representing one active role and 26 participated as (mostly observing) journalists.

### Playing the Game in Different Configurations: Constants, Experienced Game Masters

For each course section being discussed in this study, the game master was a Humanities teacher who had run the *Modernism* vs. *Traditionalism* game four or more times. All of the instructors had previously implemented the game in smaller sections that align more closely with the game authors' self-stated optimal enrollment numbers. Furthermore, the instructors fully believe in the benefits of the RTTP model for our students, which is an important consideration, given the added responsibilities and time demands of utilizing gameplay rather than traditional course content.

The variations we have introduced to the original game stem from our desire to open up the positive educational experiences of the RTTP to a wider range of students at our institution, those who enroll in typical core courses taught during standard semesters, rather than only subsets of students who have access to smaller sections, such as Honors program students or summer session students. In our average Humanities courses, we simply have too many students to be able to implement the game in its standard iteration. Unlike some other RTTP games that can be expanded to accommodate 40 or more students, this is not the case with this particular game in which all roles are documented historical figures. Nevertheless, as experienced *Modernism* vs. *Traditionalism* game masters, we wanted to determine if there could be a workaround that allowed us to implement this particular game (as its content meshes so well with our course content) in a way that preserved its most important features while not generating too complicated a model to expect a busy instructor to be able to deploy. The results are the Paired Configuration and the Journalist Configuration, which are explained below.

### Standard Configuration

In the Standard Configuration (section H), students experienced the game as it was originally conceived. The only exception was that because they were subsets of one larger class, both sets of game players were together for the first day of unit, while the game was introduced, and for about half of the last day for debriefing.

### Paired Configuration

Students in the Paired Configuration (section E) were assigned to work together in one role from the original RTTP game. Above all, this teamwork meant giving the character introduction and oral presentation together; it also meant that any in-class discussions, negotiations, or debates between artists, dealers, and/or critics were to be conducted by teams, not individuals. Team members were expected to keep one another informed about any outside-of-class discussions and negotiations, and any agreements—such as signing a contract with an art dealer—had to be ratified by both partners. However, written work (such as the argumentative essay) was to be done individually, as separate essays allowed the instructors to judge each student's performance individually and provided more data points for this study.

### Journalist Configuration

The Journalist Configuration perhaps generated the more radical departure from the standard configuration. In this configuration, students who were assigned an active-role-playing character (such as an artist, critic, or dealer) experienced the game in standard playing conditions. Students playing the roles of journalists participated in the game in a more passive way as they did not, for the majority of the game, adopt a persona to inhabit in class or execute moves, form alliances, or otherwise directly shape the development of the game play. Their responsibilities were to listen to and document the speeches, debates, and interactions that unfolded among the active-role-playing characters and produce a record for future class meetings.

The journalists were divided into two teams (journal staffs), each headed by its own editor. The journalists were assigned randomly. The editors were selected randomly, or they volunteered from those in the section assigned to be journalists. Each team was instructed to produce and distribute to the rest of the class a journal that summarized and commented on the events of the game generated by the active role-players. The teams were responsible for reporting on events on alternating days. For instance, if one team reported on game events that took place on a Monday, the next team was responsible for reporting on Wednesday's events. Just like with real-world news, the events and happenings of each game day varied and had the potential to be dramatic or at least surprising. Each student-editor assigned journalists to cover specific artists or critics. It was the editor's job to organize the contributions and distribute them. Editors could also solicit opinion pieces as well as advertisements or announcements from role-playing characters actively engaged in the game.

The *Modernism* vs. *Traditionalism* game as originally formulated is complex, with many interlocking and interacting components. Rather than potentially weakening its structural integrity by trying to shoehorn in more moving parts, we created the journalistic component. The journalists have the potential to indirectly affect the twists and turns of the game, but they have no direct power to shape its outcome. In addition to our desire to maintain the game's essential nature was our curiosity about whether the addition of less-active components would significantly alter the enhanced learning experiences typical of RTTP game play. Given that some students engage with their characters and personas much more than others, it did not seem counterintuitive to develop a role that is aligned with very active game play although not requiring or desiring the same degree of theatricality, assertiveness, and decision-making expected of artists, critics, and dealers.

Students' journalistic duties primarily consisted of generating a "paper of record". To generate more parity in responsibilities (and within grading models), each journalist (and each editor) also completed a four- to five-page journalistic profile of an assigned historical figure, such as Gustav Eifel or Stéphane Mallarmé. As time permitted, students gave three- to five-minute oral presentations on their figures (from a third-person perspective, not as the historical figures themselves) during class. In line with the interdisciplinary design of the course, these figures included writers and composers, as well as other figures prominent in cultural affairs during the period. (See Appendix C for a list of these figures.) Though all active-role game players are required to have oral presentation components, within the constraints of our semester schedule and the other units we needed to cover, dedicating even more class time to additional required oral presentations that did not move the game play forward—that is, journalists' third-person presentations—was impractical and, truly, unfeasible. On the final formal day of game play, in order to gain a taste of the active role-playing other students were enjoying, student journalists adopted the personas of their researched historical figures for the World Exposition. At this point, their journalistic duties had concluded as no time remained in the unit schedule to generate articles based on their observations of the World Exposition, and they were able to transition into historical characters and immerse themselves in the milieu of 1889 Paris, interacting not only with artists, critics, and dealers but with special guests who included influential art buyers.

## METHOD

To compare the effect of the two new configurations, we collected data from sections implementing the Standard, Paired, and Journalist Configurations on student performance, student engagement, and perceived learning from three different sources: argumentative essays submitted by students as part of their assigned work for the game (see rubric in Appendix B), a quiz administered at the end of the game (see Appendix C), and a survey asking about student engagement and perceived learning, administered at the end of the unit (see Appendix A). The students also gave oral presentations during the unit; however, since the argumentative essay and the oral presentation were generally submitted on the same day, the two items had very similar content, and the essays could be graded more reliably; no effort was made to capture separate data from the oral presentations for this study, though, in terms of satisfying the course's learning outcomes, the oral presentations were significant.

In order to assess student acquisition of basic knowledge about historical context and the works of specific artists or artistic movements, we created a short quiz that consisted of 19 multiple-choice questions (see Appendix C).

### *Argumentative Essay*

Students were required to submit a three- to five-page essay. For students with standard, active historical roles (i.e., artist, critic, dealer), this was an argumentative essay written in the voice of their assigned characters. Journalists completed a four- to five-page journalistic profile (written in the third person) on their assigned historical figure. To satisfy the argumentative component, profile-writers advocated for the perspective they believed, based on their research, their assigned figure would likely have held in the game-day debates about the nature of and future of art. These profile-writers were instructed to ground their judgment in the figure's opinions and work and to analyze two different paintings as examples of what the figure would (and would not) value, supporting their claims with evidence from the figure's life, education, or stated views.

With an eye to assessing the depth of knowledge and facility in visual analysis achieved by the students, the essays were evaluated using a rubric (see Appendix B) with five categories on a five-point scale. The categories are

- Character research and synthesis
- Understanding of the relevant artistic movements
- Awareness of the historical moment
- Facility in the visual analysis of a work from the movement most identified with the figure
- Facility in the visual analysis of a work from a different movement

The category of character research and synthesis assessed each essay on demonstrated knowledge of the character's biography and the essay-writer's ability to ground his or her distinct point of view within the character's training and life story. The second category evaluated how correctly and thoroughly the essay discussed two different artistic movements. The third category, awareness of historical moment, assessed each essay for the use of relevant historical information in the essay's argumentation. The two final categories are related to the second category, which looked at the under-standing of the artistic movements at the time; however, these are focused specifically on proficiency at visual analysis. We broke this into two individual categories so that we could evaluate whether a student's ability to conduct visual analysis was different when he or she applied the visual analysis to work that was not preferred by his or her characters. An explanation of the categories and the criteria used to assess the essays is found in Appendix B.

### Survey

As discussed above, we conducted a survey at the end of the unit. On the survey, students were asked to identity their role in the game. We did not ask students for identifiable information that would allow us to connect results on the quiz or the argumentative essay to the survey data. The survey instructed students to respond to prompts that asked about a number of unit and course goals. Specifically, on a 1–5-point scale (with 1 = "not at all" and 5 = "very much"), participants rated the extent to which the game helped them do the following[1]:

- Interpret a painting using formal analysis.*†
- Compare values or perspectives of two different artistic movements by analyzing representative works.*
- Understand the emergence of the avant-garde.†
- Recognize works of art as objects with both artistic and economic value.†
- Communicate ideas effectively in writing.*
- Communicate ideas orally.*
- Work collaboratively with others.*
- Weigh alternative points of view.*

The second section of the survey asked students to rate how often they engaged in certain activities that have been linked to student engagement and motivation (Handelsman et al. 2005). This included statements such as "I completed relevant readings" and "I thought about the unit between class meetings". The responses were rated again on a 5-point scale (with 1 = "almost never" and 5 = "almost always"). We also asked them to

---

[1] * identifies items related to course goals, while †identifies items related to unit or game goals.

respond to the question "How engaged were you in this unit?" on a 5-point scale ranging from "not at all" (1) to "very much" (5). Using the same scale, the final section of the survey asked students to rate how much they enjoyed and how much they felt they learned from specific components of the RTTP unit, specifically the argumentative essay, the oral presentation, the World Exposition, the reflective essay, and the unit as a whole (see Appendix D).

## RESULTS

### *Effect of Format*

To determine the effect of different configurations of the RTTP game, we conducted analyses that allowed us to examine the interaction of format and role. These analyses allowed us to consider the possibility of different format effects for different roles. Note that we were only able to include the three traditionally configured roles (artist, critic, and dealer) in these analyses because journalists were not part of all three implemented configurations (Standard, Paired, and Journalist). When there were multiple measures of one construct (e.g., components of the essay, multiple learning outcomes, multiple items assessing engagement), we conducted three (format) by three (role) MANOVAS as well as individual univariate analyses, followed by post-hoc tests. Tables 3.2, 3.3, 3.4, 3.5 and 3.6 organize the data by game-configuration format of the course. In the discussion of each table below, we point to a few differences that emerge from the data; however, it is essential to note that these differences were not statistically significant. In other words, in this study, the three different configurations of the game did not lead to significant differences in either student learning or student perception of learning and engagement. In the section below, we discuss the results of the individual analyses.

Our analysis of the data from the quiz and the argumentative essay (Table 3.2) revealed that the format had no effect on performance (learning) among students who were active role-players. The data from the end of unit survey of student perception (Table 3.3) indicate a disadvantage for the Standard Configuration for two of the eight comparisons of the effectiveness of the game at achieving the learning outcomes. However, these effects are small and few and confirm the findings that showed no significant difference in learning between the different configurations. This was also the case when we looked at the effect of configuration on perceived learning from specific game components (Table 3.4). Students in the Journalist

**Table 3.2**  Effect of configuration on learning[a]

| | Journalist n = 40 | | Paired n = 37 | | Standard n = 33 | | Total n = 110 | |
|---|---|---|---|---|---|---|---|---|
| | Mean | (SD) | Mean | (SD) | Mean | (SD) | Mean | (SD) |
| Quiz | 64.21 | (13.86) | 64.58 | (16.58) | 68.1 | (13.28) | 65.5 | (14.67) |
| Essay | n = 37 | | n = 34 | | n = 32 | | n = 103 | |
| Character research and synthesis | 3.08 | (.83) | 3.00 | (.29) | 3.34 | (.75) | 3.14 | (.84) |
| Artistic movement understanding | 2.54 | (.93) | 2.56 | (.86) | 2.78 | (.71) | 2.62 | (.84) |
| Historical-moment awareness | 2.57 | (1.07) | 1.62 | (.65) | 1.97 | (.78) | 2.07 | (.94) |
| Evidence of visual analysis facility-own style | 2.54 | (1.10) | 3.03 | (.83) | 2.81 | (.74) | 2.79 | (.93) |
| Evidence of visual analysis facility-other style | 2.08 | (1.02) | 2.26 | (.90) | 1.94 | (.76) | 2.07 | (.91) |

[a]The MANOVA revealed a significant effect of format on student scores on the argumentative essay, $F_{(10, 182)} = 2.63$, $p = .005$ (Pillai's Trace), $\eta_p^2 = .13$. Students in the class that included journalists received higher scores on the assessment of historical-moment awareness than students in the paired or standard class, $F_{(2, 94)} = 3.73$, $p = .03$, $\eta_p^2 = .07$. Although the univariate analysis revealed a significant effect for character research and synthesis, $F_{(2, 94)} = 4.91$, $p = .01$, $\eta_p^2 = .10$, the post-hoc comparisons revealed no significant differences

**Table 3.3** Effect of configuration on perceived effectiveness of game for achieving learning outcomes[a]

| | Journalist | | Paired | | Standard | | Total | |
|---|---|---|---|---|---|---|---|---|
| | n = 35 | | n = 30 | | n = 33 | | n = 98 | |
| | Mean | (SD) | Mean | (SD) | Mean | (SD) | Mean | (SD) |
| Use of formal analysis | 3.51 | (.98) | 3.6 | (1.07) | 3.51 | (.67) | 3.54 | (.91) |
| Compare artistic movements | 4.09 | (.78) | 3.77 | (.97) | 3.91 | (.91) | 3.93 | (.89) |
| Understand the avant-garde | 3.31 | (1.16) | 2.93 | (1.26) | 3.12 | (1.24) | 3.13 | (1.22) |
| Works of art as commodity | 3.57 | (.78) | 3.57 | (1.01) | 3.12 | (.99) | 3.42 | (.94) |
| Written communication | 3.6 | (1.06) | 3.47 | (.90) | 3.3 | (.98) | 3.46 | (.99) |
| Oral communication | 3.66 | (1.14) | 3.73 | (.87) | 3.67 | (1.02) | 3.69 | (1.01) |
| Work collaboratively | 3.86 | (1.12) | 3.9 | (1.16) | 3.97 | (.98) | 3.91 | (1.08) |
| Weigh alternative points of view | 4.06 | (.84) | 3.93 | (.87) | 3.7 | (1.10) | 3.9 | (.95) |

[a]Two univariate analyses of variance supported the outcome of the MANOVA, $F(16, 166) = 1.61$, $p = .07$ (Pillai's Trace), $\eta_p^2 = .14$. Students in the standard-format class reported that the game was less effective at helping them recognize works of art as commodity than students in the journalism- or paired-format classes, $F(2, 89) = 5.41$, $p = .006$, $\eta_p^2 = .11$. Students in the standard-format class also reported that the game was less effective at helping them weigh alternative points of view than students in classes with the journalism format, $F(2, 89) = 4.13$, $p = .02$, $\eta_p^2 = .09$

Configuration section showed some advantage in terms of their perceptions of how much they learned from a few components of the game; however, the effects were small and the MANOVA results were marginal. This was the same for students' reports of their engagement in general, and in terms of their behaviors and motivations (Table 3.5), as well as students' reports of how much they enjoyed the various components of the game (Table 3.6). The analyses led to the conclusion that the different configurations did not have a significant impact on the learning or the perception of learning and engagement by students involved in the games as active role-players. The analyses allow us to conclude that the Paired Configuration was as effective as the Standard Configuration.

**Table 3.4**   Effect of configuration on perceived learning from game components[a]

|  | Journalist n = 36 | | Paired n = 30 | | Standard n = 32 | | Total n = 98 | |
|---|---|---|---|---|---|---|---|---|
|  | Mean | (SD) | Mean | (SD) | Mean | (SD) | Mean | (SD) |
| Argumentative essay | 3.61 | (1.023) | 3.53 | (1.14) | 3.06 | (1.24) | 3.41 | (1.15) |
| Oral presentation | 3.81 | (1.04) | 3.83 | (.95) | 3.63 | (1.07) | 3.76 | (1.02) |
| World exposition | 3.97 | (.97) | 3.33 | (1.27) | 3.16 | (1.32) | 3.51 | (1.23) |
| Reflective essay | 3.92 | (.97) | 3.43 | (1.14) | 3.13 | (1.24) | 3.51 | (1.16) |
| The unit as a whole | 3.94 | (.83) | 3.6 | (1.07) | 3.44 | (1.08) | 3.67 | (1.00) |

[a]Two univariate analyses of variance supported the outcome of the MANOVA, $F(10, 172) = 1.64$, $p = .10$ (Pillai's Trace), $\eta_p^2 = .09$. Students in the journalism-format class reported that they learned more from the World Exposition, $F(2, 89) = 4.16$, $p = .02$, $\eta_p^2 = .09$, and the reflective essay, $F(2, 89) = 5.34$, $p = .01$, $\eta_p^2 = .11$, than did students in the standard- or paired-format classes

**Table 3.5**   Effect of configuration on engagement measured by reported behavior and motivation

|  | Journalist | | Paired | | Standard | | Total | |
|---|---|---|---|---|---|---|---|---|
|  | Mean | (SD) | Mean | (SD) | Mean | (SD) | Mean | (SD) |
| Enjoyment | 3.71 | (1.09) | 3.39 | (1.26) | 3.36 | (.93) | 3.49 | (1.10) |
| Effort | 4.15 | (.86) | 4.23 | (.72) | 4.18 | (.92) | 4.18 | (.83) |
| Completed readings | 3.82 | (1.11) | 3.68 | (1.28) | 3.61 | (1.20) | 3.7 | (1.19) |
| Listened carefully | 4.18 | (.80) | 4.13 | (.92) | 4.09 | (1.01) | 4.13 | (.90) |
| Attended class | 4.62 | (.78) | 4.48 | (.96) | 4.7 | (.64) | 4.6 | (.80) |
| Engagement outside of classroom | 3.85 | (1.18) | 3.87 | (1.12) | 3.45 | (1.25) | 3.72 | (1.19) |
| Desire to learn | 3.74 | (1.16) | 3.84 | (1.00) | 3.12 | (1.27) | 3.56 | (1.18) |
| Understood expectations | 3.06 | (1.39) | 3 | (1.41) | 2.64 | (1.19) | 2.9 | (1.34) |
| Helped other students | 2.97 | (1.03) | 2.96 | (1.18) | 2.97 | (1.33) | 2.96 | (1.17) |
|  |  | n = 36 |  | n = 31 |  | n = 33 |  | n = 100 |
| Engagement | 3.83 | (.91) | 3.74 | (.93) | 3.55 | (1.15) | 3.71 | (1.00) |

**Table 3.6** Effect of configuration on engagement measured by reported enjoyment of components of the game[a]

| | Journalist | | Paired | | Standard | | Total | |
|---|---|---|---|---|---|---|---|---|
| | Mean | (SD) | Mean | (SD) | Mean | (SD) | Mean | (SD) |
| Argumentative essay | 2.97 | (1.18) | 2.72 | (.96) | 2.38 | (1.21) | 2.7 | (1.15) |
| Oral presentation | 3.14 | (1.15) | 3.38 | (1.24) | 2.91 | (1.38) | 3.13 | (1.26) |
| World exposition | 4.11 | (.82) | 3.45 | (1.27) | 3.31 | (1.35) | 3.65 | (1.20) |
| Reflective essay | 3.72 | (1.03) | 3.28 | (1.10) | 3.16 | (1.19) | 3.4 | (1.12) |
| The unit as a whole | 3.64 | (.87) | 3.52 | (1.15) | 3.22 | (1.18) | 3.46 | (1.07) |

[a]Three univariate analyses of variance supported the outcome of the MANOVA, $F(10, 170) = 1.66$, $p = .10$ (Pillai's Trace), $\eta_p^2 = .09$. Students in the journalism-format class reported that they enjoyed the argumentative essay, $F(2, 88) = 3.22$, $p = .05$, $\eta_p^2 = .07$, and the reflective essay more than did students in the standard-format classes. They also reported that they enjoyed the World Exposition more than students in either the paired or standard classes, $F(2, 88) = 3.78$, $p = .03$, $\eta_p^2 = .08$

## Effect of Role

To look at whether the students who participated as journalists had different outcomes in terms of learning, engagement, and the perception of learning, we had to conduct further analyses of the data. In this analysis, we looked at data by role for students in the two classes in which students were assigned all four roles (artists, critics, art dealers, and journalists). As was the case with the previous analyses, we conducted MANOVAs when there were multiple measures of one construct (e.g., components of the essay, multiple learning outcomes, and multiple items assessing engagement), subsequent univariate analyses, and follow-up post-hoc analyses allowed us to examine the effect of role on specific measures. As we did above, in the discussion below we point to a few differences that emerge from the data; however, it is essential to note that these differences, while noticeable, were not statistically significant (Table 3.7). Importantly, the roles the students were assigned, including the role of journalist that we created for our larger sections, did not lead to significant differences in student learning or student perception of learning and engagement.

Our analyses of student learning (Table 3.7) revealed that format had no effect on quiz performance. The MANOVA revealed a significant effect of role on student scores on the argumentative essay, and subsequent univariate analyses revealed that students in the art-dealer role scored higher on character research and synthesis than students in the art critic role. This finding, however, draws a distinction between students engaged in active

**Table 3.7**  Effect of role on learning[a]

| | Artist | | Critic | | Dealer | | Journalist | | Total | |
|---|---|---|---|---|---|---|---|---|---|---|
| | Mean | (SD) | Mean | (SD) | Mean | (SD) | Mean | (SD) | Mean | (SD) |
| Quiz | n = 27 | | n = 9 | | n = 4 | | n = 21 | | n = 61 | |
| | 66.08 | (14.40) | 58.48 | (12.47) | 64.47 | (13.84) | 58.65 | (13.55) | 62.29 | (13.96) |
| Argumentative essay | n = 26 | | n = 9 | | n = 2 | | n = 24 | | n = 61 | |
| Character research and synthesis | 3.31 | (.74) | 2.33 | (.71) | 3.5 | (.71) | 2.94 | (.52) | 3.02 | (.72) |
| Artistic movement understanding | 2.5 | (1.03) | 2.56 | (.73) | 3 | (.00) | 2.15 | (.77) | 2.34 | (.89) |
| Historical-moment awareness | 2.69 | (1.16) | 2.22 | (.83) | 2.5 | (.71) | 2.54 | (.66) | 2.56 | (.92) |
| Evidence of visual analysis facility-own style | 2.58 | (1.21) | 2.33 | (.87) | 3 | (.00) | 2.04 | (.75) | 2.34 | (1.00) |
| Evidence of visual analysis facility-other style | 2.06 | (1.10) | 1.89 | (.78) | 2 | (1.41) | 1.71 | (.81) | 1.89 | (.95) |

[a]The MANOVA revealed a significant effect of role on student scores on the argumentative essay, $F(15, 165) = 1.95$, $p = .02$ (Pillai's Trace), $\eta_p^2 = .15$. Subsequent univariate analyses revealed that students in the art-dealer role scored higher on character research and synthesis than students in the art critic role, $F(3, 57) = 5.51$, $p = .002$, $\eta_p^2 = .23$

roles. It did not reveal any significant difference between those with active roles and those acting as journalists. Similarly, the analyses of the effect of role on perceived learning on learning outcomes revealed no meaningful effects of role (Table 3.8). When we considered the effect of role on perceived learning from the various components of the game (Table 3.9), there was some evidence that students who played the critic role may have perceived less advantage in learning from the World Exposition than other students. However, these effects are small and relatively weak.

The students' reports of their engagement in general and in terms of their behaviors and motivations (Table 3.10) revealed no meaningful differences due to role in the game and neither did the students' reports of how much they enjoyed the various components of the game (Table 3.11). Therefore, while there are some minor differences in student perceptions of learning and engagement, there are no significant differences between the learning and experiences of the students playing active roles and those acting as journalists.

## DISCUSSION

Overall, the data discussed above support the conclusion that the two alternative and expanded configurations can be employed successfully to extend the use of *Modernism* vs. *Traditionalism: Art in Paris, 1888–89* into sections with up to 40 students while maintaining student learning and engagement.

### Instructor Experience

While the study focused on student learning and student perceptions of learning and engagement in the different configurations of the game, we would like to comment on the instructors' experiences with the new game-playing configurations. This is especially important because engaging in an RTTP game already requires different input and preparation from an instructor than a traditional teaching experience, and the logistical implications of running simultaneous games in a section or adding in the journalist components are worth considering.

### Paired Configuration Players

When utilizing a Paired Configuration model, one could employ a variety of methods to pair students. We have used two; in one method, we drew

**Table 3.8** Effect of role on perceived learning on learning outcomes

| | Artist n = 25 | | Critic n = 7 | | Dealer n = 3 | | Journalist n = 16 | | Total n = 51 | |
|---|---|---|---|---|---|---|---|---|---|---|
| | Mean | (SD) | Mean | (SD) | Mean | (SD) | Mean | (SD) | Mean | (SD) |
| Use of formal analysis | 3.56 | (.82) | 3.29 | (.95) | 3.67 | (2.31) | 3.44 | (.82) | 3.49 | (.92) |
| Compare artistic movements | 4.08 | (.86) | 3.86 | (.38) | 4.67 | (.58) | 3.81 | (.83) | 4.00 | (.80) |
| Understand the avant-garde | 3.36 | (1.08) | 2.86 | (1.46) | 4.00 | (1.00) | 3.56 | (1.10) | 3.39 | (1.13) |
| Works of art as commodity | 3.40 | (.71) | 3.71 | (.76) | 4.67 | (.58) | 3.88 | (1.02) | 3.67 | (.86) |
| Written communication | 3.52 | (1.04) | 3.86 | (1.07) | 3.67 | (1.53) | 3.81 | (.83) | 3.67 | (.99) |
| Oral communication | 3.72 | (.98) | 3.43 | (1.27) | 3.67 | (2.31) | 3.56 | (1.04) | 3.63 | (1.09) |
| Work collaboratively | 3.84 | (1.03) | 4.00 | (1.00) | 3.67 | (2.31) | 4.06 | (.85) | 3.92 | (1.04) |
| Weigh alternative points of view | 3.88 | (.83) | 4.29 | (.76) | 5.00 | (.00) | 3.81 | (1.11) | 3.98 | (.93) |

**Table 3.9** Effect of role on perceived learning from components of the game[a]

| | Artist n = 25 | | Critic n = 7 | | Dealer n = 4 | | Journalist n = 12 | | Total n = 48 | |
|---|---|---|---|---|---|---|---|---|---|---|
| | Mean | (SD) | Mean | (SD) | Mean | (SD) | Mean | (SD) | Mean | (SD) |
| Argumentative essay | 3.64 | (1.08) | 3.43 | (.79) | 3.75 | (1.26) | 4.5 | (.67) | 3.83 | (1.02) |
| Oral presentation | 3.68 | (1.07) | 4.23 | (.76) | 3.75 | (1.26) | 3.92 | (1.09) | 3.83 | (1.04) |
| World exposition | 4.00 | (.82) | 3.29 | (1.25) | 5.00 | (.00) | 3.58 | (1.51) | 3.87 | (1.12) |
| Reflective essay | 3.76 | (.97) | 3.86 | (.90) | 5.00 | (.00) | 3.58 | (1.44) | 3.83 | (1.10) |
| The unit as a whole | 3.88 | (.83) | 4.00 | (.82) | 4.25 | (.96) | 3.75 | (1.06) | 3.90 | (.88) |

[a]Two univariate analyses of variance supported the outcome of the MANOVA, $F(15, 126) = 2.18$, $p = .01$ (Pillai's Trace), $\eta_p^2 = .21$. Students in the journalist role reported that they learned more from the argumentative essay than students in the critic or artist roles, $F(3, 44) = 2.65$, $p = .06$, $\eta_p^2 = .15$. Students in the dealer role reported learning more from the World Exposition than students in the critic role, $F(3,44) = 2.60$, $p = .06$, $\eta_p^2 = .15$

**Table 3.10** Effect of role on perceived learning on learning outcomes

|  | Artist n = 23 | | Critic n = 7 | | Dealer n = 4 | | Journalist n = 15 | | Total n = 49 | |
|---|---|---|---|---|---|---|---|---|---|---|
|  | Mean | (SD) | Mean | (SD) | Mean | (SD) | Mean | (SD) | Mean | (SD) |
| Enjoyment | 3.83 | (.94) | 3.14 | (1.35) | 4.00 | (1.41) | 2.87 | (1.19) | 3.45 | (1.17) |
| Effort | 4.17 | (.83) | 4.14 | (.69) | 4.00 | (1.41) | 4.27 | (.46) | 4.18 | (.75) |
| Completed readings | 3.70 | (1.06) | 4.14 | (1.21) | 4.00 | (1.41) | 4.13 | (.92) | 3.92 | (1.06) |
| Listened carefully | 4.17 | (.72) | 4.29 | (.76) | 4.00 | (1.41) | 4.33 | (.90) | 4.22 | (.82) |
| Attended class | 4.65 | (.78) | 4.29 | (.95) | 5.00 | (.00) | 4.60 | (.83) | 4.61 | (.79) |
| Engagement outside of classroom | 3.87 | (1.01) | 3.29 | (1.70) | 4.75 | (.50) | 3.40 | (1.24) | 3.71 | (1.21) |
| Desire to learn | 3.74 | (.92) | 3.57 | (1.51) | 4.00 | (2.00) | 3.13 | (1.25) | 3.55 | (1.21) |
| Understood expectations | 3.09 | (1.28) | 2.71 | (1.60) | 3.50 | (1.91) | 3.00 | (1.20) | 3.04 | (1.32) |
| Helped other students | 2.87 | (.97) | 2.86 | (.90) | 3.75 | (1.50) | 3.60 | (1.12) | 3.16 | (1.09) |
|  | Artist n = 25 | | Critic n = 7 | | Dealer n = 4 | | Journalist n = 15 | | Total n = 51 | |
| Engagement | 3.96 | (.61) | 3.57 | (1.13) | 3.5 | (1.95) | 3.38 | (.89) | 3.69 | (.92) |

**Table 3.11** Effect of role on engagement measured by reported enjoyment of components of the game[a]

| | Artist n = 25 | | Critic n = 7 | | Dealer n = 4 | | Journalist n = 13 | | Total n = 49 | |
|---|---|---|---|---|---|---|---|---|---|---|
| | Mean | (SD) | Mean | (SD) | Mean | (SD) | Mean | (SD) | Mean | (SD) |
| Argumentative essay | 2.92 | (1.26) | 2.86 | (1.07) | 3.50 | (1.00) | 2.85 | (1.14) | 2.94 | (1.16) |
| Oral presentation | 3.12 | (1.13) | 2.86 | (1.21) | 3.75 | (1.26) | 2.31 | (1.03) | 2.92 | (1.17) |
| World exposition | 4.12 | (.78) | 3.86 | (.90) | 4.50 | (1.00) | 3.15 | (1.21) | 3.86 | (1.02) |
| Reflective essay | 3.60 | (1.15) | 4.00 | (.58) | 4.00 | (.82) | 3.31 | (1.03) | 3.61 | (1.04) |
| The unit as a whole | 3.72 | (.54) | 3.14 | (.58) | 4.00 | (1.41) | 3.23 | (1.17) | 3.53 | (.96) |

[a]The results of the MANOVA revealed no effect of role on student enjoyment. One univariate analysis revealed that students in the role of art dealer reported that they enjoyed the World Exposition more than students in the journalist role, $F(3, 45) = 3.66$, $p = .02$, $\eta_p^2 = .20$

student names randomly and assigned them to a character. (Adjustments were made during the process to account for known or likely personality conflicts.) In the other method (and the one used in the section included in this study), we allowed students to select their partners. Of the two methods, the latter seemed to work best. Since students chose partners, they felt responsible for making the partnership work without the instructors' mediation. Furthermore, since most partners already interacted with each other outside of class, they generally found it easy to contact each other and find time to work on the course material outside of class, so instructors spent less time trying to solve issues directly related to teamwork.

To give us more data points for the study and to be able to better distinguish between the performances of the individual students, each student in this section submitted an individual essay. Although it was evident that pairs were working together during the study, no incidents of collusion or plagiarism were detected in the papers submitted in this section.

In our institutional context, the paired-player (Paired Configuration) model has a maximum of 20 game roles. With only 20 roles, the instructors can find time during the game sessions to introduce additional material or spend time with the class as a whole clarifying procedures and resolving issues. The paired-player model does have one clear advantage over the individual-player model: student absences can be less disruptive to the flow and outcome of the game. On the other hand, during the World Exposition held during the final game session, you have two students playing one character, which can be confusing for visitors and lead to a number of students standing around being rather disengaged. We tried to reduce this by requiring one partner to be stationed somewhere—such as in one of the art galleries—while the other partner was to walk around and engage visitors and other players. Halfway through the exposition, the partners switched activities.

### *Journalist Configuration*

HUMN 2002 is designed as an interdisciplinary course in World Humanities that includes music, art, and literature, as well as some philosophical and religious texts. Journalists effectively expand the scope of the RTTP game beyond the art world to report on the work of composers, authors, and other cultural figures, meaning this configuration of the game actually aligns more closely to the goals and concept of our course. However, in practice, it was difficult to carve out the class time to accommodate all the student presentations on these figures. In both Journalist Configuration sections, we used a substantial portion of the class session intended to be dedicated to post-World-Exposition debriefing and also took an additional class meeting from the next unit in order to complete the journalists' presentations. In courses where extending the time allotted for the game unit would not be an issue, this configuration could certainly present a viable alternative to traditional implementation of the game. The journalist and editor roles (as well as their journals and reports) do add more moving parts to a situation that already requires close attention to scheduling, detail, and time management. If an instructor is comfortable with this expansion of the components, the journalism configuration adds some excitement and verisimilitude to the game-playing conditions. Furthermore, there is room for expanding and refining the role of the journalists so that students in these roles become more integrated into, and possibly more integral to, the fabric of game.

## Conclusion

Curricular restrictions led us to choose *Modernism* vs. *Traditionalism: Art in Paris, 1888–1889* and to modify the game using the configurations described above. These local restrictions created the impetus for this study, which poses a more general question: can an RTTP game such as *Modernism* vs. *Traditionalism: Art in Paris, 1888–1889* be successfully modified to accommodate bigger class sizes in ways other than having each student take on a unique role? Our experiences and the data we collected attest to an answer in the affirmative. Without sacrificing student learning and engagement or student perception of learning, the two new models we generated—the Journalist Configuration and the Paired Configuration—allowed for flexibility in enrollment levels while preserving the most pedagogically attractive features of an RTTP game. The results of our study should be encouraging to those who have been interested in extending the use of RTTP games into courses with enrollments larger than those foreseen by the game developers: after all, our class sizes were in some cases nearly double what might by some be considered the ideal enrollment for the game. Differences between these modified versions of the RTTP and the traditionally configured deployment of the game were statistically negligible, according to our data, suggesting that it is not only feasible but, in fact, pedagogically responsible to utilize the RTTP game in courses of expanded size. The desirability and the viability of efforts to scale up the pedagogy into classes larger than ours is a question that only further debate and study can answer.

Our findings, of course, pertain to a particular RTTP game, *Modernism vs. Traditionalism: Art in Paris, 1888–1889.* Though we have demonstrated that expansion can successfully be implemented, our conclusions about increasing the scope of an RTTP game may be tied to the format and particular parameters of this game. The range of RTTP games is diverse in historical moments and far from homogenous in mechanics, though the games' focus on immersive experiences and player engagement argue for their deployment in college classrooms whenever possible. Our findings show that one game, at least, can be adjusted and adapted to make its wealth of experiences available to a wider swath of students and instructors. The avenues of 1880s Paris, via the modern classroom, are broad enough to accommodate *flâneurs* and learners alike.

## Appendix A: Roles in Modernism Versus Traditionalism: Art in Paris, 1888–89

William Adolphe Bouguereau
Jean-Louis Ernest Meissonier
Pierre Auguste Renoir
Edgar Degas
Vincent Van Gogh
Puvis de Chavannes
Gustave Moreau
Paul Cézanne
*G. -Albert Aurier*
*Joséphin Péladan*
**Georges Petit**
Claude Monet
Jean-Léon Gérôme
Georges Seurat
*Félix Fénéon*
**Paul Durand-Ruel**
*Joris–Karl Huysmans*
*André Michel*
Paul Gauguin

Jules Adolphe Aimé Louis Breton
Mary Cassatt
John Singer Sargent
Paul Signac
Camille Pissarro
Berthe Morisot
Henri Toulouse-Lautrec
James McNeil Whistler

The roles are listed in the order of allocation. The game developers assume a minimum of 11 players (Bouguereau to Petit) Dealers are in **bold**. Critics are in *italics*. All other roles are artists.

Figures assigned to students playing journalists. This figures are given in order of allocation, although these only represent the authors' own inclinations.

### Historical figures assigned to journalists
Nadar (Gaspard-Félix Tournachon)
Emile Zola
Claude Debussy
Eric Satie
Stephane Mallarme
Arthur Rimbaud
Paul Verlaine
Gustav Eifel
Georges Melies
Gustave Caillebotte
Auguste Rodin
Charles-Camille Saint-Saëns
Edmond de Goncourt
Maurice Maeterlinck
Frédéric Auguste Bartholdi
Cesar Franck
Alphonse Daudet
Guy de Maupassant
Augustus Saint-Gaudens

## APPENDIX B: CATEGORIES FOR RTTP RUBRIC USED TO ASSESS ARGUMENTATIVE ESSAY

In order to assess *depth of knowledge*, we will focus on the following categories:

Does the paper offer *fluid discussion of the assigned character?*

Does the paper provide *productive and purposeful comparisons of philosophies/schools, artists, and artworks?*

Does the paper demonstrate *relevant contextual knowledge of the period/ historical moment?*

Does the paper provide *evidence of directed and specific visual analysis* correctly and appropriately incorporating *terminology* found on pages 57–58 of the game manual?

---

### Character Research and Synthesis
1 = Only cursory gestures toward the assigned character's perspective
2 = Some (but insufficient) indications of the character's unique and individual point of view
3 = Frequent inclusion of references to the character's point of view; some of these may be misapplied or too rudimentary
4 = Frequent inclusion of references to the character's point of view with some gestures toward the elements of the character's training or biography that would lead to this position
5 = Fluid discussion from the perspective of the assigned character, correctly indicating the character's preferences, training, and ideas

### Artistic Movement Understanding
1 = Only cursory (name-checking) gestures toward competing artistic ideas and movements
2 = Some (but insufficient) indications of the writer's awareness of basic components of competing artistic ideas and movements
3 = Passable discussion of basic components of at least two relevant artistic movements/schools with some directly comparative analysis

4 = Detailed discussion of components of at least two relevant artistic movements, with well-organized comparison and some specific examples

5 = Thorough discussion of at least two relevant artistic movements, with well-chosen examples, offering analysis and synthesis to explain clearly how this situates the assigned character

## Historical Moment Awareness

1 = No historical information beyond the most basic (such as dates) is included

2 = Very little historical information is included; some may be irrelevant or incorrect

3 = Some historical information is included; more (or more relevant) is needed and/or there are errors in the writer's understanding.

4 = Historical information is included frequently; some choices might not be as effective

5 = Relevant historical information is included in an effective and purposeful way, leaving no gaps in understanding for the reader

## Evidence of Visual Analysis Facility

1 = Little to no visual analysis offered; perhaps some broad generalization

2 = Insufficient or incorrect visual analysis

3 = Efforts made toward visual analysis; some vocabulary from game manual utilized; some errors in analysis and usage or too shallow an analysis

4 = Detailed analysis of visual elements of artwork, using vocabulary from game manual in a generally appropriate way

5 = Thorough analysis of composition, color, scale, and imagery using vocabulary/terminology from game manual effectively

## Appendix C: Unit Quiz

Name _____

      Role_____

(1) The most prestigious artists during the time of the game were members of which organization?
   A. **Académie des Beaux-Arts (Academy of Fine Arts)**
   B. Société des Artistes Indépendants (Society of Independent Artists)
   C. Salon des Refusés, (Salon of Rejects)
   D. Jury des Salon des Artists Francais (Jury of the Salon of French Artists)

(2) Which artist's work best represents the art of Neo-Impressionism?
   A. Cezanne
   B. Moreau
   C. Renoir
   D. **Seurat**
   E. Van Gogh

(3) The work of the Avant-garde tends to exhibit which characteristics?
   A. A disregard to natural color
   B. Use of color to create an emotional impact
   C. Fine line and shading
   D. **1 and 2**
   E. 2 and 3

(4) Which movement is marked by short, broken brushstrokes that barely convey forms, the use of pure unblended color, and an emphasis on the effects of light?
   A. **Impressionism**
   B. Post-Impressionism
   C. Symbolism
   D. Expressionism
   E. None of the above

(5) Which kind of painting did the Academics value the most because it required imagination, education, and technical proficiency?
   A. Portraiture

B. Still lifes
C. Genre Scenes
D. **History Paintings**
E. Landscapes

(6) The following group of artists were interested in capturing the momentary aspects of light shifts to capture scenes of modern life in urban and suburban settings:
A. Academic artists
B. Symbolists
C. **Impressionists**
D. Neo Impressionists
E. All of the above

(7) The French Royal Academy of Painting and Sculpture was established by:
A. William-Adolphe Bouguereau in 1875
B. **King Louis XIV in 1648**
C. Jacques-Louis David in 1774
D. Theodore Gericault in 1618
E. Jean-Louis-Ernest Meissonier in 1776

(8) The annual Salon was sponsored by:
A. **The Academy**
B. Society of Independent Artists
C. Salon of Rejects
D. Jury of the Salon of French Artists

(9) The Medal of Honor winner at the 1888 salon was:
A. Georges Seurat
B. Claude Monet
C. Paul Cezanne
D. Mary Cassatt
E. **Edouard Detaille**

(10) Which group of artists believed that art did not have to have a moral message, make the viewer live a better life, or educate the viewer about French history?
A. Neoclassicists
B. Classicists

C. **Impressionists**
D. The Academy
E. Divisionists

(11) Which one of the individuals below was not a prominent art critic during the 1880s:
A. G-Albert Aurier
B. **Léon Bonnat**
C. Félix Fénéon
D. Joris –Karl Huysmans
E. Joséphin Péladan

(12) The Avant-garde:
A. Embraced the Salon as necessary in the promotion of artists
B. Embraced the Academy as the authority on aesthetic value
C. 1 &2
D. **None of the above**

(13) Which group of artists had eight independent exhibitions between 1874–1886 and demonstrated that artists could sell work on their own:
A. Classicists
B. **Impressionists**
C. The Academy
D. Divisionists
E. None of the above

(14) Which of the following is not a formal quality of a work of art?
A. **Attitude**
B. Line
C. Perspective
D. Style
E. Texture

(15) The 1889 Salon was held in:
A. Versailles
B. Luxembourg
C. Marseille
D. **Paris**
E. Saint-Etienne

16–19 are to be answered using images projected on the board.

(16) Who most likely painted this work?
    A. Gerome
    B. Puvis de Chavannes
    C. Monet
    D. **Seurat**
    E. Van Gogh

(17) Who most likely painted this work?
    A. Bouguereau
    B. Gérôme
    C. **Meissonier**
    D. Moreau
    E. Whistler

(18) Who most likely painted this work?
    A. Cezanne
    B. Gérôme
    C. **Moreau**
    D. Puvis de Chavannes
    E. Renoir

(19) Who most likely painted this work?
    A. Cassatt
    B. Gauguin
    C. Moreau
    D. Seurat
    E. **Van Gogh**

## Appendix D: Survey

Role (circle one): **Artist Critic Dealer Journalist** HUMN 2002 Section:

Please answer the following questions about your experience with the Art in Paris unit.

| To what extent did the game help you be able to... | Not at all | | | | Very much |
|---|---|---|---|---|---|
| 1. Interpret a painting using formal analysis | 1 | 2 | 3 | 4 | 5 |
| 2. Compare values or perspectives of two different artistic movements by analyzing representative works | 1 | 2 | 3 | 4 | 5 |
| 3. Understand the emergence of the avant-garde | 1 | 2 | 3 | 4 | 5 |
| 4. Recognize works of art as objects with both artistic and economic value | 1 | 2 | 3 | 4 | 5 |
| 5. Communicate ideas effectively in writing | 1 | 2 | 3 | 4 | 5 |
| 6. Communicate ideas orally | 1 | 2 | 3 | 4 | 5 |
| 7. Work collaboratively with others | 1 | 2 | 3 | 4 | 5 |
| 8. Weigh alternative points of view | 1 | 2 | 3 | 4 | 5 |

| To what extent are the following behaviors, thoughts, and feelings characteristic of you for this unit? | Almost never | | | | Almost always |
|---|---|---|---|---|---|
| 9. I enjoyed the unit. | 1 | 2 | 3 | 4 | 5 |
| 10. I put forth effort for my role in this unit. | 1 | 2 | 3 | 4 | 5 |
| 11. I completed relevant readings. | 1 | 2 | 3 | 4 | 5 |
| 12. I listened carefully in class. | 1 | 2 | 3 | 4 | 5 |
| 13. I came to class. | 1 | 2 | 3 | 4 | 5 |
| 14. I thought about the unit between class meetings | 1 | 2 | 3 | 4 | 5 |
| 15. I really wanted to learn the material. | 1 | 2 | 3 | 4 | 5 |
| 16. I felt as if I understood expectations for the unit. | 1 | 2 | 3 | 4 | 5 |
| 17. I helped other students with this unit. | 1 | 2 | 3 | 4 | 5 |

| | Not at all | | | | Very much |
|---|---|---|---|---|---|
| 18. How engaged were you in this unit? | 1 | 2 | 3 | 4 | 5 |

**PLEASE TURN PAGE OVER AND COMPLETE THE SURVEY.**

**This unit included several components. Please evaluate the components as to how much you enjoyed them and how much they helped you learn.**

| Components | Enjoyed experience | | | | | Learned | | | | |
|---|---|---|---|---|---|---|---|---|---|---|
| | not at all | | | | Very much | not at all | | | | Very much |
| Argumentative essay | 1 | 2 | 3 | 4 | 5 | 1 | 2 | 3 | 4 | 5 |
| Oral presentation | 1 | 2 | 3 | 4 | 5 | 1 | 2 | 3 | 4 | 5 |
| World exposition | 1 | 2 | 3 | 4 | 5 | 1 | 2 | 3 | 4 | 5 |
| Reflective essay | 1 | 2 | 3 | 4 | 5 | 1 | 2 | 3 | 4 | 5 |
| The unit as a whole | 1 | 2 | 3 | 4 | 5 | 1 | 2 | 3 | 4 | 5 |

## REFERENCES

Carnes, M. C. (2014). *Minds on fire: How role-immersion games transform college.* Cambridge, MA: Harvard University Press.

Handelsman, M. M., Briggs, W. L., Sullivan, N., & Towler, A. (2005). A measure of college student course engagement. *Journal of Educational Research, 98*(3), 184–191.

McKay, G., Proctor, N. W., & Marlais, M. A. (2014). *Modernism vs. traditionalism: Art in Paris, 1888–89. Player game manual version 6.0.* New York: W.W. Norton and Company.

Offutt, B. (2015). *Instructor's guide for "patriots, loyalists, and revolution in New York City, 1775–1776."* (2nd ed.). New York: W.W. Norton and Company.

Popiel, J., Carnes, M. C., & Kates, G. (2015). *Instructor's guide for "Rousseau, burke, and revolution in France, 1791"* (2nd ed.). New York: W.W. Norton and Company.

# CHAPTER 4

# Strengthening Students' Self-Efficacy Through Reacting to the Past

*Carolyn A. Schult, April Lidinsky, Lisa Fetheringill Zwicker, and Elizabeth E. Dunn*

At the end of a semester studying the politics of early twentieth-century America in the Reacting game *Greenwich Village, 1913: Suffrage, Labor, and the New Woman*, one student testified that she had discovered new abilities and new strength within herself. In her memorable words, "I learned to take charge of my education." This study of Reacting to the Past at IU South Bend provides suggestive evidence that many students share this experience. Students who took Reacting courses described measurable improvements in their confidence about their ability to make speeches, argue positions, understand differing perspectives, and write a research paper. Intriguingly, our research has also pointed to significant differences in the increases in self-efficacy in our male versus our female students, findings that suggest Reacting pedagogy might be most powerful for students who find traditional classrooms least empowering. The personal and political implications of Reacting, then, may have positive effects on students' self-efficacy beyond the classroom.

This study measures the impact of Reacting courses on students' self-efficacy or their confidence about their capability to perform a specific task or skill (Bandura 1986). Self-efficacy is different from self-esteem or self-confidence. Both self-esteem and self-confidence are judgments about

---

C.A. Schult (✉) • A. Lidinsky • L.F. Zwicker • E.E. Dunn
Indiana University South Bend, South Bend, IN, USA

© The Author(s) 2018
C.E. Watson, T.C. Hagood (eds.), *Playing to Learn with Reacting to the Past*, DOI 10.1007/978-3-319-61747-3_4

personal self-worth and generalized feelings about the likelihood of succeeding. In contrast, self-efficacy is based on people's judgments that they can succeed on specific tasks. Educational psychologists argue that self-efficacy plays a crucial role in academic success and personal adjustment to college life, especially in the first year of college (Bandura 1986; Chemers et al. 2001; Vuong et al. 2010). Students who report high levels of academic self-efficacy tend to hold themselves to high standards, use effective cognitive strategies in learning, and approach difficult tasks as challenges rather than threats (Chemers et al. 2001). Many studies have found that academic self-efficacy is a fairly strong predictor of college GPA (Vuong et al. 2010; Zajacova et al. 2005). Students with confidence in their abilities or high self-efficacy can more easily move beyond roadblocks like poor test performance or the inability to immediately grasp a concept than students who approach their classwork wondering if they will meet their professors' expectations.

## REACTING TO THE PAST AT INDIANA UNIVERSITY SOUTH BEND

Reacting to the Past was introduced to IU South Bend in 2010 by the new Dean of the College Liberal Arts and Sciences and Reacting veteran, Elizabeth Dunn. Indiana University South Bend offers Bachelor's and Master's degrees in a variety of fields and enrolls about 5500 full-time undergraduates. Overall, IU South Bend is similar to many other medium-sized regional public universities across the country and shares similar kinds of challenges. In the last five years, IU South Bend has focused renewed attention on retention, persistence, and graduation of students. In comparison with peer institutions with similar student demographics, IU South Bend has lower retention and graduation rates. For the IU South Bend campus, Reacting is an innovative pedagogy that connects with other student success initiatives.

At IU South Bend, Reacting courses fit well in the interdisciplinary General Education curriculum. Reacting courses are offered by Psychology, Women's and Gender Studies, Philosophy, and World Languages. The Department of History also began to weave Reacting courses into its advanced courses. Because Reacting courses combine several high-impact practices and offer students multiple opportunities to practice leadership, teamwork, independent research, and persuasive speaking, they have potential to combine the skill development that students need with academic content. In addition, new students build useful networks of fellow classmates in Reacting classes—an important factor in retention (Carnes 2014; Turner and Thompson 2014).

Research on Reacting pedagogy tends to focus on its use of high-impact strategies and the ways this approach creates a classroom in which students are the primary knowledge-makers (Kuh 2008). The collaborative projects and risk-taking of Reacting classrooms exemplify the types of college experiences that can help create engaged students and deep learning (Carnes 2014). The role of the professor as "gamemaster" and the structures and rules of Reacting games create some limits on students' freedom. At the same time, Reacting connects pedagogical practices that have long focused on empowering students, such as Freire's (2007) "problem-posing" mode of education or bell hooks' (1989) concept of education as "the practice of freedom." These confidence-building pedagogical approaches are also foundational to feminist pedagogy (Weiler 1991), important to this study because it helps explain the ways Reacting courses foster learning environments that may be especially helpful for students who often feel marginalized by a traditional classroom structure—one that reinforces the model of the instructor as expert, student as vessel to be filled with knowledge.

Reacting classrooms rely on the same dynamics feminist scholars have fostered for decades in classrooms, that of students as members of a community of empowered learners. Feminist scholars have encouraged teachers to incorporate dialogic, participatory, and experiential teaching and learning into the classroom—all elements that are part of the Reacting pedagogy (Chow et al. 2003). In comparison to a traditional classroom, in a Reacting course authority is decentered. Students work together to create knowledge, with a focus on students' skills and understanding of concepts as opposed to mastering a set of facts imparted by the expert professor (Shrewsbury 1993). Consistent with feminist pedagogy, Reacting courses create space for personal growth, connections between students, and the possibility of bringing personal views, passions, and experiences to the fore in course debates. While only one of the courses in this study is explicitly feminist (a Women's and Gender Studies course based around the Progressive Era *Greenwich Village 1913* game), these findings suggest that the creative, collaborative space of Reacting classrooms might be particularly empowering for women. The suggestive findings of this study show that the implications for deeper engagement within the classroom and on campus are significant for all students.

Our study includes courses newly designed for a first-year experience that use Reacting as part of a course that engages students not only in the specific classroom but in college life more generally. Because Reacting is intended to challenge students in multiple, unexpected ways, we argue it is an especially useful approach for strengthening academic self-efficacy, in the way that it motivates students to persist and master complex academic challenges. Unlike efforts to strengthen self-esteem, which often assume a one-way direction of causality (students will do better if they feel better about themselves), efforts to strengthen academic self-efficacy recognize that behaviors and beliefs operate reciprocally (Pajares and Schunk 2001). For example, students gain trust in their ability to give a speech by successfully giving a speech. The resulting increased confidence, in turn, leads them to approach new challenges rather than avoid them and work harder to attain their goals, making future success more likely (Dweck 2006).

Quantitative and qualitative data suggest Reacting courses encourage academic risk-taking that elicits higher student confidence. This is especially true for women. While previous research has shown male college students report higher academic self-efficacy than female college students (D'Lima et al. 2014), this study shows that female students have much to gain from courses early in their college careers that use RTTP, particularly as they gain confidence in public speaking, forming arguments, and understanding other perspectives.

## METHOD

We collected data over three semesters from eight sections of Literary and Intellectual Traditions Reacting courses. These courses are interdisciplinary, 100-level General Education courses that share several characteristics: they explore theories of conflict; they require an analysis of at least one primary text; they address ethical issues; and they include instruction in writing. Although the courses were intended for first-year students, they were open to all students during the period covered by this study as the first-year experience was phased in on campus. Table 4.1 shows the games used for each course.

This survey was conducted during the first and last weeks of the semester. A total of 198 students filled out at least part of the survey, and we have both pre-test and post-test surveys from 134 students (80 women, 53 men, 1 unidentified). This group included 38 first-year students, 41 sophomores, 34 juniors, and 21 seniors.

To assess the impact of the Reacting pedagogy on student engagement and academic self-efficacy, we adapted Barry and Finney's (2009) College

**Table 4.1** Department, courses, and Reacting games used in the study

| Department | Course | Reacting games |
|---|---|---|
| Philosophy | Socrates, Galileo, and Darwin | *The Threshold of Democracy: Athens in 403 B.C.* *The Trial of Galileo: Aristotelianism, the "New Cosmology," and the Catholic Church 1616–33* *Charles Darwin, the Copley Medal and the Rise of Naturalism, 1861–64* |
| Psychology | Democracy, conflict, and equality | *The Threshold of Democracy: Athens in 403 B.C.* *Patriots, Loyalists and Revolution in New York City, 1775–76* |
| World Languages | Revolutions in science, love, and politics | *Rousseau, Burke, and Revolution in France, 1791* |
| Women's and Gender Studies | Sex wars and other social revolutions | *Greenwich Village, 1913: Suffrage, Labor, and the New Woman* |
| History | Darwin's World | *Charles Darwin, the Copley Medal and the Rise of Naturalism, 1861–64* |

Self-Efficacy Survey, which measures students' confidence in their ability to successfully accomplish various tasks, both social (make new friends, work well with other students) and academic (do well on exams, participate in class discussions, write course papers). Fewer than 10% of the student body live on campus, so we removed six of the questions that seemed less relevant to students, for example, divide chores with others you live with and divide space in your residence. We replaced these with tasks important in Reacting courses, such as make speeches, engage in classroom debates, and argue a position effectively. The students rated their confidence that they could successfully complete each task on a 1–10 scale (not at all confident to extremely confident). For the post-test only, we also asked "What is the most important way in which you have changed as a result of this course?"

## RESULTS

At the end of the semester, students showed increased self-efficacy for the majority of the tasks. The greatest gains came from items specifically geared toward Reacting classes: making a speech in class (+1.65 increase), arguing your position effectively (+0.89), and understanding the perspective of someone you don't agree with (+0.75) (see Table 4.2). The other three Reacting tasks (identify important points in reading, engage in debates, and use evidence to support your point of view) also showed significant increases

**Table 4.2**  Pre-test/post-test comparisons for RTTP questions

| Question | Pre-test | | Post-test | | Mean difference | t (133) | |
|---|---|---|---|---|---|---|---|
| | M | SD | M | SD | | | |
| Make speech | 6.19 | 2.83 | 7.84 | 1.93 | 1.65 | 7.30 | *** |
| Argue position | 7.31 | 2.01 | 8.19 | 1.55 | 0.88 | 5.56 | *** |
| Understand different perspective | 7.63 | 1.99 | 8.38 | 1.41 | 0.75 | 4.75 | *** |
| Identify important points in reading | 7.40 | 1.79 | 8.10 | 1.45 | 0.70 | 4.71 | *** |
| Engage in debates | 7.35 | 2.32 | 8.00 | 1.91 | 0.65 | 3.78 | *** |
| Use evidence to support POV | 7.91 | 1.51 | 8.35 | 1.30 | 0.44 | 3.64 | *** |

*Note: n = 134; ***p < .001*

in self-efficacy. For the more general academic skills, students reported higher self-efficacy for five out of the seven tasks at the end of the semester (see Table 4.3). The tasks that did not show increases were related to perennial student concerns about workload (managing time effectively, keeping up with work). Students had low confidence in their time management skills from the beginning. It was the third lowest rated item in the pre-test, behind joining a student group and making a speech.

Students reported higher self-efficacy for the social items as well. Five of the seven items were significantly higher at the post-test (see Table 4.4). The two tasks that showed no improvement (ask a professor a question, get along well with others) were the two highest rated tasks in the pre-test, suggesting students already possessed substantial self-efficacy for these skills.

We added the scores for all 20 items to create a confidence scale for the pre-test and post-test (*range* = 20–200). We tested whether the number of Reacting games in a semester (single vs. multiple) or class standing (first-year students vs. sophomore or higher) had an effect on self-efficacy gains and found no significant effects. When we tested for sex differences with a 2 (sex: male vs. female) × 2 (test: pre-test vs. post-test) mixed ANOVA, however, we did find a significant interaction, $F(1, 131) = 7.02, p = .009$, partial $\eta^2 = .051$. Post-hoc Tukey HSD comparisons found that both female and male students reported feeling significantly more self-efficacy at the post-test than they did at the pre-test ($p < .01$) (see Fig. 4.1). At the beginning of the semester, female students felt less confident than male students ($p < .01$). By the end of the semester, however, women's confidence had grown to match the men's confidence.

**Table 4.3** Pre-test/post-test comparisons for the academic questions

| Question | Pre-test | | Post-test | | Mean difference | t (133) | |
|---|---|---|---|---|---|---|---|
| | M | SD | M | SD | | | |
| Research a paper | 7.49 | 1.82 | 8.15 | 1.69 | 0.66 | 4.32 | *** |
| Ask question in class | 7.22 | 2.52 | 7.87 | 1.99 | 0.65 | 3.49 | ** |
| Write papers | 7.72 | 1.77 | 8.32 | 1.56 | 0.60 | 3.90 | *** |
| Understand readings | 7.72 | 1.63 | 8.18 | 1.34 | 0.46 | 3.29 | ** |
| Do well on exams | 7.69 | 1.61 | 8.06 | 1.51 | 0.37 | 2.93 | ** |
| Manage time | 6.97 | 1.95 | 7.25 | 1.77 | 0.28 | 1.75 | |
| Keep up with work | 7.99 | 1.55 | 7.96 | 1.68 | −0.03 | 0.20 | |

*Note:* $n = 134$; ** $p < .01$; *** $p < .001$

**Table 4.4** Pre-test/post-test comparisons for social questions

| Question | Pre-test | | Post-test | | Mean difference | t (133) | |
|---|---|---|---|---|---|---|---|
| | M | SD | M | SD | | | |
| Make friends | 7.17 | 2.24 | 7.90 | 2.02 | 0.73 | 4.02 | *** |
| Join student group | 5.55 | 3.00 | 6.23 | 2.77 | 0.68 | 2.92 | ** |
| Work well in group | 7.86 | 1.94 | 8.47 | 1.61 | 0.61 | 3.18 | ** |
| Join class discussion | 7.34 | 2.32 | 7.94 | 1.93 | 0.60 | 3.63 | *** |
| Talk to staff | 7.67 | 2.07 | 8.19 | 1.84 | 0.52 | 3.14 | ** |
| Ask professor a question | 8.60 | 1.61 | 8.68 | 1.45 | 0.08 | 0.63 | |
| Get along with others | 8.96 | 1.18 | 8.97 | 1.19 | 0.01 | 0.07 | |

*Note:* $n = 134$; ** $p < .01$; *** $p < .001$

### Open-Ended Responses

The quantitative results provide strong evidence that students in Reacting courses experience significant changes in their academic self-efficacy, particularly in the skills related to Reacting games. The qualitative results reveal similar changes in response to the question: "What is the most important way in which you have changed as a result of this course? (This change could be a fact, concept, theory or skill that you have learned, but it could also be a change in attitude or belief.)"

In their open-ended reflections, students described improved confidence in a number of academic skills and in some cases improved confidence overall. One student in her qualitative remarks noted, "I gained a lot more self-confidence." As we know, such improvements in self-confidence

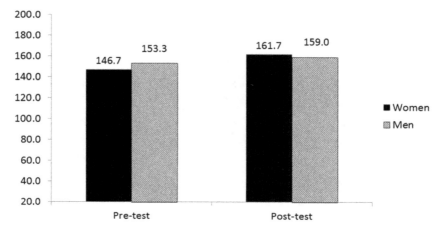

**Fig. 4.1**    Increases in confidence for women and men students

connect in diverse ways to college success and can lead to improvements in persistence and retention (Lotkowski et al. 2004). Yet, when considering the specific academic skills that students discuss, it is worth remembering that this study measured students' self-efficacy or confidence that they could successfully complete a task rather than measuring improvements in the skill itself. Although we do not have direct evidence of student outcomes for these skills, in certain areas like participating in a debate, improvements in confidence would logically transfer directly to improved ability. A confident debater is often a more persuasive debater.

Both in the results and in the review of students' open-ended feedback, improved confidence in public speaking saw the largest changes between the pre- and post-tests. Students' qualitative feedback connects public speaking with debating and in general the sense that they could make their own views an integral part of the class. In the words of one student, "The game really taught me how to speak up because my opinion and thoughts could make a positive change." Students in these Reacting courses see other students modeling effective and persuasive speaking and have many chances to practice this skill. Some students saw real improvements in their ability to participate in debates and make arguments. In the words of a male student in the study, "I know how to debate instead of just argue."

As students practiced public speaking and debating, they also gained confidence in their abilities to think critically about the primary source material, find the errors in their opponents' positions, and construct their own persuasive claims based on their character roles. Students' pre- and post-test results reveal strong improvements in their confidence in constructing arguments. In the quantitative data, this area, "arguing a position," saw the second strongest change after "making a speech." In their reflections on how they had changed, students expressed confidence about their ability to find their voice and make powerful claims. According to one woman, "This course helped me so much [in] speaking in front of a classroom of people and constructing an argument that is effective."

By requiring that students debate ideas in character, Reacting provides students the opportunity to construct and deliver arguments on issues that do not necessarily reflect their own beliefs. The quantitative data reveals strong change in the category "understanding a different perspective," which is also supported by written comments. One student noted that this game allowed him "to step into the shoes of others and really try to understand their positions." Another student reported that "the game has encouraged me to be able to hear other opinions other than my own, and to knowledgeably [counter] with my views." Students described the games as helping them develop skills and attributes that would lead them to listen carefully to others, even others with whom they disagree. In the words of one student, "I learned how to listen to everyone's point of view," or another, "I am more open to different perspectives."

In order to present these ideas effectively and persuasively, students needed to read primary sources carefully and closely. As a result, it makes sense that "identifying points in readings" and "researching a paper" ended up among the top five skills that saw the most improvement in confidence. The results offer additional evidence that for at least some students, Reacting provides a spur to intense engagement in course materials. One student reported that she "used to just do the minimum amount of work or research to get a good grade in class, but I found I couldn't do that in this class, and so I have learned to really research and immerse myself in the learning process." Students reported an increased sense of interest and enthusiasm about learning course materials.

In the right context, passion about history can be infectious and the close work with classmates required in Reacting builds a sense of the importance of historical subjects and the stakes in classroom debates. As students strategized together to achieve shared aims, they practiced teamwork skills that helped them achieve game objectives. The complex skills related to group work might include listening carefully, explaining clearly, interpreting non-verbal communication, reflecting on group progress, encouraging fellow students, or sensing the feelings or ideas of fellow group members. These skills are not explicitly measured by the Barry/ Finney self-efficacy scale. At the same time, our data showed statistically significant improvements overall in confidence related to working in teams. Students described improvements in their confidence about "working in a group" or "making friends." Students already rated themselves very high on the confidence scale for "getting along with others." As a result, this area both began and ended as one of the highest in the whole study.

One of our more striking findings is the significant increase in women's confidence, in particular. Their self-efficacy scores rose more than twice as much as men's scores on the quantitative measures. Given the truly open-ended nature of our question about how students believed the course changed them, it is especially interesting how frequently women explicitly refer to increased confidence, as students—particularly in relation to public speaking, researching, and writing—but also more generally. For example, one woman claimed, "I gained confidence with public speaking and working with others that will help me in my life." Perhaps because several of the games focus on aspects of democracy, many women connected increased confidence with a new sense of political engagement and responsibility. Another woman who noted "The game made me realize how important it is to vote, I felt proud that I could vote. It made me think a lot harder w/politics" concluded her comments with "I now gained a lot more self-confidence." One woman mentioned learning "to stand up for what I believe to be true"; another claimed, "I have become more outspoken and bold."

Other remarks from women that reflect confidence outside the classroom include: "The game really taught me how to speak up because my opinion and thoughts could make a positive change in some way"; "I have become more of an activist and aware of my community"; and "I am also more aware of what is going on in our current society, and have more inclination and drive to stand up for what is right." The levels of enthusiasm that these qualitative remarks reveal—"the game...taught me how to speak up;" "I have become an activist;" "I ... have more inclination and drive to stand up for what is right"—suggest a high level of engagement with the course that for these students transferred to community and political engagement more broadly.

## DISCUSSION

Our students gained substantial confidence in their academic abilities during the semester, particularly for skills important to Reacting courses. While the quantitative results can only provide a measure of how much their self-efficacy improved over time, the qualitative data make clear that students are crediting their experiences in Reacting games for their increased confidence. While both men and women demonstrated gains, the effect was especially strong for women. While the temptation to say Reacting is responsible for all these benefits is strong, we must exercise caution in our conclusions. We only assessed students in Reacting courses, and our study did not include a non-Reacting course comparison. We also have no direct measures of student outcomes. While students clearly felt more confident about their public speaking and ability to defend a position, this study does not demonstrate that they actually gave better speeches or crafted better arguments. Still, the literature on academic self-efficacy and its link to student persistence and success suggests that increased self-efficacy is valuable in its own right. Students with high academic self-efficacy set higher goals for themselves, put more time and effort into difficult tasks, show more flexibility in their problem-solving strategies, and perform better than students of equal ability with low academic self-efficacy (Chemers et al. 2001; Vuong et al. 2010).

A small number of students in our study were students in their first year of college. At the same time, as the research has demonstrated the importance of self-efficacy for first-year students, our study provides promising evidence for the potential uses of curriculum like Reacting for first-year experiences (Bandura 1986; Chemers et al. 2001; Vuong et al. 2010). As research has demonstrated, success in the first year of college is crucial to degree completion. Significantly, a successful first *semester* of college strongly predicts eventual graduation. (D'Lima et al. 2014). Thus, incorporating Reacting pedagogy may strengthen students' ability to persist as they transition to the university environment.

Carnes (2014) discussed the sometimes problematic relationship between self-esteem and student success. Having been praised and protected from failure from a young age, today's college students as a group have high self-esteem but also a tremendous amount of anxiety and doubt. Criticism or failure can cause overwhelming stress and despair. While higher self-esteem is not a desirable outcome when based on empty praise, higher self-esteem as a result of higher self-efficacy most definitely is. As students' self-efficacy rises, their self-esteem may also rise. A parallel increase might easily occur when students value the skills in which they are gaining confidence and competence—here, the increase in self-esteem would be based on actual skill development and performance (Pajares and Schunk 2001). Thus, as Carnes (2014) argued, the risk-taking of Reacting classrooms can be an antidote to one of the unintended consequences of the self-esteem movement: undercutting students' resilience through over-praise and learning environments that do not reward actual achievement or allow failure.

As we have argued, the most dramatic results of our research are the increases in self-efficacy for women. This is important for a number of reasons. First, our study documents intriguing evidence that women and men respond differently to Reacting, a finding that previous assessments did not fully address. The most comprehensive study to date of Reacting did not test for sex differences, or even report the number of women and men in their studies (Stroessner et al. 2009). The majority of their sample came from all-female institutions, so perhaps these institutions did not include enough men to make valid comparisons. Second, self-efficacy has a stronger relationship to academic achievement for women than for men (D'Lima et al. 2014), so finding methods to eliminate the gender gap in self-efficacy is of particular significance to our students' success.

These findings suggest Reacting has the potential to significantly strengthen students' self-efficacy outside the classroom, particularly for women, based on their open-ended responses. Given the relatively low ratio of women represented in US public life (19.4%) (CAWP 2015), this study offers hope that the confidence-building skills in Reacting courses can help women see themselves as agents of change in the public sphere. The students' written responses speak to the empowerment goals of feminist pedagogy inside and beyond the classroom and suggest both that Women's and Gender Studies courses might look to Reacting courses to meet these goals and that Reacting can particularly be effective for increasing confidence of female students in any course.

Reacting classrooms encourage hooks' feminist pedagogical vision of playful intellectual risk-taking that unsettles assumptions about class, race, gender, and sexuality differences (hooks 1989), as the students' character identities often become as meaningful in their relationships to one another as their "real life" identities. (Tellingly, students often continue to use their character names for one another, playfully, long after the semester is over.) This helps students see identities as socially constructed and inspiringly malleable. In so doing, Reacting entwines the goals of longstanding feminist pedagogy, as well as a growth-mindset (Dweck 2006) that conceives of the self as a site of potentiality.

Reacting may be particularly suited to fostering a growth mindset. A growth mindset involves embracing risks and challenges, which are always a part of Reacting. If students understand challenges as important to stretching and improving themselves, they can embrace the unexpected and unusual learning opportunities of Reacting courses without worrying that the occasional failure (which is part of any game) will chip away at their self-esteem or self-worth. In their comprehensive assessment of Reacting, Stroessner et al. (2009) found that in contrast to students in control groups, students who completed Reacting courses reported higher self-esteem and substantiated the idea that traits were malleable.

The students' responses about the impact of this increased self-confidence, including specific ideas about using Reacting skills outside of the classroom, further build on feminist approaches to meaning-making that focus on moving from theory (or ideas) to action. So, for example, confidence in speech-making in the classroom, according to our students, often inspires them to have a stronger voice in the public sphere. This is a feminist pedagogical goal that is, of course, important to all students' sense of agency, not just women's.

These findings suggest Reacting to the Past pedagogy provides students—particularly women—opportunities for significant growth in self-confidence and self-efficacy over the course of a single semester. This research could usefully enrich current findings on self-efficacy and college performance, particularly if considered in light of D'Lima et al.'s (2014) finding that self-efficacy is more predictive for college performance for female students than for male students. At a time when many institutions—particularly public universities—are facing shrinking resources and in some cases shrinking pools of students, the stakes are high in conversations about student retention and success since state legislatures expect proof of the "value" of education (Fish 2010; Sinclair 2012). The rising student debt crisis, too, has led students to become concerned about the payoff of courses like the Reacting classrooms studied here. In the popular press, the liberal arts face particular scrutiny in an anxious economic climate that has fostered public critiques about whether an "investment" in a liberal arts education is a wise one. Those who teach in the liberal arts have seen how the skills and insights students gain can help them lead meaningful lives and become critical thinkers and engaged public citizens. Students in this study reported that they experienced these benefits from Reacting courses. This research provides evidence that the specific pedagogical approach studied here—Reacting to the Past—has a measurable impact on students' self-efficacy, with positive implications for students' college careers and beyond.

## REFERENCES

Bandura, A. (1986). *Social foundations of thought and action: A social cognitive theory.* Englewood Cliffs: Prentice Hall.

Barry, C. L., & Finney, S. J. (2009). Can we feel confident in how we measure college confidence? A psychometric investigation of the college self-efficacy inventory. *Measurement & Evaluation in Counseling & Development, 42,* 197–222. doi:10.1177/0748175609344095

Carnes, M. C. (2014). *Minds on fire: How role-immersion games transform college.* Cambridge, MA: Harvard University Press.

CAWP. (2015). *Women in US congress 2015.* Retrieved from http://www.cawp.rutgers.edu/women-us-congress-2015

Chemers, M. M., Hu, L., & Garcia, B. (2001). Academic self-efficacy and first-year college student performance and adjustment. *Journal of Educational Psychology, 93,* 55–64. doi:10.1037/0022-0663.93.1.55

Chow, E., Fleck, C., Fan, G., Joseph, J., & Lyter, D. (2003). Exploring critical feminist pedagogy: Infusing dialogue, participation, and experience in teaching and learning. *Teaching Sociology, 31,* 259–275.

D'Lima, G. M., Winsler, A., & Kitsantas, A. (2014). Ethnic and gender differences in first-year college students' goal orientation, self-efficacy, and extrinsic and intrinsic motivation. *Journal of Educational Research, 107*(5), 341–356. doi:10.1080/00220671.2013.823366

Dweck, C. S. (2006). *Mindset: The new psychology of success.* New York: Random House.

Fish, S. (2010). *The crisis of the humanities officially arrives.* Retrieved from http://opinionator.blogs.nytimes.com/2010/10/11/the-crisis-of-the-humanities-officially-arrives/

Freire, P. (1970/2007). *Pedagogy of the oppressed.* New York: Continuum.

hooks, b. (1989). *Talking back: Thinking feminist, thinking black.* Boston: South Bend Press.

Kuh, G. D. (2008). *High-impact educational practices: A brief overview.* Retrieved from https://www.aacu.org/leap/hips

Lotkowski, V. A., Robbins, S. B., & Noeth, R. J. (2004). *The role of academic and non-academic factors in improving college retention.* Iowa City: ACT.

Pajares, E., & Schunk, H. D. (2001). Self-beliefs and school success: Self-efficacy, self-concepts, and school achievement. In R. Riding & S. Rayner (Eds),

*Perception* (pp. 239–266). London: Ablex. Retrieved from http://www.uky.edu/~eushe2/Pajares/PajaresSchunk2001.html

Shrewsbury, C. M. (1993). What is feminist pedagogy? *Women's Studies Quarterly, 21*(3/4), 8–16.

Sinclair, S. (2012). *Confronting the criticisms: A Survey of attacks on the humanities.* Retrieved from http://4humanities.org/2012/10/confronting-the-criticisms/

Stroessner, S. J., Beckerman, L. S., & Whittaker, A. (2009). All the world's a stage? Consequences of a role-playing pedagogy on psychological factors and writing and rhetorical skill in college undergraduates. *Journal of Educational Psychology, 101*, 605–620. doi:10.1037/a0015055

Turner, P., & Thompson, E. (2014). College retention initiatives meeting the needs of millennial freshman students. *College Student Journal, 48*, 94–104.

Vuong, M., Brown-Welty, S., & Tracz, S. (2010). The effects of self-efficacy on academic success of first-generation sophomore students. *Journal of College Student Development, 51*, 50–64. doi:10.1353/csd.0.0109

Weiler, K. (1991). Freire and a feminist pedagogy of difference. *Harvard Educational Review, 61*, 449–475.

Zajacova, A., Lynch, M. S., & Espenshade, J. T. (2005). Self-efficacy, stress, and academic success in college. *Research in Higher Education, 46*, 677–706. doi:10.1007/s11162-004-4139-z

# CHAPTER 5

# Scaling a Reacting Game for Use at a Large Public University

*Keri Watson and Patsy D. Moskal*

What is the best way to teach today's students the history of art? How can art historians leverage new pedagogies and technologies to reach twenty-first-century students? Research conducted over the past 30 years has shown that it is impossible for students to absorb and process all the information presented during a typical one-hour lecture, and as colleges and universities continue to expand, an increasingly large number of students are less adept at navigating the traditional classroom (Freeman 2014). In an effort to embrace more effective methods of knowledge transfer, in fall 2015, an upper-level art history course at the University of Central Florida (UCF) was redesigned to incorporate a Reacting to the Past (RTTP) game. The game, *Modernism vs. Traditionalism: Art in Paris, 1888–89,* was played over the course of four weeks and culminated in a restaging of the 1889 Universal Exhibition in the UCF Art Gallery (McKay et al. 2014). Although past research has been conducted on the use of Reacting games in first-year seminars at small liberal arts colleges (Stroessner et al. 2009), little scholarship has addressed the applicability of this pedagogy to the teaching of art history or its use at large public universities and in larger courses. This chapter provides information to help fill this lacuna by discussing the deployment of an RTTP game in ARH 4430: Nineteenth-Century Art, an

K. Watson (✉) • P.D. Moskal
University of Central Florida, Orlando, FL, USA

C.E. Watson, T.C. Hagood (eds.), *Playing to Learn with Reacting to the Past*, DOI 10.1007/978-3-319-61747-3_5

upper-level course offered by the School of Visual Arts & Design at UCF, and by relating its use to best practices in undergraduate education.

UCF is among the largest universities in the United States with an enrollment of over 63,000 students, and it is quickly approaching Hispanic Serving Institution (HSI) status. Many of UCF's courses are technology enhanced, with fully online, blended, and lecture capture courses comprising a significant amount of the offerings. In 2015–16, 40% of the total university student credit hours were in online instruction and 79% of all students (81% of undergraduates) took at least one online (web, blended, or lecture capture) course. UCF students are comfortable with technology and familiar with the utilization of creative instructional resources and techniques that are frequently used in their courses.

Within UCF, the School of Visual Arts & Design has the largest enrollment in the College of Arts and Humanities with 2,674 students. For approximately 250 of these students, primarily art history majors and minors, ARH 4430 is a required course. However, many art, film, and digital media students take ARH 4430 as an elective. The class is designed to offer an overview of art in the nineteenth century, to introduce students to the major artists of the period, to raise questions about the sources and authority of art history, and to familiarize students with key terms and methods employed by art historians. The chosen topics are discussed from a variety of perspectives, including style, artists' techniques and materials, potential interpretations, and socio-historical contexts.

Art history courses at UCF have an enrollment of 50–500 students, with the average class size being approximately 100 students. Most upper-level core requirements, such as ARH 4430, are capped at 60 students. Lecturing is the dominant method used to teach these classes, and most art history professors rely on projections of digitized images of major works of art. The professor lectures about the artwork, its style, artist, and historical period, covering approximately 15–20 major works of art in an hour and 15-minute lecture. Exams often are a mixture of slide identifications, during which an image is projected for a few minutes while students write down the memorized artist, title, and date, and essay questions that ask students to compare and contrast two works of art, or discuss the ways in which a single artwork is emblematic of a historical or stylistic period, although for large classes some faculty employ multiple choice tests as well. In all cases, a successful student is one who takes good and detailed notes and memorizes the course material. Three tests over the course of the semester and possibly a term paper are the methods of assessment one can usually expect.

This model of teaching and learning has proven to be effective for motivated students, particularly those who excel in memorization, but it is usually not as successful with studio art majors and others from outside the discipline. Students at UCF have become accustomed to the lecture nature of instruction that is typical of art history courses at the university, and the use of a Reacting game was dramatically different from what they had experienced in the past. Moreover, relatively few games have been developed for art history, but as Klopfer (2008) points out, "Through game playing, students learn how to collaborate, solve problems, collect and analyze data, test hypotheses, and engage in debate." Reacting to the Past serves as an example of the potential impact of intentionally designed classroom games on student engagement. This study focuses on the issues and challenges faced by both faculty and students when scaling a RTTP game to large classes; the impact of the game on student learning; and, how students responded to the more active interaction demanded by the game.

## METHOD

The RTTP game, *Modernism vs. Traditionalism: Art in Paris, 1888–89*, (McKay et al. 2014) was integrated as part of the course instruction. ARH 4430 had only one section offered in the fall 2015 semester with 57 enrolled students. UCF utilizes Instructure Canvas, branded Webcourses, for the course learning management system (LMS), which allowed for easy download and examination of student learning outcomes for the graded game elements, final exam score, and overall course grade. Upon course completion, gradebook data was downloaded and de-identified for analyses.

Several surveys were used to evaluate student reactions to their engagement with the game. The student perception of instruction (SPI) form is administered by the university each semester in every course taught at UCF. This form (see Appendix) has nine Likert and two open-ended items requesting student feedback on what they liked best about the course and their suggestions for improving the course and how it was taught. These ratings can provide a good indication of student reactions to implemented instructional changes. The surveys are administered electronically to students via the campus portal, accessed via authenticated login, de-identified and aggregated with the class as a whole. Faculty and departments receive the summarized results of the surveys for each class at the completion of each semester.

In addition to this automated survey, student surveys specific to the game were developed and administered at the beginning and the end of the course. These anonymous pre- and post-game surveys, designed to capture student reactions and gather feedback specific to the RTTP game and its integration into the course, provided data on student expectations prior to participation in the game and also their reactions to their experiences with the game at course completion. Chi-square contingency analysis was used to compare results to five questions which were common in pre- and post-iterations. Open comments in these student surveys provided rich data on student perceptions, including identifying issues that might be addressed in future iterations of the game.

Other valuable sources of information, both qualitative and quantitative, were offered through assignments required as part of the game-play by students including a reflective paper and data on course assignments. The reflective paper offered insight into students' perceptions and interaction with the game and its incorporation into their art history experience. In addition to game-play, students' performance in the course was measured by quizzes and a final exam. Comparing the scores on the quiz and exam taken after game-play to the pre-game-play scores also provided information regarding the game's impact on student learning, student success (A, B, or C grade), and withdrawals in this course compared with recent course iterations without an RTTP component. While there are differences across the various faculty and students through different semester course iterations, monitoring overall student success and withdrawal is valuable. Incorporating major changes to instruction motivated the researchers to attempt to document a complete look at the implications of these changes on our students, including possibly impacting those who withdrew or did not succeed.

Finally, valuable information is provided by the faculty perspective. While the game had been taught by this instructor on a smaller scale at a liberal arts college, it required significant planning and modification in order to implement the game in a large class setting. Documenting the process of scaling an RTTP game to a large course provides valuable information for others who might be considering this method of instruction at large public universities or in a large class environment.

## Procedures

In the fall 2015, ARH 4430: Nineteenth-century Art, met for 1 hour and 15 minutes twice a week. The course material was presented in five modules: Neoclassicism; Romanticism; Realism; Impressionism and Neo-Impressionism; and the Fin de Siecle (Symbolism and Art Nouveau). Each module was covered over a three- to four-week period followed by a quiz. The course concluded with a cumulative final exam. Modules one, two, three, and five were presented via traditional lecture and assigned textbook readings. For the fourth module, Impressionism and Neo-Impressionism, the material was taught through the immersion of the class into the Reacting to the Past game, *Modernism vs. Traditionalism: Art in Paris, 1888–89*.

In the original game, *Modernism vs. Traditionalism: Art in Paris, 1888–89*, students play the role of artists, critics, and dealers in late-nineteenth-century Paris. The game begins at the Salon of 1888 and culminates in a restaging of the 1889 Exposition Universelle de Paris. Existing RTTP game materials include an instructor's manual, pedagogy manual (Carnes 2005), student game book, and a PowerPoint presentation. The instructor's manual provides historical background, suggestions for class exercises, and role sheets for 35 characters. Twenty-eight of these roles are designed to be played by students enrolled in the course and include academic and avant-garde artists, art dealers, and critics; the other seven demi-roles are for faculty or other students not in the class who play the role of secret buyers at the 1889 World Fair. Role sheets include biographical information and instruct students on their character's objectives. The student game book includes an introductory vignette and provides historical background, a glossary of terms, a game schedule, a list of the roles in the game, translated excerpts of contemporary art criticism, and a bibliography of primary and secondary sources. The accompanying PowerPoint presentation includes a selection of images indicative of the work shown at the 1888 Paris Salon.

The original game includes roles for 21 artists, 2 dealers, 5 critics, and 9 buyers (see Table 5.1). However, to be used in the current class of 57 students, the game needed to be altered and expanded so that each student could participate in the game. One adjustment was that the buyers were played by students enrolled in the class rather than by guests recruited from outside the course's enrollment. These roles had to be expanded and provided with objectives. Another adjustment was the addition of roles. The

**Table 5.1**    Role distribution in game—New characters in **Bold**

| Traditional artists | Modern artists | Critics | Dealers | Demi-roles (buyers—Played by students in class) |
|---|---|---|---|---|
| Bouguereau | Monet | Aurier | Petit | William Waldorf Astor |
| Meissonier | Renoir | Péladan | Durand-Ruel | Richard Wallace |
| Gérôme | Degas | Fénéon | | Henry LeRolle |
| Puvis de Chavannes | Cézanne | Huysmans | | Henry Tate |
| Moreau | Van Gogh | Michel | | Philip Lehman |
| **Bonnat** | Seurat | **Dujardin** | | William T. Walters |
| **Cazin** | Gauguin | | | Sir Frederic Leighton |
| **Detaille** | Breton | | | Roger Marx—Governmental buyer |
| **Knight** | Cassatt | | | Pierre Muston—Museum official |
| | Sargent | | | **Louisine Havemeyer** |
| | Signac | | | **Gustave Caillebotte** |
| | Pissarro | | | **Henri Rouart** |
| | Morisot | | | **Henry Clay Frick** |
| | Redon | | | **J. P. Morgan** |
| | Toulouse-Lautrec | | | **Isabella Stewart Gardner** |
| | Whistler | | | |
| | **Forbes** | | | |
| | **Dupré** | | | |
| | **Gay** | | | |
| | **Bernard** | | | |
| | **M. Bracquemond** | | | |
| | **F. Bracquemond** | | | |
| | **Forain** | | | |

faculty member created additional characters depending on availability of historical information and overall balance of role types. The additional characters that were added are highlighted in bold in Table 5.1, and include 13 artists, 1 critic, and 6 buyers. The new game, scaled for a larger class enrollment, features 34 artists, 2 dealers, 6 critics, and 15 buyers—all of whom were students in the class.

Prior to the start of the game, the game's mechanics, schedule of play, and grading scheme were explained to students. This material was available to students on Webcourses for their reference throughout game-play. A course Pinterest page was created so that the various characters could upload images of artwork. The students' homework was to study their characters and review the historical material available in their textbooks and on Webcourses. On the first day of game-play, the students introduced themselves to the class while in character. These were brief introductions (three to five minutes) during which the characters said a little bit about themselves, for instance where they were from, their role in the art world, and what type of art they preferred. The second day the classroom was transformed into the Salon of 1888 and students playing members of the French Academy of Painters and Sculptors led the class, presented awards, and gave speeches on the future of art. Characters, such as William-Adolphe Bouguereau, Jean-Louis-Ernest Meissonier, Jules Breton, Jean-Léon Gérôme, and Leon Bonnat used their speeches to attempt to persuade the class on the value of Academic painting and the worthiness of their personal aesthetic. Written versions of speeches were posted on Webcourses for reference throughout the game. The future of art was debated during the next class period. Artists such as Claude Monet, Mary Cassatt, Edgar Degas, Vincent Van Gogh, and Paul Gauguin, who supported newer styles of art and condemned the Academy as outdated, gave speeches and presented their work.

During this class period, it was announced that a seat had opened in the Academy and elections were held to fill the vacant seat. The role sheets for Gustave Moreau, Auguste Renoir, John Singer Sargent, James McNeill Whistler, Pierre Puvis de Chavannes, Jean Charles Cazin, Édouard Detaille, and Julien Dupré instructed students who portrayed these characters to vie for the newly available seat. Speeches were given and members of the Academy voted. After the induction of the new member, the Academy met to decide how to organize the Salon of 1889. The following class period was led by students playing art critics Albert Aurier, André Michel, Joséphin Péladan, Joris-Karl Huysmans, Félix Fénéon, and Jean Dujardin, as well as students playing art dealers Georges Petit, and Paul Durand-Ruel, who gave speeches endorsing artists and expounding on their views of art. The critics awarded "critic tickets," which guaranteed sales for those artists who received them. During the next class period, buyers gave speeches in which they introduced themselves and discussed the type of work they like or might like to buy. The next class period was reserved as a planning day. Members of the Academy had to decide who to include in the official Salon of 1889, dealers Petit and Durand-Ruel had to solicit artists for their booths at the Exposition Universelle of 1889, and others had to plan whether they

**Fig. 5.1**    French theme restaging of 1889 exposition Universelle de Paris

would band together for group shows, set up alternate exhibitions, show their work alone, or boycott the Fair. Students also had to determine how they would exhibit their work, advertise their shows, and lure buyers to the World Fair.

The game culminated with the 1889 Exposition Universelle de Paris. This occurred in the UCF Art Gallery. To help transform the gallery, a model of the Eiffel Tower was erected, Thomas Edison's film of the Fair projected, music by Claude Debussy played, and French pastries served (see Fig. 5.1). Faculty and staff were recruited to come as contemporary celebrities, including Oscar Wilde, Buffalo Bill, Rosa Bonheur, and Annie Oakley. Others were invited to attend by posters hung around campus and through social media advertising; tickets were distributed to attendees (see Fig. 5.2). The Academy projected the paintings included in their Salon via an LCD projector and large screen in the main gallery (see Fig. 5.3). The dealers were set up in alcoves with laptops to show their artists' images. Independent artists were allowed to show their work on iPads, tablets, or laptops (see Fig. 5.4). The students' presentations of their character's work and their ability to persuade visitors to buy their art determined the winners

**Fig. 5.2**  Tickets to the 1889 Exposition Universelle de Paris

of the game. Points were awarded for being elected to the Academy, for critic tickets, and for sales. There were several winners: the artist who sold the most work; the critic who endorsed the artist who sold the most work; the dealer who made the most sales; and, the buyers who bought work by the winning artist. These winners each received three bonus points.

The day following the restaging of the World Fair was reserved for what Carnes (2014) terms the "post mortem." During this class period, winners were announced and presented with certificates. A brief lecture on the actual circumstances of the 1889 Paris World Fair and fate of some of the artists was delivered. Students were then asked to share their thoughts and reflections on the game as a whole in a class discussion.

Students were assessed on the quality and persuasiveness of their speeches, the clarity, accuracy, and elegance of their written products, their performance at the Paris World Fair, and their overall participation in the game. The game was worth 30 points, which translated to 30% of the students' final grade. The following elements of the game were assessed: introduction in character (two- to three-minute speech worth three points); persuasive speech delivered in character (five-minute speech worth five

**Fig. 5.3**   Projection of Thomas Edison's film of the Fair displayed in the UCF Art Gallery during restaging of 1889 Exposition Universelle de Paris

points); persuasive paper posted to the course blog (approximately 500–750 words, five points); participating in the game and demonstrating historical understanding and embodiment of character (demonstrated through in-class discussions, tweets, blogging, and creation of didactic and promotional materials and worth seven points); and, a reflective essay (750–1000 words worth ten points). The reflective essay asked students to answer the following questions: how well did your character meet his/her objectives; what did you do in the game to try to meet these objectives; what research did you do to help you understand your character and the historical time period; what would you do differently if you had the chance to play the game again; and, was the game an interesting and effective way to learn about nineteenth-century French art? There also was a quiz after the game (Quiz Four: 10%) and a cumulative final exam that included material addressed in the game (Final Exam: 20%).

**Fig. 5.4**   Student artists displaying their art (via slideshow) to attendees and potential buyers

## Results

From the faculty perspective, the scaling and use of the RTTP game in a large upper-level art history course was successful. Class assessments, student surveys, student reflections and instructor observation indicated a positive learning experience for students. And, generally, students and the faculty were positive regarding the use of the game within the course. Presented here are specific findings as well as instructor recommendations and observations in the course.

### *Student Performance: Quiz and Test Scores*

Fifty-six students were enrolled in ARH 4430, with 68% of the course being female. The majority of students (70%) were seniors, with 27% juniors, and 4% sophomores. Table 5.2 presents results of the quizzes that students had to complete throughout the course. Quiz Four tested students on aspects learned through the game itself. The students' performance on this quiz was

**Table 5.2**   Quiz and final exam scores ($n = 56$)

|  | Mean score (%) | Std dev | High score (%) | Low score (%) |
|---|---|---|---|---|
| Quiz 1 | 88 | 9.30 | 100 | 65 |
| Quiz 2 | 79 | 20.13 | 100 | 0 |
| Quiz 3 | 83 | 22.51 | 105 | 0 |
| Quiz 4 | 80 | 15.33 | 100 | 45 |
| Final exam | 98 | 4.26 | 100 | 80 |

comparable to the other quiz averages. Quiz scores were also similar to past semesters. The final exam scores, however, demonstrated a slight increase over prior semesters, suggesting the pedagogy may help improve long-term comprehension of material.

Past iterations of this course, without RTTP, had success rates (C or better grade) ranging from 75 to 96%, depending on the semester, and withdrawal rates from 0 to 9%. With the RTTP game, the course resulted in 97% of students succeeding with at least a C grade and only 2% (or one student) withdrawing from the course. This is certainly on the high end of typical student performance in recent semester offerings of ARH 4430. This course is typically taught in lecture format. Given the first semester of a major instructional change, the researchers were pleased with the students' success as a result of the game implementation.

### Pre- and Post-game Surveys

Pre- and post-game survey results (see Table 5.3) suggest that the majority of students were positive about playing games (72% pre-game; 67% post-game) both before and after the game. Interestingly, a higher percentage of students indicated they enjoyed acting/role playing (38% pre-game; 58% post-game). The percentage of students who were positive about the game's ability to improve their understanding of course content increased (61% pre; 71% post), as did the percentage of those who were negative (15% pre; 25% post). Finally, there was a slight increase in students who believed that working in a group was a valuable skill, although most of the students saw this as important prior to participating in RTTP. Student surveys were anonymous which precluded matching responses to compare changes in attitudes from pre-game to post-game. Chi-square analysis was used to examine the variation of pre- and post-group survey responses on the five

**Table 5.3**   Pre ($N = 39$) and post ($N = 24$) survey results by percent

| Question | Student response | | | | | $\chi2$ | p |
|---|---|---|---|---|---|---|---|
| | Strongly agree | Agree | Neither | Disagree | Strongly disagree | | |
| Enjoy playing games | | | | | | | |
| Pre | 31 | 41 | 13 | 13 | 3 | 1.10 | .89 |
| Post | 29 | 38 | 13 | 13 | 8 | | |
| Enjoy role playing | | | | | | | |
| Pre | 10 | 28 | 23 | 13 | 26 | 5.82 | .21 |
| Post | 33 | 25 | 17 | 4 | 21 | | |
| Role playing will/did increase understanding of nineteenth-century art | | | | | | | |
| Pre | 10 | 51 | 23 | 5 | 10 | 4.19 | .38 |
| Post | 29 | 42 | 4 | 17 | 8 | | |
| Enjoy working in group | | | | | | | |
| Pre | 3 | 21 | 33 | 26 | 18 | 9.93* | .04 |
| Post | 4 | 54 | 13 | 25 | 4 | | |
| Ability to work with others is a valuable skill | | | | | | | |
| Pre | 49 | 49 | 3 | | | .73 | .70 |
| Post | 54 | 46 | | | | | |

*$p < .05$; percentages rounded

common questions. Although the post-game attitudes were generally more positive for students, results indicated that the only significant relationship in attitude change from pre- to post-game was in those who enjoyed working in groups at the end of the game (58%) compared to those who were positive about group work prior to participating in the RTTP game (24%).

Additionally, student attitudes regarding participating in the RTTP game were captured at the end of the course through more specific questions regarding the game and the students' interaction with it. Twenty-four students completed the post-game survey for a response rate of 42%. Sixty-eight percent of students felt that participating in the game reinforced their understanding of the course content contained in the lectures, modules, and textbook. Half of those responding indicated they preferred the game-based format compared to traditional content delivery. Another 21% had no preference. Still, 13% of the respondents were very negative and strongly disagreed to using the game over traditional course delivery. When asked how the game impacted their learning, 63% indicated that they learned more about, 62% felt they had gained a better appreciation of, and 71% felt they had a better understanding of the complexities of classifying nineteenth-century art than through traditional lectures and exams. In terms of interaction, 67% of respondents thought the game fostered cooperation among students and 75% indicated that the game fostered competition among students. Overall, students recognized positive aspects of the game and the majority appreciated its use in instruction. However, there were students who were not as comfortable with the use of the RTTP game for instruction as the traditional lecture format with which they were more familiar.

### *Student Perception of Instruction*

The University of Central Florida utilizes a standardized, five-point Likert style (Excellent to Poor) Student Perception of Instruction (SPI) form to gather student data and evaluate course and teaching effectiveness. The SPI is automatically administered to students through the online portal during a two-week period near the end of each semester. Each time students log in to Webcourses during this period, they see requests to complete the SPI for each course in which they are enrolled. These requests stop once students have completed the SPI, or upon completion of the SPI time window. This was the first iteration of the course utilizing a RTTP game and the first semester the course was taught by this instructor. Overall, 33 students provided feedback (57% response rate). Generally, student ratings were slightly lower this semester than in the past two iterations of the course (see Table 5.4) but were comparable to the department average of 4.13 and university average of 4.12. Forty-eight percent of students rated the overall effectiveness of the instructor as excellent, with 24% very good and 18% good.

**Table 5.4** Mean for students' overall ratings of instruction for ARH 4430

| Semester | N | Mean |
| --- | --- | --- |
| Spring 2014 | 29 | 4.59 |
| Fall 2014 | 36 | 4.28 |
| Fall 2015 | 33 | 4.09 |

In addition to Likert response, 20 students provided open-ended comments regarding the course, responding to the questions: what did you like best about the course and/or how the instructor taught it? And, what suggestions do you have for improving the course and/or how the instructor taught it? Of the 20 students who responded, 19 mentioned the game specifically in their responses. Many comments were positive. Students responded "I loved this class. The lectures were a little boring in the beginning but when we went to the role playing game I was very interested and learned a lot about my artist and the time period." Another student said,

> I love this class, because we get to interact a lot and I believe that is a great way to learn. The lectures are brilliant and also our projects. The best part is that we did a role play for The Salon of 1888 & 1889. This was a great experience and I got to learn better this way.

Other student responses included: "The RTTP role game was quite fun and such a different learning experience in comparison to the traditional lecture;" "I enjoyed the lecture aspect of the class, but it was the game that really made this class stand out. I learned the most from the game, and I wish other classes would use this tool for learning;" and "The lectures did not help me learn as much as the game, so perhaps if more games were incorporated into the class it would help the students learn more." Two students replied that they did not like the game. One wrote, "I wasn't a big fan of RTTP, I wasn't able to grasp the expected concepts as well as I would have wanted to" and one simply requested "fewer games." Still others provided suggestions for improving the game such as, "For RTTP I think some students had to do way more work (for e.g., as a member of the Academy) than others. As a buyer, my interaction was somewhat limited due to my character's limited influence;" "better expectations dialogue for the RPPG [sic], many were lost with what was happening through the course of the game;" and "Put the RTTP game more towards the end of the semester to allow more time for course material to be lectured."

Although the response rate was only 57%, the SPIs provided a reliable gauge of student interest in the game. The comment regarding the level of engagement depending on the role was particularly helpful, as the buyer roles need to be more fully developed for future iterations.

## *Reflective Essays*

As part of the course assignments related to the RTTP game, students were required to write reflective essays in which they were asked to evaluate how well their character met their objectives, what strategies they employed, what resources they used to conduct their research, what they would do differently if they could play again, and how the game enhanced their understanding of late nineteenth-century French art. All but one student wrote the reflective essay (98% response rate). While qualitative, this rich data provided insights as to why some students liked the game and why it did not resonate with others.

Student responses in the essays were overwhelmingly positive. Comments included: "I would love to participate in some other kind of game like this in the future. This game really made learning about 19th century French art really fun;" and "I felt this particular Reacting to the Past game helped me understand the complex relationships between artists, dealers, critics, and buyers during late 19th century France;" and "I was immersed in the experience and learned a great deal." Some students admitted they were skeptical at first, but came to appreciate the game. One student wrote:

> I was admittedly nervous about how seriously everyone, including myself, would take the game, and how successful we would be in unraveling the desires and motivations of late nineteenth-century artists. As everyone got into the rhythm of the game, I was pleasantly surprised at how much fun I was having, and how well we all seemed to understand the goals of the game.

Another said, "I was skeptical at first as to how the game would work and if students would actually react to the past. . . but what a success! Each time we met in class the game became increasingly more convincing and real;" and, a third replied, "I came to really enjoy learning from my fellow students. It took some getting used to, but by being more readily involved and interactive with my peers I came to have a stronger understanding of the material."

Still, there were students who never warmed to the game. One student wrote, "I guess you can call me a traditional student, but I feel I learn Art History best from lecture and a slide show displaying the artist, title, and date," while another said, "The game itself and games of this nature are not in line with how I, personally, learn best. I learn best under a lecture scenario."

Most students recognized and appreciated the level of research required by the game. One student noted, "I feel like I learned and connected with my character and his contemporaries in a deeper way that I would not have through lecture or reading solely," while another said, "I was very excited every time I found new information about my character, especially when I found a very old photograph of his private collection." A particularly insightful comment was provided by a student who wrote, "I fought myself the entire time I played this game. I thought it was pointless, until one day outside of class I started rambling on about Impressionism and Sir Richard Wallace."

Reflective essays provided a larger pool of respondents, because they were required for a grade. At the same time, however, students may have given more positive responses because they felt their grade depended on it.

### *Faculty Perception of RTTP Instruction*

Despite Walter Benjamin's 1939 treatise on the political power of art in the age of mechanical reproduction, Jacques Derrida's emphasis on the visible in *Of Grammatology* (1967), and W. J. T. Mitchell's 1995 arguments for a "pictorial turn," many pundits, politicians, and administrators discredit the importance of art history in contemporary social and political life. From President Barak Obama's 2014 exhortation that, "Folks can make a lot more potentially with skilled manufacturing or the trades than they might with an art history degree," to Florida Governor Rick Scott's declaration that, "I want that money to go to degrees where people can get jobs in this state. Is it a vital interest of the state to have more anthropologists? I don't think so," disciplines in the humanities, such as art history, are under fire (Steinhauer 2014; Jaschik 2014). In 2012, Consumer Reports listed fine arts, drama, film, photography, graphic design, and architecture as "useless" majors, and in 2016 Kiplinger listed art and photography among the worst college majors for a lucrative career (Rapacon 2016).

The lion's share of education funding goes to STEM fields (Science, Technology, Engineering, and Math), and despite significant effort, STEAM ("A" is for Art) never really took off, so what can art historians do to justify their place in the university curriculum? Art history is an integral part of a liberal arts education that provides students with the skills they need to navigate an increasingly visual world, and the use of a Reacting game provided an interesting and exciting way to leverage new pedagogies and technologies to reach twenty-first-century students. *Modernism* vs. *Traditionalism* was not only effective at teaching students content, it created opportunities for cooperation and competition, and increased students' oral and written communication skills. The game introduced the students to the significant issues surrounding art in the late nineteenth century and enabled them to put these issues into a broader context through a variety of exercises. The use of *Modernism* vs. *Traditionalism* leveraged students' interest in games to transform the classroom, achieve learning goals, and increase student success.

Despite its success, some revisions could be made to increase its efficacy at this scale. Whereas Twitter worked great in a class of 25, it did not work well in a class of 57. Too many students tweeting distracted from their ability to follow the speeches, and it was time consuming to sort through Twitter to read and record the number and quality of the students' tweets, even with the help of TweetDeck. More artists should be added to the roles of the game, and the roles of buyers should be reserved for guests recruited from outside the class, unless the buyer roles are more developed (i.e., given more objectives to create agency and competition among buyers such as active competitive bidding at the Fair). The use of Pinterest could be expanded as well. In the scaled iteration, a class Pinterest page was created for the game, but if buyers and critics made pages, too, they could re-pin their favorite art, thereby "buying" it and curating online exhibitions.

Some students noted that the roles were uneven in the amount of work each one required, leading to some working harder than others, so this should be addressed in future iterations. Harder to overcome is the seeming unwillingness of some UCF art history students to embrace non-lecture-based learning. There is a persistent culture of passive learning as well as a perception among some students that games are for fun, but not appropriate for the college classroom. While many students came to appreciate the game and understand its value and the use of it in instruction, a vocal minority clearly would have preferred the typical didactic lecture class format.

The game also was time consuming to scale and manage, and with a 3–3 teaching load and classes that range from 60 to 300 students without teaching assistants, this was challenging. Despite the extra time and effort required, however, the game proved to be a valuable addition to instruction and increased student success. Instead of relying solely on lectures, we propose that art historians consider integrating game-based learning and other interactive approaches that have been shown to reach more students and to enhance comprehension and retention. Instead of telling students

the relevant "facts" about an art object, we propose that professors experiment with new, innovative teaching and learning strategies such as
Reacting games.

## CONCLUSION

Overall, teaching nineteenth-century art using a Reacting game was effective and added interactivity to the class that typically is not present. Some
students' responses were negative and there are some adjustments that need
to be made to optimize the game as well as equalize the students' experience
at this scale. Students wanted to win the game, and they worked hard to
meet their characters' objectives. They researched the historical circumstances of their characters and the artwork that they created, supported,
or disliked. The game encouraged competition, but it also promoted teamwork as the students had to build alliances and work cooperatively to solve
problems. This research found that students were generally positive,
succeeded in learning the material, and that generally their views regarding
the benefits of the game were higher after participating in RTTP.

Research on the Reacting pedagogy indicates that students participating
in role-playing games "showed elevated self-esteem and empathy, a more
external locus of control, and greater endorsement of the belief that human
characteristics are malleable" and that students who played the game
increased their rhetorical skills (Stroessner 2009, p. 605). The use of *Modernism* vs. *Traditionalism* at UCF supports these assessments.

## APPENDIX: STUDENT PERCEPTION OF INSTRUCTION

Instructions: Please answer each question based on your current class
experience. You can provide additional information where indicated.

All responses are anonymous. Responses to these questions are important to help improve the course and how it is taught. Results may be used in
personnel decisions. The results will be shared with the instructor after the
semester is over.

Please rate the instructor's effectiveness in the following areas:

1. Organizing the course:
   (a) Excellent          (b) Very Good          (c) Good
   (d) Fair               (e) Poor

2. Explaining course requirements, grading criteria, and expectations:
   (a) Excellent            (b) Very Good            (c) Good
   (d) Fair                 (e) Poor

3. Communicating ideas and/or information:
   (a) Excellent            (b) Very Good            (c) Good
   (d) Fair                 (e) Poor

4. Showing respect and concern for students:
   (a) Excellent            (b) Very Good            (c) Good
   (d) Fair                 (e) Poor

5. Stimulating interest in the course:
   (a) Excellent            (b) Very Good            (c) Good
   (d) Fair                 (e) Poor

6. Creating an environment that helps students learn:
   (a) Excellent            (b) Very Good            (c) Good
   (d) Fair                 (e) Poor

7. Giving useful feedback on course performance:
   (a) Excellent            (b) Very Good            (c) Good
   (d) Fair                 (e) Poor

8. Helping students achieve course objectives:
   (a) Excellent            (b) Very Good            (c) Good
   (d) Fair                 (e) Poor

9. Overall, the effectiveness of the instructor in this course was:
   (a) Excellent            (b) Very Good            (c) Good
   (d) Fair                 (e) Poor

10. What did you like best about the course and/or how the instructor taught it?
11. What suggestions do you have for improving the course and/or how the instructor taught it?

## References

Carnes, M. C. (2005). *Reacting to the past: Pedagogy manual.* Upper Saddle River: Pearson Education.

Carnes, M. C. (2014). *Minds on fire: How role-immersion games transform college.* Cambridge, MA: Harvard University Press.

Freeman, S. (2014). Active learning increases student performance in science, engineering, and mathematics. *Proceedings from the National Academy of Sciences, 111*(23), 8410–8415. doi:10.1073/pnas.1319030111.

Jaschik, S. (2014). *Obama vs. art history.* Retrieved from https://www.insidehighered.com/news/2014/01/31/obama-becomes-latest-politician-criticize-liberal-arts-discipline

Klopfer, E. (2008). *Augmented learning: Research and design of mobile educational games.* Cambridge, MA: MIT Press.

McKay, G., Proctor, N. W., & Marlais, M. A. (2014). *Modernism vs. traditionalism: Art in Paris, 1888–89. Player game manual version 6.0.* New York: W.W. Norton and Company.

Rapacon, S. (2016). *10 worst college majors for your career.* Retrieved from http://www.kiplinger.com/slideshow/college/T012-S001-worst-college-majors-for-your-career-2016-2017/index.html

Steinhauer, J. (2014). *Obama loves art history but thinks it's (economically) useless.* Retrieved from http://hyperallergic.com/106217/obama-loves-art-history-but-thinks-its-economically-useless/

Stroessner, S., Beckerman, L., & Whittaker, A. (2009). All the world's a stage? Consequences of a role-playing pedagogy on psychological factors and writing and rhetorical skill in college undergraduates. *Journal of Educational Psychology, 101*(3), 605–620.

# CHAPTER 6

# Eliciting Meaningful Engagement in an Art History Survey Course: Reacting to the Past and Active Learning

*Marie Gasper-Hulvat, David M. Dees, and Anthony V. Shreffler*

In the introductory art history survey course, Reacting to the Past (RTTP) pedagogy provides a vehicle for students to actively engage with large questions of context, meaning, materials, and processes of creation that are inherent to critical, abstract thinking in the discipline. The purpose of this chapter is to discern if significant differences in meaningful engagement occurred between art history students who participated in an RTTP game and students who participated in other active learning exercises.

The phrase "meaningful engagement" is used in this study to denote deep, internalized learning relevant to the discipline of art history. The use of this term pertains to student interest but extends far beyond that to include deep understanding of course material and practice of discipline-relevant skills. In order to answer the research question, this study compared two sections of an art history survey course covering Renaissance to Modern art. Each section completed a unit on fifteenth-century Italian art. Participants in the study were all taught the unit over five class meetings, with one

M. Gasper-Hulvat (✉)
Kent State University at Stark, North Canton, OH, USA

D.M. Dees • A.V. Shreffler
Kent State University, Kent, OH, USA

© The Author(s) 2018
C.E. Watson, T.C. Hagood (eds.), *Playing to Learn with Reacting to the Past*, DOI 10.1007/978-3-319-61747-3_6

section playing the RTTP *Duomo* game and the other section completing five active learning modules covering the same material. Students wrote essays prior to and following the unit, which were scored using a rubric specifically developed for this study. Data was analyzed by conducting a series of repeated measures analysis of variance (ANOVA) in order to examine differential growth in meaningful engagement between students in the two different sections.

## INTRODUCTION

Although traditional methods of teaching the survey in a slide-lecture format persist in art history (Yavelberg 2014), a handful of scholars have published literature documenting active learning practices in art history survey courses. Researchers have demonstrated how dialogue-based pedagogy facilitates increased ability to analyze art (Baxter 2012; Gioffre 2012). Sowell has qualitatively documented how experimental manipulation of concrete objects can teach art historical concepts and skills (Sowell 1991; Sowell 1993), and Allen has documented a case study using debate to prompt discussion in online survey students (2008). Although not within the sphere of higher education, it is pertinent to this study that elementary-level art educators have noted positive outcomes for role-playing activities related to art historical objects (Szekely 1997; Venable 2001).

Perhaps the most extensive developments in facilitating active learning in art history have manifested within digital technologies. A number of interactive multimedia programs have been developed to augment or replace the art history lecture (Cason 1998; Donahue-Wallace 2008; Gleeson 1997; Hoffmann and Cavalier 2008). At least two online, multi-user, virtual environment art history games have been developed and tested within classrooms: ARTEMIS (Janet and Miles 2009) and ThIATRO (Froschauer et al. 2013). As museum educators Burnham and Kai-Kee conclude, "play, it turns out, is a way to learn about art" (2012, p. 128). This study reaffirms their conclusion.

## METHOD

The pedagogical treatments examined in this study were administered in the spring 2016 semester during the fourth, fifth, and sixth weeks of the semester. During the first three weeks of the semester, prior to the treatments, course content covered art of the fourteenth century, primarily in

Italy and France, and art of the fifteenth century in Northern Europe, primarily in Flanders and France. During these introductory weeks, students practiced basics of visual and iconographical analysis as well as taking slide quizzes and writing essays discussing the significance of artworks. Pedagogical methods during these three weeks included lecture, instructor and student-led discussions, and laboratory activities in which students working in groups manipulated images and materials to explore formal properties of works of art.

Following the introductory weeks, the experimental pedagogical treatment employed an RTTP game that places students in Florence, Italy in the year 1418. It begins with the historically accurate announcement of a competition to build the largest dome Italy has ever seen upon Florence's long-unfinished Santa Maria del Fiore Cathedral, also known as the Duomo (Lazrus 2015). At the time of this study, the Duomo game was an unpublished, Level 2 game only available to experienced instructors directly from the author, but not yet posted for download on the main RTTP instructors' website. The instructor in this study has play-tested and provided feedback to the author of this game since its inception in 2013. This study investigated the eighth playtest of this game that the instructor conducted.

In the Duomo game, three competing factions (one each for rival goldsmiths Brunelleschi and Ghiberti, and one from the town of Arezzo) must each develop a design plan for the dome; indeterminates represent contemporary humanist, artistic, economic, and religious values. Important themes for an art history survey that emerge include individual artists' diverse skills in media such as sculpture, painting, and architecture; the development of linear perspective; and the role of humanistic thought in shaping art and architecture.

On the other hand, the control pedagogical treatment employed a series of five modules with activities sandwiched between dialogic setup and debriefing for each module. Prior to the experiment, all students in both groups received instruction in a manner similar to the control treatment. The modules included a debate between teams supporting either Brunelleschi's or Ghiberti's sculptures, student led discussions on the Duomo, an experimental manipulation of concrete objects and geometry to analyze linear perspective, a primary source-based scavenger hunt, and a concluding module using a well-documented pedagogy known as the Question Formulation Technique (Rothstein and Santana 2011). The investigators chose to employ these methods of active learning due to

**Table 6.1**    Comparison of pedagogical treatments

|  | *RTTP treatment (8 students)* | *Modules treatment (6 students)* |
| --- | --- | --- |
| Assigned resources | Game manual, role sheet, Slide bank of images | Textbook chapter, slide bank of images |
| Primary textual sources | 3 sources, 31 pages total | 7 sources, 7 pages total |
| Homework | 7 game-related short answer questions | 10 interactive multimedia assignments, 12 primary-source-related short answer questions |
| Quizzes | None | 1 slide quiz |
| In-class activities | 2 days of game setup using dialogic pedagogy, 3 days of role playing | 5 days using dialogic pedagogy and modules including debate, student led discussion, lab exercise, and problem-based learning activity |

their support in previous literature (Allen 2008; Baxter 2012; Gioffre 2012; Sowell 1991, 1993) (Table 6.1).

The differences in student experiences between these two treatments are noteworthy. Within the RTTP treatment, the instructor actively facilitated in-class discussions only on the first two days of the unit, whereas in the control treatment, this occurred every day. Students in the control group received significantly more instruction on how to read and interpret the primary sources used. Students in the control group were never tasked with occupying an identity other than their own, whereas students in the RTTP group took on historical identities in character. Both groups received instruction and secondary materials that were carefully designed by professional experts (Lazrus and the instructor, who holds a PhD in art history) to elicit meaningful engagement with the material. However, debriefing discussions about student learning and content occurred in every class for the control group, whereas they occurred only on the final day of the RTTP unit.

It should be noted that neither the experimental nor control interventions of this study can be considered traditional art historical pedagogy. The authors chose an array of different active learning approaches as a control for a representative sample of how it is possible to incorporate non-RTTP active learning into a survey course. Although a comparison of traditional slide lecture pedagogy with the RTTP and non-RTTP groups may have been instructive, time constraints for the study precluded such a research design;

during the semester of the study, the instructor only taught two sections of the course. Furthermore, based on the parameters of this edited volume, it was imperative that the study includes a comparison of RTTP with other active learning techniques.

## Research Design

Quality scholarship of teaching and learning projects (Berstein 2010, Bishop-Clark and Dietz-Uhler 2012; Hutchings et al. 2011) can provide powerful insight into practices that actually work. However, true experimental designs are tremendously difficult, if not impossible, to create in a college setting. This study utilized a quasi-experimental design (Creswell 2002) that was modeled after a pre-posttest framework. An experimental and control group format (Torgerson and Torgerson 2008) was utilized in an attempt to limit the misinterpretation of the data.

## Participants

Students who participated in this study all attended an open-admission, larger regional campus of a mid-sized major university in the Northeast. Given the fact that the quality of the essay responses may be affected by the interplay between historical and artistic knowledge as well as writing ability, basic information on these prior experiences in college-level coursework was gathered from participants. What follows are characteristics of the research participants and the research groups:

- One male and seven females participated in the RTTP group versus two males and four females in the control group.
- One student in each group was over the age of 35.
- One student in each group had a prior art history course.
- One student in each group had five or more art courses.
- Two students in the RTTP group had one art course, whereas three students in the control group had two to four art courses.
- Two students in the RTTP section had two or more history courses compared to only one student in the control group.
- Seven of the eight students (88%) in the RTTP section had two or more writing courses versus four of the six students (67%) in the control group.
- The average grade point average of the RTTP group was 3.22 compared to 3.36 of the control group.

The researchers concluded that due to the small sample size and the minor differences between the groups that none of these prior experiences suggested removing any participant from the study.

### *Measures*

Prior to baseline data collection, all students practiced writing two mini-analyses in order to understand the expectations of the professor and the study. Both essays were due at the beginning of week 3, one week prior to the beginning of the experimental and control treatments. One essay prompted students to explain the significance of two works of art from fourteenth-century Italy, both discussed at length in class and in homework assignments. The other essay prompted students to explain the significance of a painting which would not be discussed in the course until week 15 of the semester. These essays gave students the opportunity to practice writing about works with which they presumably had engaged and about a work with which they had not engaged in the context of the course. After they submitted these essays, the instructor provided in-class feedback on their quality and content.

At the end of week three, students received a short lecture on the study design and their voluntary participation in the study. The study required each participant to write two critical responses to images of art, with choices for both essays including a sculpture and a building. The instructions given for both essays were, "Explain the significance of one or both of these works of art in approximately 300–500 words. Your grade on this assignment will be based only on your completion of it, not on the quality or accuracy of what you write." The paired image format mimicked a traditional art history slide comparison exam, although students could choose if they wished to write about one or both images, as well as if they wished to compare the two. This format did not mimic the traditional slide exam in that essays were written outside of class time using a learning management system, and students were given no instructions regarding their use of outside resources. Because their essays were graded as pass/fail based only on completion, the quality of students' responses depended entirely on their internal motivation. As such, the responses may suggest insight into the students' depth of learning as well as their commitment to the material. This grading policy was necessary to keep the essays anonymous to the instructor, who served as one of the evaluators for the study.

The first essay response was written prior to any intervention, as a pretest due at the beginning of week 4, and the second essay response was written after the intervention as a posttest due three classes following the end of the treatment, at the end of week 7. Both essays focused on works important for fifteenth-century Italy: the Baptistery of San Giovanni in Florence (1059–1128) and Donatello's *David* (1446–1460) for the pretest; the Duomo (1420–1436) and Ghiberti's *Sacrifice of Isaac* (1401–1402) for the posttest. The pretest essays prompted students to review objects that had not yet been covered in the course and the posttest essays prompted students to review objects that were covered extensively in the unit.

### Essay Scoring Procedures

Each individual essay was rated by four evaluators, including the principal investigator. All essays were de-identified, and the evaluators did not know which essay belonged to which student, or even which intervention group. All evaluators utilized the same agreed-upon rubric to assess meaningful engagement in art historical thinking as evidenced through writing. The rating scale from the rubric was applied to four separate categories of engagement within each essay: (1) Art Vocabulary; (2) Visual Evidence; (3) Historical Evidence; (4) Critical Thinking. The following five-point rating scale was used for each category: (1) F—Failure to engage; (2) D—Minimal engagement; (3) C—Surface engagement; (4) B—Measurable engagement; (5) A—Meaningful engagement. Within the rubric, characteristics for each rating were provided for each category to encourage consistency.

### RESULTS

Data analysis began with an examination of the intraclass correlation coefficients (ICC). Because four reviewers were used to rating student essays, this analysis provided a measure for inter-rater reliability. Intraclass correlation coefficients were analyzed for each of the four categories at both the pretest and posttest and were computed using SPSS, analyzing absolute agreement for a two-way random model with a confidence interval of 95% and a test value of zero. Table 6.2 presents the intraclass correlation coefficients.

There was strong agreement among the four reviewers on six of the eight ratings as evidenced by ICC values above .70 (LeBreton and Senter 2008,

**Table 6.2** Intraclass correlation coefficients (ICC) for all categories at pretest and posttest

| Category of engagement | Pretest ICC(2,4) | Posttest ICC(2,4) |
| --- | --- | --- |
| Art vocabulary | .469 | .874 |
| Visual evidence | .752 | .759 |
| Historical evidence | .816 | .821 |
| Critical thinking | .424 | .815 |

p. 836). However, for the two categories of art vocabulary and critical thinking, there was weak agreement among the reviewers on the pretest essays (values of .469 and .424, respectively), meaning that even though a mean score was computed based on the raters' reviews, it may not represent the true level of engagement. This presents a limitation to the results of the two-way repeated measures ANOVA. Overall, however, there was strong agreement among the raters, allowing us to proceed with the analyses. Thereby, a mean rating was computed for each pretest and posttest category for all students.

Differential growth in the depth and analysis of student essays between the intervention and control groups was investigated by conducting a series of two-way repeated measures analysis of variance (ANOVA), one for each of the four categories of engagement. These analyses were performed on the mean ratings of the four reviewers, and the results are described herein.

When examining the engagement in art vocabulary, the intervention group received a mean rating of 2.34 ($SD = .801$) on the pretest essays and a mean rating of 3.28 ($SD = 1.39$) on the posttest. The control group received a mean rating of 2.67 ($SD = .832$) on the pretest essays and a mean rating of 3.71 ($SD = 1.28$) on the posttest. For engagement in historical evidence, students in the intervention group received a mean rating of 1.78 ($SD = 1.02$) on the pretest essays and a mean rating of 3.25 ($SD = .791$) on the posttest. The control group received a mean rating of 1.88 ($SD = .802$) on the pretest and a mean rating of 3.50 ($SD = .354$) on the posttest. Tables 6.3 and 6.4 present the results of the two-way repeated measures ANOVA for art vocabulary and historical evidence, respectively. For both of these categories, results indicated that there was a significant main effect for time but no main effect for group and no interaction effect. Students, on average, received higher ratings on the posttest than the pretest, regardless of which intervention they received.

**Table 6.3** Two-way repeated measures ANOVA on art vocabulary

| Source | df | MS | F | p |
|---|---|---|---|---|
| Within-subjects | | | | |
| Time | 1 | 6.715 | 12.497 | .004 |
| Time × group | 1 | .019 | .035 | .856 |
| Error | 12 | .537 | | |
| Between-subjects | | | | |
| Group | 1 | .964 | .501 | .493 |
| Error | 12 | 1.926 | | |

**Table 6.4** Two-way repeated measures ANOVA on historical evidence

| Source | df | MS | F | p |
|---|---|---|---|---|
| Within-subjects | | | | |
| Time | 1 | 16.408 | 46.201 | < .001 |
| Time × group | 1 | .042 | .118 | .737 |
| Error | 12 | .355 | | |
| Between-subjects | | | | |
| Group | 1 | .203 | .216 | .651 |
| Error | 12 | .938 | | |

For engagement in visual evidence, students in the intervention group received a mean rating of 3.03 ($SD$ = .850) on the pretest essays and a mean rating of 3.03 ($SD$ = .901) on the posttest. Students in the control group received a mean rating of 3.08 ($SD$ = .465) on the pretest essays and a mean rating of 3.17 ($SD$ = .683) on the posttest. For engagement in critical thinking, students in the intervention group received a mean rating of 2.56 ($SD$ = .623) on the pretest essays and a mean rating of 2.91 ($SD$ = 1.18) on the posttest. Students in the control group received a mean rating of 2.67 ($SD$ = .342) on the pretest and a mean rating of 3.13 ($SD$ = .971) on the posttest. Tables 6.5 and 6.6 present the results of the two-way repeated measures ANOVA for visual evidence and critical thinking, respectively. For both of these categories, results indicated that there were no significant mean differences within-subjects or between-subjects (Fig. 6.1).

## DISCUSSION

This study demonstrated the use of quasi-experimental design principles in the context of an introductory art history survey course and can serve as a framework for future studies on this issue. By examining student

**Table 6.5** Two-way repeated measures ANOVA on visual evidence

| Source | df | MS | F | p |
|---|---|---|---|---|
| Within-subjects | | | | |
| Time | 1 | .012 | .031 | .863 |
| Time × group | 1 | .012 | .031 | .863 |
| Error | 12 | .384 | | |
| Between-subjects | | | | |
| Group | 1 | .060 | .076 | .788 |
| Error | 12 | .796 | | |

**Table 6.6** Two-way repeated measures ANOVA on critical thinking

| Source | df | MS | F | p |
|---|---|---|---|---|
| Within-subjects | | | | |
| Time | 1 | 1.103 | 1.745 | .211 |
| Time × group | 1 | .023 | .036 | .853 |
| Error | 12 | .632 | | |
| Between-subjects | | | | |
| Group | 1 | .179 | .211 | .654 |
| Error | 12 | .848 | | |

performance on written essays, the authors sought to uncover if instructing students using RTTP had a different effect on meaningful engagement than instructing students using other active learning techniques. Results indicated that there was no statistically significant difference between the two groups on their growth in meaningful engagement. For the categories of art vocabulary and historical evidence, students performed significantly better on the posttest than on the pretest, regardless of which teaching technique they received. That the categories of visual evidence and critical thinking did not elicit significant learning gains in either group raises further research questions to understand what learning activities encourage development in these areas, if this study's findings would be different if a longer duration of class sessions was studied, and if the rubric was adequate for measuring gains in these areas. Overall, students performed similarly whether they received the RTTP intervention or other active learning techniques, perhaps because many of these other techniques employed methods similar to RTTP.

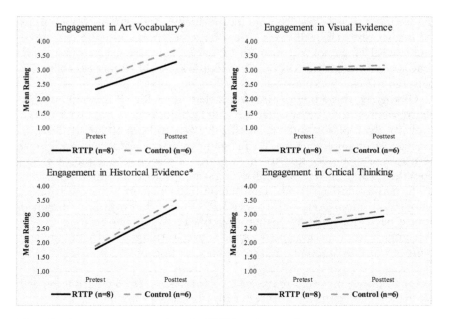

**Fig. 6.1** Engagement over time for RTTP and control groups

## Limitation of Study

One limitation of this study is that it did not investigate which of the various active learning techniques most profoundly affected the control group's learning. Moreover, the authors acknowledge that the small sample size and limited scope of a single five-class unit for this study limits the generalizability of results, and readers should not conclude that utilizing RTTP is no more effective than utilizing other active learning techniques. This study provides a framework for future research to apply these methods to larger samples in order to truly evaluate the effectiveness of RTTP.

Another limitation of the study may have been that the control group and intervention group might be considered unequal. Students in the control group were already familiar with the treatment they were receiving. On the other hand, with the RTTP group, almost all of the class time on the first days of the unit was spent introducing the concept of RTTP, fielding questions related to game mechanics and grading, and addressing anxieties about giving speeches. For this reason, in the RTTP treatment, only three of the five class days focused on significant disciplinary content. Implications for further research in this vein would be to compare classes which played multiple RTTP games with non-RTTP classes, comparing a later unit when time spent on content, as opposed to logistics, would be more comparable between the two treatments.

Ultimately, this study demonstrates that using RTTP in an art history classroom instead of other active learning techniques does not disadvantage students. Such play is, indeed, an effective way to learn about art. Despite the fact that employing an RTTP game requires significant additional course time to be devoted to the logistics of playing the game, students nonetheless appear to learn similarly important skills and content regardless of the pedagogical approach. This demonstrates that art history instructors who wish to adopt a relatively short RTTP game within an already-designed course need not radically change the course. RTTP can be used as one pedagogical tool among many other active learning tools with similarly positive learning outcomes in introductory art history.

**Acknowledgement** Special thanks to Dr. Nancy Ross, Dr. Steven Rugare, and Albert Reischuck for their assistance in analyzing data for this study.

# References

Allen, E. (2008). Tradition and innovation: Using new technology in online art history surveys. In K. Donahue-Wallace, L. La Follette, & A. Pappas (Eds.), *Teaching art history with new technologies: Reflections and case studies* (pp. 98–108). Newcastle: Cambridge Scholars Publishing.

Baxter, K. (2012). The role of family snapshots in teaching art history within a dialogic pedagogy. *Art Education, 65*(1), 11–18.

Berstein, D. (2010). Finding your place in the scholarship of teaching and learning. *International Journal for the Scholarship of Teaching and Learning, 4*(2), 1–6.

Bishop-Clark, C., & Dietz-Uhler, B. (2012). *Engaging in the scholarship of teaching and learning.* Sterling: Stylus.

Burnham, R., & Kai-Kee, E. (2012). *Teaching in the art museum: Interpretation as experience.* Los Angeles: The J. Paul Getty Museum.

Cason, N. (1998). Interactive multimedia: An alternative context for studying works of art. *Studies in Art Education, 39*(4), 336–349.

Creswell, J. W. (2002). *Research design: Qualitative, quantitative, and mixed methods approaches* (2nd ed.). Thousand Oaks: Sage Publications.

Donahue-Wallace, K. (2008). A tale of two courses: Instructor-driven and student-centered approaches to online art history instruction. In K. Donahue-Wallace,

L. La Follette, & A. Pappas (Eds.), *Teaching art history with new technologies: Reflections and case studies* (pp. 109–118). Newcastle upon Tyne: Cambridge Scholars Publishing.

Froschauer, J., Merkl, D., Arends, M., & Goldfarb, D. (2013). Art history concepts at play with ThIATRO. *Journal on Computing and Cultural Heritage, 6*(2), 7.

Gioffre, P. (2012). *An investigation of interactive, dialogue-based instruction for undergraduate art history.* Retrieved from http://eric.ed.gov/?id=ED531704

Gleeson, L. (1997). An interactive multimedia computer program on art history. In D. C. Gregory (Ed.), *New technologies and art education: Implications for theory, research, and practice* (pp. 87–94). Reston: The National Art Education Association.

Hoffman, E. R., & Cavalier, C. (2008). ARTIFACT: Mapping a global survey of the history of art. In K. Donahue-Wallace, L. La Follette, & A. Pappas (Eds.), *Teaching art history with new technologies: Reflections and case studies* (pp. 79–96). Newcastle upon Tyne: Cambridge Scholars Publishing.

Hutchings, P., Huber, M., & Ciccone, T. (2011). *The scholarship of teaching and learning reconsidered: Institutional integration and impact.* San Francisco: Jossey-Bass.

Janet, J., & Miles, M. (2009). ARTEMIS: Reinvigorating history and theory in art and design education. *Journal of Art & Design Education, 28*(1), 52–60.

Lazrus, P. (2015). *Santa Maria del Fiore's Dome – Who shall build it? Art and architecture in 1418 Florence (version 3.1).*

LeBreton, J. M., & Senter, J. L. (2008). Answers to 20 questions about interrater reliability and interrater agreement. *Organizational Research Methods, 11*(4), 815–852.

Rothstein, D., & Santana, L. (2011). *Make just one change: Teach students to ask their own questions.* Cambridge, MA: Harvard Education Press.

Sowell, J. (1991). Learning cycles in art history. *College Teaching, 39*(1), 14–19.

Sowell, J. (1993). A learning cycle approach to art history in the classroom. *Art Education, 46*(2), 19–24.

Szekely, G. (1997). Instructional resources: The art educator as artist: George Szekely's new art. *Art Education, 50*(1), 29–32. 57–60.

Torgerson, C., & Torgerson, D. (2008). *Designing randomized trials in health, education and the social sciences: An introduction.* New York: Palgrave Macmillan.

Venable, B. B. (2001). Using role play to teach and learn aesthetics. *Art Education, 54*(1), 47–51.

Yavelberg, J. (2014). Questioning the survey: A look into art history survey and its pedagogical practices. *Journal of Mason Graduate Research, 1*(1), 23–48.

# CHAPTER 7

# Reconvening the Senate: Learning Outcomes after Using the *Reacting to the Past* Pedagogy in the Intermediate Latin Class

*Christine L. Albright*

## INTRODUCTION

In an attempt to rethink how intermediate Latin classes are taught, a few years ago, I incorporated the *Reacting to the Past* (RTTP) game *Beware the Ides of March: Rome in 44 BCE* (Anderson and Dix 2008) into the first course of our intermediate Latin sequence at the University of Georgia. The game is set during the period immediately following the assassination of Julius Caesar, and students play Roman senators contending for power in the political vacuum left after Caesar's death. Intermediate-level Latin classes in particular can be challenging to teach. Not only do students frequently read real Latin texts for the first time, but most approach these texts without knowing much about their literary or historical context, often resulting in less-than-exciting class meetings in which students slowly pick their way through Latin sentences with little appreciation for what they are actually reading.

I had two primary goals in adopting the *Reacting to the Past* pedagogy for my Latin class. First, I wanted to break up the monotony of the traditional routine of daily translation and parsing of grammatical constructions and

C.L. Albright (✉)
University of Georgia, Athens, GA, USA

© The Author(s) 2018
C.E. Watson, T.C. Hagood (eds.), *Playing to Learn with Reacting to the Past*, DOI 10.1007/978-3-319-61747-3_7

give students the opportunity to learn Latin through a more multifaceted approach. Second, I wanted to help students understand the larger historical significance of the Latin they were translating. To ensure that students continued to develop their language skills while they played the game, I required students to compose and deliver two formal speeches in Latin. At the end of that first experiment with *Reacting to the Past*, students in the class reported that the game was their favorite activity of the semester, that they learned a significant amount about Roman history by playing the game, that they became more engaged with the Latin texts they were reading in class, and that their Latin skills improved during the semester despite the time spent playing the game (Albright 2013). Because the endeavor was so successful, I since have restructured my first-semester intermediate Latin course so that the *Reacting to the Past* game is the focal point of the class. During fall term, 2014, I once again attempted to measure the effectiveness of using the game in this capacity, this time by comparing my own students' responses to a questionnaire to those of students in two other sections of the same course. Results of this study suggest that *Reacting to the Past* can be effective in helping students better understand what they are reading in Latin and also in helping them improve their Latin translation skills.

### Game-Based Learning in Latin Courses

In general, although it is used more extensively in teaching modern languages, game-based pedagogy has been used with success in Latin classrooms, often providing valuable opportunities to situate language acquisition within lessons about culture and history. For at least forty years, students studying Latin in middle and high schools have participated in *Certamen* tournaments, and for some time, computer games have offered students simulations of the ancient world as well as platforms for practicing vocabulary and grammar (see Reinhard 2012). In recent years, seventh graders at the Harvard-Westlake School in Los Angeles have learned Latin via a gamified curriculum (Pike 2015); students studying at middle schools, high schools, and at least one college have used Operation LAPIS, a two-year introductory game course focusing on Latin and Roman civilization (Sapsford et al. 2013), and students at Earlham College have approached

Vergil's *Aeneid* through role-playing games (Paule 2016).[1] T.H.M. Gellar-Goad has taught upper-level Latin composition using an extended role-playing game at Wake Forest University with encouraging results (2015), and Bret Mulligan has experimented successfully with the use of his chapter-length *Reacting to the Past* game *The Crisis of Catiline: Rome, 63 B.C.* in his elementary Latin course at Haverford College (2014).[2] To my knowledge, Mulligan's write-up and my own original study (2014) are the only available discussions about using the *Reacting to the Past* pedagogy in Latin classes. However, *Reacting to the Past* games generally have been used with positive outcomes in foreign language education as well as in the teaching of English as a second language.[3]

## METHOD

### *Restructuring Around the Game*

In the first of our intermediate Latin classes, we typically read Julius Caesar and Ovid. Most instructors divide the semester into two parts, with the first half devoted to prose and the second half devoted to poetry. In restructuring my course, I focused on the same authors but divided the fifteen-week semester into three sections. For the first six weeks, we read Caesar; for the next four weeks, we played the game; and we read Ovid for the last five weeks of the term. On the first day of the semester, I introduced the game and assigned individual roles. When I first used the game in the course, I had taught many of the students in elementary Latin and thus could assign roles with students' personalities in mind. I did not know any of the students in this second class, so I assigned roles randomly. While I could only hope that I was choosing the right students for important roles such as Marc Antony, Octavian, and Cicero, the random assignment provided an

---

[1] For more information about Operation LAPIS, see Slota et al. (2013) as well as Travis (2011). For general discussions about the use of games in education, see, for example, Slota and Young (2014); Wouters et al. (2013); and Young et al. (2012). Bogost (2014) offers a discussion of problematic aspects of gamification.

[2] Mulligan's chapter-length game is designed to be played over just a few class sessions rather than for an extended period. He describes using it at the end of the term in his elementary Latin course.

[3] For discussions about using *Reacting to the Past* games in language classes other than Latin, see Dolmays (2015); McKinley (2013); Schaller (2012); and Davison and Goldhaber (2007).

opportunity for fostering a sense of community early in the class. As I announced which character each student would play and handed out the role sheets, excitement grew in the classroom. The students clapped when they recognized a figure from history, and many of them started talking to each other about their new identities. Students started to refer to each other using their characters' names, and this practice continued for the entire term (during the course of the semester, I frequently received emails signed Catullus or Cleopatra, for example). To set the stage for the course, I also offered a brief lecture on the history of the late Republic and early Empire. Thus, students not only started to bond with each other but also focused on history on the very first day of the course.

After the initial setup, students began translating selections from Caesar's *Bellum Civile*. In previous classes, including the first time I used RTTP in the course, students read parts of Caesar's *Bellum Gallicum*, which is an easier text. I decided to read *Bellum Civile* despite its more difficult material because its content provides a natural bridge into the game. As usual, most students had not looked at Latin since the previous spring semester, so we spent some time during the first few classes reviewing elementary forms and constructions. In general, I taught this portion of the class in a traditional format, asking students to translate and parse words from passages they had prepared at home. Many students struggled with the Latin, and our progress through the text was slow. Several of the passages which we read described meetings of the senate. These sections were especially challenging for the students because they contained advanced constructions such as indirect discourse governed only by the implication of speech as well as technical terms for senatorial procedure. We spent most of our time picking apart complicated Latin sentences, but I allowed time in every class for discussing content, making sure that the students understood what they had just translated. I also frequently asked students to discuss more general aspects of the text. We talked about textual elements which might provide insight into how Caesar felt about a political opponent or Caesar's larger political agenda, for example. For the first third of the term, then, students practiced their Latin skills while at the same time developing an understanding of Caesar as a historical figure, basic Roman institutions, and senatorial procedure—all of which are important things to know for the game.

After we read Caesar, for the next four weeks of the semester, we actually played the game. There were twenty-one students in the class. One graduate student who wanted to learn more about the *Reacting to the Past* pedagogy joined us for this part of the course. In keeping with the recommendations of the game's authors, there were twice as many Caesarians as Republicans. The issues students debated in our game included whether to give Caesar a state funeral or to throw his body into the Tiber River, whether to attack the Parthians, relations with Egypt, and the possible deification of Caesar. Although *Reacting to the Past* games strive for historical accuracy, the outcomes of the games are often not in keeping with history. This has certainly been the case in my classes. The first time I used the game in a Latin class, Lepidus marched on Rome and set Marc Antony up as Dictator. This second time, Sextus Pompeius, played by the graduate student who had joined us, marched on Rome and successfully set himself up as Dictator. He then claimed to have acted only in the manner of Cincinnatus and resigned the office, becoming for the rest of the game a voice of reason and authority. Later, Mark Antony and Lepidus failed in their own attempt to march on Rome and were condemned to death.[4]

The primary challenge I have faced in using the game in a Latin class is bringing Latin into it. The first time I used the game, I had the students compose two long, formal speeches in Latin—350–400 words each. I found that, although students in that first class reported that the compositions very much helped them with their Latin skills (Albright 2013, p. 11), the length of these speeches was somewhat overwhelming for most students. (Latin composition is quite difficult, and students usually do not attempt anything more than short sentences until reaching an advanced level of study.) Moreover, there were long periods of time during the game when students were not working directly with the language, which resulted in a slower transition back into reading Latin after the game. For this second experiment, I instead had the students compose four 100-word speeches—they turned in one for each week we played the game. The shorter length and increased frequency of the compositions made certain that students were engaged with Latin throughout the game. Also, this second time around, I allowed the students to rewrite each speech after receiving general comments from me, which of course resulted in better final speeches.

Students regularly delivered a few lines of their speeches to their fellow senators in Latin as part of the game. The first time I used the game, most students simply went to the podium and read their speeches with little emotion or emphasis, often stumbling over and mispronouncing words.

---

[4] Mark Carnes discusses how "getting it wrong" in *Reacting to the Past* games can help students better understand historical events (2014, pp.246–270).

Eventually, a few students delivered more polished speeches which did inspire others to practice their speeches before making them in class. This second time, the graduate student who played Sextus Pompeius was one of the first students to deliver a speech in Latin. He had practiced his delivery and spoke clearly with drama and gravity. His performance set the bar for the rest of the students, and, although many students had expressed anxiety about making speeches in Latin, in general, students in the class delivered their speeches as real orations. Thus, during the game, students experienced Latin as a living language rather than only as ancient text.

The first time I used the game, the formal speeches served as the only language exercises during the game. For this second experience, I brought Latin into the game in other ways as well. First, students who wish to convene the senate in the game compose a formal *relatio*, following a formula provided in the game manual. I required students to compose the *relatio* for each session in Latin before sending it to me. I then corrected any mistakes and posted it on the class website for everyone to translate. Second, during the course of the game, I required students to compose and make public three political graffiti in Latin. So, students were regularly translating short bits of Latin as part of the game. Third, I had students translate passages from Cicero's *In Catilinam I* as well as excerpts from a few of Pliny the Younger's letters. Our class met on Tuesdays and Thursdays for seventy-five minutes, and our senate meetings usually lasted for 50 to 60 minutes. So, I used the last few minutes of class sessions to go over these texts. Cicero's speech against Catiline provided an example of a real Roman speech for the students, and I assigned the excerpts from Pliny's letters as examples because some characters who were sent away on military campaigns as part of the game were writing letters to the senate in lieu of making speeches.

After the final session of the game, we spent one class examining our *Reacting to the Past* experience. First, we talked about what had happened in our game. The students revealed to each other what their individual goals had been as well as the deals they had made with each other to accomplish those goals. After we discussed the various events which had taken place in our historical simulation, I announced the winners. In general, the students had worked diligently on their strategy and speeches during the game, and thus they had become heavily invested in the outcome. Also, to inspire competition in the game, I had offered two bonus points toward the final course grade for the winner or winners of the game, so everyone was quite eager for my announcement. I chose three students as winners, and the rest of the class cheered so loudly for them as I called their names that we disturbed the other classes around us. After looking back at what had happened during our game, I talked about the actual events which occurred following the assassination of Caesar. The students were all anxious to learn what really happened to their individual characters. Although our game did not directly follow history, it focused the students' attention on the period and on certain historical figures. So, when we did talk about the actual history, the students were much more interested in the subject.

For the final part of the semester, we turned to Latin poetry and translated Ovid's description of the apotheosis of Caesar in Book Fifteen of *the Metamorphoses*. Again, I ran the class in the traditional format, asking students to translate and to parse. As usual, the Latin text was challenging for the students, but, because students had been translating Latin regularly throughout the game, the transition back to the traditional class format was much less bumpy than the first time I incorporated the game into the course. In general, as we made our way through the Latin, students were eager to discuss the passage as a work of literature, and they were better prepared to consider the historical references and possible political implications of the passage than most students in intermediate Latin classes. Students reacted to Ovid's long list of Caesar's political and military achievements as if still in character, which generated robust discussion about Ovid's account. Because Octavian had been a major player in our game, everyone was particularly interested in Ovid's references to Augustus. Every time we encountered a reference, the student who had played Octavian stood up with authority and pretended to accept praise from his fellow classmates. It was clear that the students were approaching Latin as a text with historical significance rather than simply as a linguistic code to be deciphered.

### Measures

I assigned three five-to-seven page papers during the semester which were designed to deepen the students' understanding of the texts they were translating in class and also to facilitate preparation for and performance in the game itself. For the first exercise, I asked students to read all of Caesar's *Bellum Civile* in translation and to write about how their character would respond to a public reading of the work. In preparing their essays, students had to think deeply about their own characters, and our class discussion about the project allowed the students to learn more about other figures in the game. The exercise, then, not only helped students appreciate Caesar's work as something larger than a series of gerundives and ablative absolutes but also allowed students to acquire useful knowledge for the game.

The second paper was designed to introduce students to classical texts they might use in constructing arguments for the game. For this assignment, I showed students the collection of Loebs in our departmental library and asked them to write about three Latin or Greek texts their characters in the game would be most likely to possess. A few students in the class had taken classical culture courses and thus had read a survey of authors, but most students had only been exposed to classics by taking Latin. I frequently saw students sitting in the library, browsing the collection, and many students told me that they did not realize how many classical authors existed before doing research for the assignment. The exercise thus also served to introduce students to the larger field of classics.

The students' final writing assignment focused on the *Metamorphoses*. For this paper, I required students to read the entire poem in translation, and I asked them to focus on Ovid's treatment of Roman history in the epic, especially on stories such as Aeneas' wanderings after the fall of Troy, the deification of Romulus, Cipus' refusal to become a Roman king, and Caesar's apotheosis. Students once again considered the work from the perspective of their characters in the game and wrote about how their characters would react to reading the poem for the first time. In general, students wrote strong papers for all three assignments; their papers showed deeper thought and more effective argumentation than papers in previous Latin classes I had taught which did not use a *Reacting to the Past* game.

### Questionnaire

For the formal study, students in the three sections of first-semester intermediate Latin which were offered during fall, 2014 were asked to complete a simple questionnaire by their instructors. The questionnaire included three questions which asked students to quantify their own learning during the semester. Of course, one section was my own class; the other two sections were taught by faculty members who did not use a *Reacting to the Past* game. These instructors conducted their classes in a traditional format for the whole term, asking students in class to translate and to parse words from passages they had prepared as homework. All three classes used the same textbook for prose: *Finis Rei Publicae: Eyewitness to the End of the Roman Republic* by Robert Knapp and Pamela Vaughn (Knapp and

Vaughn 2003), which features a large amount of historical material in its commentaries. For Ovid, the two other instructors used Richard LaFleur's *Love and Transformation: An Ovid Reader* (LaFleur 1994) while, again, my students read about the apotheosis of Caesar in the *Metamorphoses* using a commentary I provided.

### Participants

Students in all three classes read selections from the same epic, although they read different individual stories. The study relied on students' voluntary and anonymous self-reporting. Twenty out of twenty-one students in my class participated, and twenty-eight students total in the two other classes participated (twelve in one and sixteen in the other). This number constituted almost all of the students enrolled in the first semester of intermediate Latin at the time. The study produced the following results.

## RESULTS

First, students were asked to rate their general understanding of the history surrounding the Latin authors and texts they read during the semester. I asked them to use a scale from 1 to 10, with 10 indicating that they understood a great deal about the history. In my class, the average response was 7.6. The average response in the other two classes combined was 5.19. So, students in my class definitely felt that they understood the history surrounding the Latin texts they were reading better than students in both of the other classes.

Second, I asked students to rate using the same scale how much Roman history they had learned in class during the semester. Students' responses in my class averaged at 8.18. The average in the other two classes combined was 5.6. Thus, students in my class felt that they had learned significantly more about history in the class than students in the other two sections. I asked students in all the classes to indicate from which activity or activities they had learned the most about history during the semester. A few students in my class reported that they had learned from activities such as daily translation, writing assignments, and lectures, but an overwhelming majority of students (eighteen out of twenty) reported that they had learned the most from playing the *Reacting to the Past* game.

Finally, I asked students to rate how much their Latin skills improved during the semester. For this question, I asked them to use a scale of 1 to 5, with 5 indicating that their Latin skills had improved very much during the term. The average response in my class was 3.43. In the other two classes combined, the average response was 3.0. One of my concerns about using *Reacting to the Past* in a Latin class has been that the time spent playing the game might negatively affect the development of students' skills in Latin. Thus, it was particularly noteworthy to me that my own students' responses indicated that they felt more positive about the improvement of their skills in Latin than students in the other two classes which did not use the game.

## *Assessment*

Students' grades were based on weekly quizzes (10%), regular homework assignments (9%), a midterm exam (15%), the three writing assignments (15%), the four Latin speeches (20%), the three political graffiti (3%), a political pamphlet composed in English (3%), and a final exam (20%). I did not assign a specific letter grade for performance in the game, but, to encourage active participation in it, students received a grade for class participation (5%). Most quizzes required students to translate and parse words from Latin passages they had prepared that week; one quiz tested students on historical material necessary for the game. Homework assignments were basic exercises in grammar and were graded for accuracy. For the midterm exam, students were required to translate and to parse words from passages they had prepared for class and to translate one passage at sight. Writing assignments were evaluated for both content and the quality of the writing. The Latin speeches were graded according to the accuracy of the Latin, the content of the speech, and the effectiveness of the argument. Political pamphlets were evaluated for the appropriateness of the propaganda, and the graffiti were graded for the accuracy of the Latin. The final exam was similar in format to the midterm but included longer Latin passages. To earn a high grade for class participation, students were expected to come to class having prepared the assigned Latin text, to contribute to class discussions, and, during the game itself, to be active players.

My own assessment of students' work was in keeping with their responses in the formal study. Most students showed significant improvement on quizzes during the course of the semester, which often happens as students become more familiar with grammatical constructions as the term progresses. Not surprisingly, almost all of the students showed real improvement in composing Latin from the first speech to the fourth. Most students showed noticeable improvement from the midterm to the final exams in terms of skills in translation and in recognizing grammatical constructions. The exercises in original composition of the speeches no doubt contributed to the overall development of language skills during the course of the term. Also, that students had a better understanding of the history behind the Latin texts they read seemed to help them remember for the exams vocabulary and grammatical details. Students seemed more concerned about improving their skills in Latin, and general overall performance in the class was slightly better than in my previous intermediate Latin classes which did not use the game.

## CONCLUSION

I will continue to use the game in my intermediate Latin class. The game not only breaks up the monotony of the traditional routine and helps keep daily class dynamics fresh but also serves to focus the class. It provides historical context for Latin texts and motivates students to learn more about Roman history. *Reacting to the Past* has been shown to facilitate student-bonding and the development of communities (Carnes 2014; Webb and Engar 2016), resulting in increased motivation and engagement among students (Lazrus and McKay 2013). A strong learning community certainly developed in my class, and students were clearly engaged with the material.[5] Students became invested in their own performance and also in each other early in the semester, and many have remained close friends since taking the class. One student seemed to capture this idea well in his response to a question which asked students to describe their experience with *Reacting to the Past*: "I was really looking forward to class and was upset if I had to miss it. Every day was a lot of fun, and I got to know my classmates while learning *a lot!*"

Most importantly, the game seems to enhance learning while still allowing for the development of Latin language skills. It offers excellent opportunities for learning new vocabulary and grammar as well as for meaningful exercises in composition. In fact, the game provides a matrix for incorporating all of the goal areas outlined in the *World-Readiness*

---

[5] For discussions about the positive effect of learning communities on students' motivation, learning outcomes, and general success in college, see Kuh et al. (2005); Laufgraben and Shapiro (2004); Smith et al. (2004); Zhao and Kuh (2004); Shapiro and Levine (1999); and Gabelnick et al. (1990).

*Standards for Learning Languages* (*2015*), especially the goal area of communities. This goal area often is quite difficult to address when teaching ancient languages, but at least one study has shown that students value it most of all when learning a foreign language (Magnan et al. 2012, p. 176). Through the *Reacting to the Past* game, students had the opportunity to learn Latin within a microcosm of late-Republican Rome, experiencing firsthand many of the interwoven linguistic and cultural threads which make up the complex tapestry of language acquisition. Finally, it is worth mentioning that most of the students in my class were taking Latin to satisfy a language requirement. At the end of the semester, eight students talked to me about majoring or minoring in Latin or Classical Culture, and many of these students reported that the experience of playing the game had inspired their interest in the subject.

## REFERENCES

ACTFL. (2015). *World-readiness standards for learning languages*. Alexandria: American Council on the Teaching of Foreign Languages.

Albright, C. L. (2013). Reimagining Latin class: Using the reacting to the past pedagogy in the intermediate Latin class. *Teaching Classical Languages, 5*(1), 1–14.

Anderson, C. A., & Dix, T. K. (2008). "Reacting to the past" and the classics curriculum: Rome in 44 BCE. *The Classical Journal, 103,* 449–455.

Bogost, I. (2014). Why gamification is bullshit. In S. Waltz & S. Deterding (Eds.), *The gameful world: Approaches, issues, applications* (pp. 65–79). Cambridge, MA: MIT Press.

Carnes, M. C. (2014). *Minds on fire: How role-immersion games transform college.* Cambridge, MA: Harvard University Press.

Davison, A., & Goldhaber, S. L. (2007). Integration, socialization, collaboration: Inviting native and non-native English speakers into the academy through "reacting to the past.". In J. Summerfield & C. Benedicks (Eds.), *Reclaiming the public university: Conversations on general and liberal education* (pp. 143–161). New York: Peter Lang Publishers.

Dolmays, J. M. (2015). Reacting to translations past: A game-based approach to teaching translation studies. *Translation and Interpreting Studies, 10*(1), 133–152.

Gabelnick, F., MacGregor, J., Matthews, R. S., & Smith, B. L. (1990). *Learning communities: Creating connections among students, faculty, and disciplines.* San Francisco: Jossey-Bass.

Gellar-Goad, T. H. M. (2015). World of wordcraft: Foreign language grammar and composition taught as a term-long role-playing game. *Arts & Humanities in Higher Education, 14*(4), 368–382.

Knapp, R., & Vaughn, P. (2003). *Finis rei publicae: Eyewitness to the end of the republic* (2nd ed.). Newburyport: Focus Publishing.

Kuh, G. D., Kinzie, J., Schuh, J. H., Whitt, E. J., & Associates. (2005). *Student success in college: Creating conditions that matter.* San Francisco: Jossey-Bass.

LaFleur, R. (1994). *Love and transformation: An Ovid reader* (2nd ed.). New York: Scott Foresman-Addison Wesley.

Laufgraben, J. L., & Shapiro, N. (2004). *Sustaining and improving learning communities.* San Francisco: Jossey-Bass.

Lazrus, P. K., & McKay, G. K. (2013). The reacting to the past pedagogy and engaging the first-year student. In J. Groccia & L. Cruz (Eds.), *To improve the academy: Resources for faculty, instructional, and organizational development* (Vol. 32, pp. 315–416). San Francisco: Jossey-Bass.

Magnan, S., Murphy, D., Sahakyan, N., & Kim, S. (2012). Student goals, expectations, and the standards for foreign language learning. *Foreign Language Annals, 45*(2), 170–192.

McKinley, J. (2013). Reacting to the past: A CLIL pedagogy. *The Language Teacher, 37*(5), 69–71.

Mulligan, B. (2014). Coniuratio! Ethopoeia and "reacting to the past" in the Latin classroom (and beyond). *The Classical Journal, 110*(1), 107–123.

Paule, M. T. (2016). Companions of Aeneas: Gamifying intermediate Latin. *Teaching Classical Languages, 6*(2), 1–16.

Pike, M. (2015). Gamification in the Latin classroom. *Journal of Classics Teaching, 16*, 1–7.

Reinhard, A. (2012). Learning Latin via gaming. In T. Thorsen (Ed.), *Greek and Roman games in the computer age* (pp. 127–153). Trondheim: Tapir Academic Press.

Sapsford, F., Travis, R., & Ballestrini, K. (2013). Acting, speaking, and thinking like a Roman: Learning Latin with operation LAPIS. *Journal of Classics Teaching, 28*, 13–16.

Schaller, P. (2012). Can role-playing the French revolution *en Français* also teach the eighteenth century? *Digital Defoe: Studies in Defoe and His Contemporaries, 4* (1), 41–60.

Shapiro, N. S., & Levine, J. (1999). *Creating learning communities: A practical guide to winning support, organizing for change, and implementing programs.* San Francisco: Jossey-Bass.

Slota, S. T., & Young, M. F. (2014). Think games on the fly, not gamify: Issues in game-based learning research. *Journal of Graduate Medical Education, 6*(4), 628–630.

Slota, S. T., Ballestrini, K., & Pearsall, M. (2013, October). Learning through operation LAPIS: A game-based approach to the language classroom. *The Language Educator*, pp. 36–38.

Smith, B. L., MacGregor, J., Matthews, R. S., & Gabelnick, F. (2004). *Learning communities: Reforming undergraduate education*. San Francisco: Jossey-Bass.

Travis, R. (2011). Practomimetic learning in the classics classroom: A game-based learning method from ancient epic and philosophy. *New England Classical Journal, 38*(1), 25–42.

Webb, J., & Engar, A. (2016). Exploring classroom community: A social networking study of reacting to the past. *Teaching and Learning Inquiry, 4*(1), 1–17.

Wouters, P., van Nimwegen, C., van Oostendorp, H., & van der Spek, E. (2013). A meta-analysis of the cognitive and motivational effects of serious games. *Journal of Educational Psychology, 105*(2), 249–265.

Young, M. F., Slota, S., Cutter, A. B., Jalette, G., Mullin, G., Lai, B., Simeoni, Z., Tran, M., & Yukhymenko, M. (2012). Our princess is in another castle: A review of trends in serious gaming for education. *Review of Educational Research, 82*(1), 61–89.

Zhao, C. M., & Kuh, G. D. (2004). Adding value: Learning communities and student engagement. *Research in Higher Education, 45*(2), 115–138.

# CHAPTER 8

# What Happens After Reacting? A Follow-Up Study of Past RTTP Participants at a Public Regional University

*Jeffrey L. Bernstein, Mary Grace Strasma, Russ Olwell, and Mark D. Higbee*

The pedagogical benefits of active learning in general, and Reacting to the Past (henceforth Reacting or RTTP) more specifically, have been established in the research literature to date. This paper explores the longer-term impact Reacting has upon students' competencies in (a) understanding cultural differences; (b) teamwork; and (c) public speaking, as well as in improving student retention. This study compares students in RTTP classes to students in other "humanities" general education classes at the university, matched by high school GPA and ACT score. While the survey shows that Reacting does help improve public speaking skills, students in RTTP are less likely to persist and graduate than their humanities peers, though they are more likely to do so than freshman at the university as a whole. This suggests the possibility that while RTTP can be an engaging introduction to the university, unless other equally engaging experiences

J.L. Bernstein (✉) • M.G. Strasma • M.D. Higbee
Eastern Michigan University, Ypsilanti, MI, USA

R. Olwell
Merrimack College, North Andover, MA, USA

© The Author(s) 2018
C.E. Watson, T.C. Hagood (eds.), *Playing to Learn with Reacting to the Past*, DOI 10.1007/978-3-319-61747-3_8

exist later in the curriculum, students may find their subsequent courses discouraging in comparison.[1]

## INTRODUCTION

Mark Carnes (2005, 2014) has argued that the Reacting curriculum produces an increase in student intellectual and social engagement that leads to greater integration in college life and thus to an increase in student retention. Studies of Reacting have focused on how the curriculum impacts students' worldviews and how it may lead to higher engagement both inside and outside of the classroom (Higbee 2008; Stroessner et al. 2009). A white paper produced by an RTTP team for the Teagle Foundation summarized the evaluation data on RTTP as follows:

> Assessment confirms that students in a variety of institutions are becoming more engaged in classroom discussions, more willing to work in teams, and are demonstrating improved skills in rhetorical presentation, critical thinking, and analysis. They also develop higher levels of empathy and a greater understanding of contingency in human history and thus the role of individual action and engagement. (Burney et al. 2010, p. 16)

Researchers outside the RTTP consortium concur that RTTP leads to gains in student learning, historical thinking, and freshman retention but that a subset of students found the class less engaging than more traditional classes (Olwell and Stevens 2015).

RTTP, designed to build and maintain student engagement, might naturally be expected to raise first-year retention and graduation rates. Tinto's (1993) theory of student retention and student engagement—that students will persist if they find work inside the classroom and activities outside the classroom that connects with what motivates them—suggests this would be the case. Likewise, Kuh et al.'s (2008) work on the National Survey of Student Engagement (NSSE) shows colleges successful at building experiences that compel student effort will have higher retention rates, graduation rates, and learning outcomes. However, if there is only a single

---

[1] We are grateful to Meng Chen and to Melissa Benson for their assistance in helping us with data collection on this project. We also very much appreciate those students who took our surveys, or participated in our focus groups, and in so doing helped us understand the impact of Reacting more than we did previously.

such course in a student's college experience—what Tinto (1999) calls the "vaccine" approach to retention—many interventions that would seem to have great promise for student retention may appear to be relatively ineffective, as the factors that lead to leaving college can be far more complex and difficult than a single course or method can successfully address.

Kuh (2008) has focused on "high-impact practices", those forms of engagement that lead to the most gains in student outcomes. RTTP would fit Kuh's definition of high-impact practice, making it appear more likely that utilizing it would lead to retention gains.[2] Kuh's work informs the Association of American Colleges & Universities' (AAC&U) VALUE Project, which seeks to measure how students are progressing in key areas during their college experience (Finley and Rhodes 2013). We used these categories to develop survey questions for students in RTTP classes and other General Education (Gen Ed) Humanities classes in the areas most closely related to RTTP classwork: cultural knowledge, oral communication, and teamwork.

While Reacting's results are usually impressive on student self-confidence and expression, previous studies have not dug deeply into *what* about RTTP is engaging and *how* this engagement leads to student learning gains. One exception is Lightcap (2009), who found that students in his first-year RTTP class gave the class higher ratings than comparable first-year offerings, and that RTTP students reported higher "critical thinking, teamwork, active learning, consideration of real world problems, incorporating diverse perspectives and application of theory to course material," than students in these other classes (p. 178).

Other literature is beginning to suggest that some of RTTP's most significant impact may be in student engagement. As Carnes has pointed out, the in-class playing of the game is only one part of the engagement—many students become engaged in the research process to better their speeches, work with their peers outside of class to sharpen their speeches, and negotiate/plot with other factions. In the best-case scenario, students in RTTP are highly engaged both inside the classroom and in their residence halls, the dining hall, and the library (see https://www.aacu.org/value/rubrics).

---

[2] Reacting is often used in what Kuh (2008) calls a "First Year Seminar and Experience," one of his high-impact practices. It also could be considered an example of "Collaborative Assignments and Projects" and "Diversity/Global Learning", two other high-impact practices.

This study looked at several key areas where we believed RTTP would have an impact. Using the AAC&U's VALUE rubric framework gave us a nationally validated set of skills and characteristics on which to base our work. We chose the rubrics for intercultural understanding, oral communication, and teamwork as our key areas to examine, as they are both intrinsic to the RTTP experience and because they are also key goals of general education more broadly. We expanded the definition of intercultural understanding to include historical understanding, as RTTP promises to help students develop "historical thinking" skills that allow them to empathize with those in the past or in different cultural settings (Wineburg 1999). In addition to conducting focus groups and surveys, we also collected aggregate data from our university to explore some of our research questions.

## METHOD

As a first attempt at understanding the impact of Reacting, we surveyed all students who took a RTTP first-year seminar class since 2011 at EMU.[3] These seminars, all capped at 25 students, were the university's first attempt to offer a first-year course aimed at entering students. The seminars were all based on using two or three Reacting games and were designed as a pilot intervention, by faculty members and the then Provost, acting on a mandate from the university's governing board to develop interventions aimed at increasing the university's graduation rate.[4] Students who took the Reacting seminars signed up for them as incoming students, influenced by a two minute speech by one Reacting professor who stressed the class's value for peer engagement and academic success.[5] The two-minute speech on the Reacting seminar was featured as part of a 90-minute presentation on the university's general education program and its various requirements. The Reacting seminar had been designated as fulfilling the requirement for a General Education Humanities course, a box on the Gen Ed worksheet that could be met in many ways.

---

[3] All our research was approved by the university's Human Subjects Review Committee.

[4] The six-year federally defined graduation rate for the university has always been under 40%.

[5] Incoming students visit campus to register for their first classes on various dates in the spring before starting college; at this "Fast Track" day, groups of students are quickly registered for class, have their photo IDs made, and do other activities associated with beginning college.

We also surveyed a control group of 768 students who were sampled to match the RTTP students in high school GPA and ACT scores and who had completed a separate Gen Ed Humanities course during their first year in college. Of the 381 RTTP students emailed, only 33 responded, despite several reminder attempts. Without incentives for the survey, it was clear that this 9% response rate, while anemic, was the best that was attainable. Of the 768 control students surveyed, only 39 responded, a 5% response rate. Unlike the RTTP students, control students had no connection to the survey topic and may have simply been unwilling to spend time answering questions about their general education class.[6]

While designed to be open for instructors from multiple fields, the RTTP first-year seminars actually offered were all taught by history instructors, because administrative leadership failed to carry out the actions necessary, in the university's system, to allow instructors from multiple departments to teach sections of a single course aimed at first-year students. The course was approved by the history faculty but never acted on by higher bodies; thus, the university failed to offer its first course taught by instructors from multiple sections. Indeed, the pilot project as designed and applauded by the Board of Regents and President was to have drawn on faculty from across the university, with 20 or more sections being offered for three years each fall for first-year students. The pilot, if carried out on that scale, was expected to yield substantial data on student engagement and academic success. But the pilot was never allowed to grow larger than five sections taught by historians in a given year. This was due to the Provost's resignation for health reasons as well as the indifference of other administrators, who felt relieved when members of the Board of Regents relented on the university's "60% drop out problem," to quote one former regent.

Of the RTTP students, 75% reported playing the Athens game, with Ancient Rome the second most played game (50%). Students had also played Frederick Douglass (35%), Anne Hutchinson (25%), China (15%) and Rwanda (5%) games. The history faculty had adopted Athens as its common game for RTTP at the freshman level, giving instructors wide latitude after that to use one or two other games to complete the class. Our analysis focuses on the impact of Reacting in terms of students'

---

[6] This was why we drew a larger sample for the control group, in hopes of achieving enough respondents for both groups to do data analysis.

understanding of, and appreciation for, cultural differences, as well as their skill-building in teamwork and public speaking.

## RESULTS FROM THE SURVEYS

### *Cultural Differences*

Wineburg (1999) has written extensively about how historical thinking can help students become more empathetic for people in other times and places. If students in RTTP are invited to put their own ideas aside and think through the position of someone different than themselves in culture, identity, and thinking, then students should ideally report some change in their thinking about cultural differences.

This expectation was met; 90% of RTTP students indicated that the class helped them to better understand cultural differences (yes or somewhat), 78% indicated that the class helped them think about their own culture and biases, 89% said it taught them about other cultures, 83% said it helped develop empathy, 89% said that it helped encourage curiosity about other cultures, and 94% said it helped them learn to interact with people from other cultures. These high levels indicate that RTTP games did encourage students to develop empathy across time and place, to try to see the world from the perspective of other individuals or groups.

However, intercultural learning was also indicated in the control group: 89% of the control group said that their general education class in the humanities helped them better understand cultural difference, 77% said it helped them know their own culture and biases, 93% said it helped them know about the complexity of other cultures, and 85% said it helped them develop empathy, curiosity about other cultures, and helped them interact with other cultures. Both RTTP and general humanities offerings thus work to develop student empathy for others, a positive finding for classes across the field.

### *Teamwork*

In the RTTP group, 90% of students reported that the class helped them build teamwork skills; specifically, 88% of students reported being better able to contribute to a team, 82% reported being better able to run a team meeting, 82% reported being able to work before a team meeting to ensure productivity, 90% reported being able to help build a positive team climate, and 76% reported being able to resolve conflicts among team members. This overall gain in teamwork is a result of all students in RTTP classes being forced to work together with one another. As a result of this structure, they report very high levels of teamwork and conflict management skills.

In the control group, only 58% reported that the class helped build teamwork skills, a dramatic difference in favor of Reacting. Of those who answered that they did believe they developed these skills, 100% reported learning how to contribute to a team, 88% reported learning how to effectively facilitate meetings, 75% reported learning to do pre-work for a meeting, 88% reported being able to build a positive team climate, and 100% reported being able to resolve conflicts. While students in general humanities classes who reported developing teamwork skills did so comprehensively, there were many fewer of them than in RTTP classes.

## Public Speaking

Like no other class, RTTP classes get students out of their chairs to speak, sometimes at a moment's notice. We should not be surprised, then, that 90% of RTTP students reported that the class helped them become a better and more confident public speaker. Of these students, 94% responded that they were better able to write a speech with a strong central message, 88% were better able to organize a speech, 73% reported being confident in their speaking, 88% reported being able to use evidence in a speech, and 94% reported being able to adjust a message for their audience.

Those students in Gen Ed Humanities classes report much less speaking skill development. Only 65% of control students reported feeling that their general education class helped their oral communications skills. Of those who did, 100% reported that they were better able to make an argument with a central point, better organize a speech, locate evidence, and adjust a speech for the audience, while 75% reported feeling confident in the area of speaking as a result of their class.

## Larger Issues: Choice of Major, Retention

Simply taking one class—an RTTP class or a Gen Ed Humanities course—showed little net change in students' majors or intended majors. For students in RTTP classes, the class did not impact their choice of major, either to or away from the humanities—81% of students reported no change in major, 6% moved into a humanities major, while 6% moved out. Of the control group students, 8% moved into a humanities major as a result of their class, 15% moved out, and 62% remained unchanged in major choice. There was, however, evidence that both types of classes encouraged retention: 59% of RTTP students say that the class encouraged them to keep taking classes at EMU, while 67% of the control group said the same of their humanities class. This slight difference, in a negative direction, foreshadows results we present below.

### Engagement

Finally, we explored engagement with humanities classes. Students in RTTP classes reported feeling engaged with their classwork—37% of RTTP students reported being engaged with their RTTP class, 36% reported engagement with other students in class, 36% reported making friends in class, and 34% reported engagement with student activities. In the control group, 24% reported feeling engaged with the class, 16% reported engagement with students outside class, 16% reported making friends with classmates, and 13% reported engagement with student activities. Students in the control reported their Gen Ed Humanities class less engaging than other freshman year classes, while RTTP students reported higher engagement with their Reacting class than other classes that term or subsequent classes at EMU. After the class ended, RTTP students were slightly more likely to remain connected to classmates—53% of RTTP students reported being still in contact with other students from their class, as opposed to 46% in the general education class. This offers yet more evidence in support of the literature's contention of Reacting's effectiveness.

## Results from Focus Groups

As a second attempt to unpack the impact of Reacting, we convened two focus groups composed of students who had taken one or more courses using RTTP, generally more than one semester prior to the time the research was conducted.[7] While these groups were somewhat self-selected based upon positive experiences with RTTP, as they consisted of students with sufficient interest in talking about the experience to attend a focus

---

[7] The students were offered pizza as compensation for their participation in the focus groups. They were also paid $15 at the beginning of the session.

group, the results are still an impressive endorsement of Reacting, even more strongly positive than in the surveys. Further, while the positive impacts reported are in the same areas as in the surveys—building public speaking, teamwork, research skills, engagement, and understanding cultural differences—the statements by students in the focus groups give us deeper data on *how* RTTP classes build these outcomes. In addition, some specific examples of the impact of RTTP on further coursework by these students may provide evidence for a positive impact on integrative learning. Lastly, some focus group participants spoke movingly of the impact on their college careers of encountering an RTTP instructor whom they perceived as being, in their experience, more engaged with student learning than instructors in their other classes.

We examined the focus group responses to identify key areas that emerged from student responses. It was difficult to separate out the responses into categories, however, as they tended to overlap and reinforce each other.

### Skilled Argumentation

Not surprisingly, students in the focus groups stated that their public speaking skills had improved. What they really described, however, was better argumentation and an understanding of evidence. One student told us that the game increased his love of argumentation:

> Sometimes since the game, I enjoy kind of playing devil's advocate. . . .[I]f like a group is on board, I'll kind of step aside and just try to poke holes in it just to make the right idea or a good idea. Maybe I can see a flaw when no one else can, or through the discussion you keep playing it, and then a flaw will come up that no one saw and it will help strengthen the whole [idea].

Focus group students also said they were now more confident in advocating a position. One student, who said that his "flaw" before taking the RTTP class was that he was too easily neutral because he likes to please everybody, now said:

> If I have an opinion on something, and I can't see any legitimate reason why I should have to falter in it, I stick more strongly to it. I have an easier time, I guess, standing up for the things I'm arguing. . ... after that game, I'm just like,

no, look, it's right here. This is why you are wrong, and this is why I'm right. If I have all the evidence in front of me.

Similarly, another student stated that she now feels:

Comfortable giving reasons and...knowing that my reasons are solid because this game makes you look for your own sources, and they have to be logical sources, because the professor I took it under, he would kill you if you were wrong. He was like nope, that's wrong, you're dead, you're this person now...So, like, I think it kind of shows you have to know what you're talking about in order to feel like you can actually talk about things, otherwise, you're just [talking] nonsense.

The impact appears to go even deeper, however. As participants discussed how they researched and put together arguments, they spoke of the impact of increased empathy and the ability to see multiple perspectives on their problem-solving and communication skills.

[S]ince I'm in a fraternity, there [are] always dissenting opinions on everything we do. I got really good at just stepping back and finding the root cause why you want to do this, why is this important to you, and it has really helped.

### *Cultural Difference: Engaging the Past*

These results go far beyond simply improved public speaking skills; they show both a deep engagement with the complexities of the past and an understanding of how to apply this insight in the present. One student related the issue of argumentation to the range of perspectives and interests that people have in any society:

People have their own individual things they want to accomplish...you get a sense of how they were living, like these aren't like tales that they are hearing now – like an actual society of people, who maybe have their own needs and wants.

Another student pointed out in the focus groups that the games help one get beyond the binary, "right/wrong" view of arguments with which many freshmen enter college. This student told the focus group:

[T]he games showed me that there's not always a good or bad but there is a ton of gray area...we might have our hearts in the right place, but our minds may have a different way of going about things.

Yet another student related this issue of argumentation to the difficult historical issues around slavery. "This class offers a really good way to see that so many different factors are really going into an argument. You know it's not just pro-slavery and anti-slavery; there's every individual person who has their own agenda." This deeper understanding of how conflict and debate functioned in the past suggested to another student a more skilled approach to politics and society in the present:

I think in America it's so easy – we're so used to if you are right you are the winner.....It's so easy when someone says something that you don't agree with, we think is stupid or whatever, we shut down listening to them and then we're just looking for ways to tell them how they are wrong...but maybe we're both wrong and right and there's a new thing that we can like create together.

## Integrative Learning

Huber and Hutchings (2004) argue that higher education institutions must consciously work to provide opportunities for integrative learning. They describe some of the elements of integrative learning as "making connections within a major, between fields...or between academic knowledge and practice," within the framework of an overall program that allows students to be more self-aware and purposeful in their own educational careers (p. 3). The focus group students, while once again describing what they believed to be skills acquired through their RTTP classes, in fact gave examples of ways in which the experience helped them integrate skills and perspectives across their programs. For example, one STEM major found that RTTP helped integrate the different classes, even though no other course was a humanities class. The student told the focus group:

I've got a bio lab, and chem lab, genetics – stuff like that, and this is peppered in the middle. Being more involved in this class and my speeches and actually looking into the history and doing research actually helped me become more involved with my other labs and my groups in there and doing research. I think that helped me solidify better grades in my other courses.

Reflecting Huber and Hutchings' perspective that skills in integrative learning continue even beyond college, we are gratified to see this expressed in student work. Specifically, beyond the research skills they gained, students saw how the same argumentation and ability to look for multiple perspectives supported them in their career paths. One student related the skills of cultural awareness and empathy gained in RTTP to the needs of the healthcare field, telling the focus group:

> I'm going into nursing, so I'll be [working with patients from] other cultures, and I had to take cultural anthropology as one of my pre-reqs. Because of Reacting, I was able to really think about more cultures and different points of view, so I did amazing in that class. . ...It will open other people's minds as well instead of just opening up your own. You'll be like 'well, have you thought about this factor?'

In summary, the focus group data provide strong examples of how students believe Reacting has improved their argumentation skills, helped them grasp cultural differences cross-sectionally, as well as over time, and enabled them to integrate their learning. While hard to quantify, these examples make clear that for at least some of our students, the impact of RTTP went well beyond the single class.

## AGGREGATE ANALYSIS OF THE REACTING EFFECT

The final place we might look to see an impact for Reacting to the Past is at the aggregate, university-wide level. We begin by suggesting five possible effects we might see in our data. First, Reacting students might be expected to return to college in subsequent years; if Reacting does, in fact, make students more engaged in their college careers, they could be more likely to return to college for their second and third years. Second, Reacting students might be expected to graduate at higher rates than non-Reacting students.[8] Third, we might expect Reacting students to earn a higher GPA (another mark of high academic performance). Fourth, given their greater exposure to different cultures and geographic areas, we expect Reacting students to be more likely to pursue opportunities to study abroad (within the

---

[8] In our case, since Reacting was only launched in 2010, and accurate graduation rates cannot be determined for all but the earliest Reacting cohorts, we focus on credits earned rather than on graduation rates.

constraints of study abroad being a financially and logistically difficult option for our students). Finally, if the history courses using Reacting are as engaging as they are purported to be, students in Reacting courses might be more likely to choose to major in history.[9]

Our data consisted of all Eastern Michigan University students who took a Reacting class between the fall 2010 and winter 2014 semesters, as well as a matched sample (with two cases selected for every one Reacting student) of students who did not take Reacting but who took a General Education Humanities course during their first year in college. (These groups were the same groups that received the surveys discussed earlier.) We also used a second control group, this one consisting of all EMU students who entered the school as first-year students during the same time period. The data were provided to us by the university's Institutional Research and Information Management Office, with identifying student data removed. These data are presented in Table 8.1.

Table 8.1 shares mixed results. In general, and in support of our arguments that Reacting brings about pedagogical benefits, the Reacting group (column one) performs better than the control group of all EMU students (column three). Reacting students were almost 2% more likely to return for their second year at EMU and were a little over 3% more likely to return for both their second and third years. Consequently, as of January 2016, the treatment group had earned almost ten credits more than the control group, on average. However, their average GPA was somewhat lower the control group of all EMU students (2.57 vs. 2.68) and they were less likely to study abroad.[10]

However, when we compare the RTTP students to the control group of students who had taken a Gen Ed Humanities course (column two), the RTTP students perform significantly worse. They were much less likely to return for their second year (76% vs. 90%) and for their third year (65% vs. 77%). They had earned six fewer credits and had a GPA that was much worse (a difference of 0.29) as compared to the Gen Ed Humanities group.

---

[9] For this variable, we considered anyone majoring in history, as well as any of the social studies-teaching programs, to be a history major (since virtually all social studies majors take a history-laden curriculum).

[10] The large number of cases in the dataset means that almost any relationship will be statistically significant, as, in fact, virtually all our relationships are. We leave it to the reader to determine, on a substantive basis, which of any relationships are large enough to warrant further consideration.

**Table 8.1**    Markers of success for Reacting versus non-Reacting students

| Metric | Experimental group (Reacting students) | Control group (non-Reacting, humanities students) | Control group (all EMU students) |
|---|---|---|---|
| % returning for second year | 75.88 | 89.72 | 74.12 |
| % returning for second and third years | 65.00 | 77.08 | 61.67 |
| Credits earned by January 2016 | 69.52 | 75.33 | 60.27 |
| GPA | 2.57 | 2.86 | 2.68 |
| % studying abroad | 0.80 | 0.74 | 1.17 |
| % majoring in history | 3.2 | 4.2 | 3.2 |
| Total number of cases | 340 | 719 | 9385 |

The control group was also one-third more likely to choose a major in history. RTTP students, on average, appear to perform better than the typical EMU students on the metrics we have used but worse than this more specifically chosen control group of students.

Why the Reacting group performed so much worse than the control group of students who took another Gen Ed Humanities course confounds us. Our close examination of the data reveals that this pattern was largely consistent across all cohorts; furthermore, when we dug deeper to see if the two samples did, in fact, match each other, we found they truly did. It is possible that the students who took Reacting might have perceived themselves at higher risk to graduate and took what they could have perceived to be a "fun" course in choosing Reacting (the two-minute speech during the Fast Track orientation did contrast the Reacting seminar to more traditional pedagogies, which often bore incoming students). Or, it is possible that students who perceived themselves stronger at the traditional text-lecture-test approach might have been scared off by the unusual, and perhaps unwelcome, innovation of the Reacting curriculum. We also wonder if students who would voluntarily choose to take a traditional humanities course early on in their college career might be "different" from the average student, in a way that our data cannot capture.

While we can take some pleasure in the fact that the RTTP students did experience some gains, their clear (and substantial) deficits as compared to students taking other humanities courses is a significant concern and warrants further study. A large number of EMU courses fulfill the humanities area of the university's general education program, ranging from foreign languages to 100-level literature courses to some introductory theater and some history courses. For instance, the children's literature course on the Harry Potter novels, or a course on Jane Austen, fulfills the same general education requirement as the Reacting first-year seminar and may well attract already highly engaged students from the entering student population, perhaps different at the outset from the RTTP students. Unfortunately, we have no way to directly address this speculation.

## DISCUSSION

Reasons for retention failure are manifold, of course, and cannot be addressed by a single approach. The failure of Reacting, at least in this case, to address this problem is cause for concern. Might there be anything inherent in the teaching method that may *cause* Reacting students to be *less* likely to persist? While speculative, we offer up this argument for others (and ourselves) to grapple with as we continue to use and refine RTTP.

We have evidence, imperfect, but evidence nonetheless, that Reacting students experience increased empathy, see multiple perspectives, and take an integrated view of their studies. Students in the focus group reported that their RTTP class made them more likely to return; it lowered their stress level, and they enjoyed having an active learning course as a change of pace from the rest of their classes. This self-selected group no doubt was more comfortable with this format and found it to be a positive toward retention. Further, their descriptions of how they later applied the experience in other courses suggest a much deeper impact than the tools that any good public speaking course might provide, moving them toward the ability to grapple skillfully with conflict in their personal, professional, and civic lives.

But, these differences between RTTP and traditional classes, which we would expect to be positives, *might* in fact be the things that lead *some* students away from a traditional program. When RTTP is successful, it confuses students and disrupts their equilibrium. That is precisely the effect a good liberal arts education should (temporarily) have. We want students to make the shift into seeing gray areas and being able to hold multiple perspectives at the same time. This change typically happens between the second and third years of a traditional liberal arts program. While it is initially unsettling for many students, by the end of the program, graduating seniors are, ideally, better prepared for the challenges and complexities of a democratic society.

Yet at EMU, and perhaps others of its institutional type, much of our student population is looking for a quick path into a career (as they understand it), rather than a broad liberal arts education. Does RTTP frustrate these students? Does it lead them to shy away from a history major? Does it lead them to be frustrated with our university and to either leave for another school or abandon higher education entirely?

Even asking these questions ascribes more power to one single course than we should. However, if we intend to offer courses like RTTP that disrupt the students, causing them to have to work harder to achieve the "answers" that they seek, we must make sure to scaffold RTTP. We must let students know this kind of work, with its inherent uncertainty, is not a "one-off" but rather is something expected across the board in college. It may well be the case that RTTP can "work" for all students but that students need to be supported so it fits within their overall education. A course with Reacting embedded should not be the *one* course that sticks out in the general education, causing students dissonance and challenging them to do things that are uncomfortable and difficult.

## References

Burney, J. M., Powers, R. G., & Carnes, M. C. (2010). Reacting to the past: A new approach to student engagement and to enhancing general education. *A white paper for the Teagle Foundation*. Retrieved from https://reacting.barnard.edu/about/special-initiatives/fresh-thinking

Carnes, M. C. (2005). Inciting speech. *Change: The Magazine of Higher Learning, 37*(2), 6–11.

Carnes, M. C. (2014). *Minds on fire: How role-immersion games transform college.* Cambridge, MA: Harvard University Press.

Finley, A., & Rhodes, T. (2013). *Using the VALUE rubrics for improvement of learning and authentic assessment.* Washington, DC: Association of American Colleges and Universities.

Higbee, M. D. (2008). How Reacting to the Past games "made me want to come to class and learn": An assessment of the reacting pedagogy at EMU, 2007–2008. *The scholarship of teaching and learning at EMU, 2*(4), 1–34. Retrieved from http://commons.emich.edu/sotl/vol2/iss1/4/

Huber, M. T., & Hutchings, P. (2004). *Integrative learning: Mapping the terrain.* Washington, DC: Association of American Colleges and Universities.

Kuh, G. D. (2008). *High impact practices: What are they, who has access to them, and why they matter.* Washington, DC: Association of American Colleges and Universities.

Kuh, G. D., Cruce, T., Shoup, R., Kinzie, J., & Gonyea, R. (2008). Unmasking the effects of student engagement on first-year college grades and persistence. *Journal of Higher Education, 79*(5), 540–563.

Lightcap, T. (2009). Creating political order: Maintaining student engagement through "Reacting to the Past". *PS: Political Science and Politics, 42*(1), 175–179.

Olwell, R., & Stevens, A. (2015). "I had to double-check my thoughts": How the Reacting to the Past methodology impacts first year college student engagement, retention and historical thinking. *The History Teacher, 48*(3), 561–572.

Stroessner, S. J., Beckerman, L. S., & Whittaker, A. (2009). All the world's a stage? Consequences of a role-playing pedagogy on psychological factors and writing and rhetorical skill in college. *Journal of Educational Psychology, 101*(3), 605–620.

Tinto, V. (1993). *Leaving college: Rethinking the causes and cures of student attrition.* Chicago: University of Chicago Press.

Tinto, V. (1999). Taking student retention seriously: Rethinking the first year of college. *National Academic Advising Association Journal, 19*(2), 5–9.

Wineburg, S. (1999). Historical thinking and other unnatural acts. *Phi Delta Kappan, 80*(7), 488–499.

# CHAPTER 9

# Playing with Learning and Teaching in Higher Education: How Does *Reacting to the Past* Empower Students and Faculty?

*Thomas Chase Hagood, Naomi J. Norman, Hyeri Park, and Brittany M. Williams*

## INTRODUCTION

Advocates and researchers of *Reacting to the Past* (RTTP) have long heralded the game-based pedagogy as an approach to teaching and learning that places, at its core, the science of active learning. As a teaching strategy, the pedagogy lends itself to both flipped classrooms and to student-centered environments and promotes essential learning outcomes, as defined by the Association of American Colleges & Universities' National Leadership Council for Liberal Education and America's Promise, "knowledge of human cultures and the physical and natural world, intellectual and practical skills, personal and social responsibility, and integrative learning" (Association of American Colleges and Universities 2007, p. 3). The pedagogy also empowers faculty to step aside from their "sage on the stage" role to cede control of the classroom to students as teaching partners whom they respect, trust, and value in liminal, yet significant, learning environments (Carnes 2004; Stroessner et al. 2009).

T.C. Hagood (✉) • N.J. Norman • H. Park • B.M. Williams
University of Georgia, Athens, GA, USA

© The Author(s) 2018                                                          159
C.E. Watson, T.C. Hagood (eds.), *Playing to Learn with Reacting to the Past*, DOI 10.1007/978-3-319-61747-3_9

RTTP finds itself in conversation with a number of high-impact practices that have received attention in the scholarship on teaching, learning, and instruction over the last decade (Kuh et al. 2013). This volume is evidence of the important interest and growing attention of faculty on measuring how RTTP impacts students' learning—a trend begun by Burney et al. (2010). This chapter departs from others in the volume as it is not an individual case study on implementation and results, but rather an examination of data collected through two national surveys of both students and instructors.

## LITERATURE REVIEW

Having experienced RTTP in our own classrooms and having conducted numerous faculty development workshops on RTTP throughout the southeastern United States, we had several presuppositions that shaped the survey designs (Appendix). Over the last five years, when we have asked faculty why they use or might consider using RTTP, the typical response has often been the resulting high and nearly inexplicable levels of student participation and commitment to class sessions using RTTP games. Students share a similar reply: the games make learning interesting and fun. As noted below, our survey data confirmed these general impressions. However, we wanted to look more closely at why these games worked as they did, thereby, following up on earlier work on the psychological motivational factors of learning in these unique environments (Stroessner et al. 2009).

Adding to the work of Stroessner, Beckerman, and Whittaker, in 2016, Webb and Engar explored similar questions regarding the evolution of student relationships by evaluating three-month-long RTTP games played in one semester of a lower division honors course at a large US public university. Driven by the dearth of scholarship on student communities, Webb and Engar sought "to develop a hypothesis about how teaching approaches emphasizing peer interaction, such as RTTP role-playing games specifically and collaborative learning more generally, impact classroom social structure" (2016, p. 2). Their findings are compelling: namely, that the collaborative learning environments necessitated by RTTP promote "dense, inclusive classroom networks by structuring opportunities for students to form ties that cut across clique boundaries" (p. 14). Such relationships "benefit students educationally not only in the classroom as they are challenged by different perspectives, but also beyond the classroom" (p. 14). Ultimately, Webb's and Engar's findings suggest that not only did students foster greater friendships and relationships with peers during RTTP games, but that previously isolated students tended to forge new and stronger relationships with individuals they would not have interacted with otherwise. Their student-focused study drew important conclusions about Reacting's ability to help create a classroom community and was an important first step in suggesting that RTTP environments promote social cohesion among students.

Unlike previous research, we utilized two models for investigating the impacts of RTTP—one on the student development side of the experience, the other, from the teaching side of the learning dynamic. On the student experience, the principles of social cohesion seem to capture what occurs in RTTP classrooms. Social exchange theory, or social cohesion, is a framework from the field of social psychology. Cook et al. (2013) examine the ways in which social exchange, social identities, and characteristics intersect. Within the contexts of higher education, their framework provides a more holistic approach to understanding the ways in which group dynamics and interactions coincide with student identities and backgrounds even when these characteristics seem neutralized or inactive in the social setting of a higher education classroom. As they suggest, power and its distribution often plays a critical role in human interaction and exchange and in how members of a social group cohere or fail to cohere. For faculty practitioners of RTTP and students who have experienced the pedagogy, this framework of social cohesion will likely ring true. The higher levels of coherence, to borrow Webb's and Engar's "ties that cut across clique boundaries" (2016, p. 14), lead to higher levels of group pride, commitment, performance, and satisfaction. Further, it is enveloped within the necessary exchange and intersection of identities in the liminal worlds of subversive play central to RTTP—an exchange and intersection that must be at least managed, if not mastered, if individual students or group factions are to win the game they are playing to learn.

Interestingly, sociologists hotly contest the principles and even the definition of social cohesion. They do not agree on a singular definition and/or set of parameters for what makes for social cohesion as it can exist across groups, among groups, intra-communally, and extra-communally, all of which contributes to the tension in ascribing a singular definition to the phenomena. Yet, Friedkin (2004) tagged both an experience grounded within group membership and the sharing of a common space as key features of social cohesion that could facilitate greater investments in the academic environment. Despite the contentions on a singular definition of social cohesion, we find Friedkin's emphases on group membership and common spaces to be persuasive, particularly in the context of RTTP game play among students.

On the faculty side of the equation, the model of relationship-driven teaching seemed the most applicable lens through which to view the unique approach to instruction provided by RTTP. Rogers and Renard (1999) conceptualized the framework of relationship-driven teaching, maintaining the belief that motivational educational environments require a mix of tools and skills including teacher recognition and awareness of students' emotional needs. Their framework sought to ensure that students actively learn what instructors aspire to teach; the intention(s) of teachers and their self-realization are key to this approach. Positive relationships, bound by context and relevance, provide opportunities for deeper learning, support, and student success.

The notion that relationship-driven teaching enables collaboration and inclusion was key to Slater's (2004) research on the meaningful ways students perceive teacher relationships when connections are built on trust. The development of trusting relationships, Salter argued, is not only necessary for learning, but also aligned with the ultimate goals of education: namely, to assist students develop critical thinking and decision-making skills. When such relationships are missing from an educational environment, the processes of learning are reduced to necessity motivated by, for example, grades, rather than by shared goals and personal connection. Slater, like other educational researchers, placed the onus of relationship-driven teaching on instructors. In Slater's view, it is up to faculty to facilitate a "relationship-first" approach in order to affirm students, allow space for learning, and create dynamics of multicultural inclusion, self-discovery, and global understanding. Indeed, it is RTTP's suspension of students' contemporary identities, realities, and self-held ideologies through the adoption of historic identities within a game that propels or at least nudges them across conflicting lines of color, class, gender, and political identity. Trust in the teacher/gamemaster sits at the crux of learning à la play.

As Beaty-O'Ferrall et al. (2010) remind us, relationship-driven teaching is not a fundamentally new concept. Rooted in research on the K-12 environment, relationship-driven teaching arose just as the inclination to focus on the totality of students' experiences to encourage engagement and desire to learn emerged in the mid-late twentieth century. Holistic student engagement is a central learning goal apparent throughout RTTP. Beaty-O'Ferrall and colleagues suggested that teachers must view classroom management as a process that depends on ongoing, positive, and responsive student-teacher relationships. In particular, they encouraged educators to share with students their place of origin and the complex notion of how they came to understand the world around them—limiting and complicating any "teacher only" perceptions students might hold of instructors. In this way, they argued, teachers could "win over" their students and make the learning environment exponentially more personable and person-first. Despite variations in the techniques employed by instructors/gamemasters within Reacting, the student-centered nature of the pedagogy aligns with the principles articulated as relationship-driven, an approach clearly influenced by Vygotsky's et al. (1978) theories of social constructivism and collaborative learning.

More recently, Bishop et al. (2014) utilized a qualitative focus group approach to examine learning-centered teaching as a means of facilitating higher impact educational experiences for students and faculty. Their findings suggest students perform at optimal levels when faculty prioritizes student learning over their own time and preparation. They found that the quality of didactic lectures should center on students' ability to process and make sense of in-class content rather than the ease of facilitation or faculty instructional preferences, an approach that is distinct from the instructional design of RTTP. Varying presentation methods, however, was a significant and consistent theme throughout their research, and their findings indicate students and faculty alike must necessarily build connections or learning relationships to foster classroom success (also see Kuh and Hu 2001; Lamport 1993; Swaner and Brownell 2008). Moreover, frequent interaction with faculty is one of the most important factors in student motivation and involvement (Chickering and Gamson 1987) and can lead students to take greater intellectual risks (Fenty 1997). The kind of variation of instructional methods situated on an axis of relational approaches to content delivery (faculty) and deep processing of information (students) continues to motivate the development and implementation of RTTP games (Proctor 2011).

## Method

Given RTTP's tremendous growth since its earliest iteration in the mid-1990s, students and faculty alike have come to view it as a transformative experience (Carnes 2014). This chapter takes seriously a research-based approach to assess both sides of the RTTP classroom. To do so, we constructed two surveys—one for faculty who had embedded RTTP within at least one course and another for students who experienced the pedagogy during their undergraduate education. With Institutional Review Board approval at the University of Georgia (UGA), we used three mechanisms to invite faculty to take the survey: e-mails to the established RTTP listservs developed by the UGA Reacting to the Past program and by the RTTP consortium at Barnard College; a notice posted on the RTTP Faculty Lounge Facebook site, a private group open only to RTTP faculty; and flyers distributed at the Annual RTTP Summer Institute hosted by Barnard College. Each invitation included an anonymous link to the survey. We asked RTTP instructors to invite their students to take the student survey.

Social cohesion theory and relationship-driven teaching influenced the construction of both surveys. Several demographic questions, followed by categorical, open-ended and Likert-type questions across five areas were posed. The five areas were learning experience/outcomes (seven questions on each survey in this area; students were asked about learning experience and faculty were asked about learning outcomes), student behaviors (six questions), student relation to faculty/faculty relation to students (seven questions), effectiveness of RTTP (six questions), kind of class/mode of delivery (six questions). See Appendix for abbreviated faculty and student survey instruments. Based on the number and sort of questions asked, Cronbach's alpha indicated that our groupings of questions were reliable (see Table 9.1).

To measure the perceived impacts of Reacting, we ran $t$-tests or ANOVA comparisons on three issues for students ("RTTP affected my learning," "I learned course content more deeply," and "Number of RTTP courses taken") and two issues for faculty ("RTTP affects how I teach" and "Is content coverage a problem"). We also conducted a $t$-test comparing students' responses with those of faculty across the survey's five categories.

The surveys were designed to gauge students' and instructors' perceptions of the myriad impacts of Reacting upon learning and teaching, the issue of content coverage, and any change in student behaviors and faculty interactions in a RTTP class. In particular, we wanted data on social cohesion within the classroom and on relationship-driven teaching—specifically, whether RTTP supports both models, given the unique environment of a Reacting class. On social cohesion, questions measuring learning experience/outcomes and student behaviors revealed that the pedagogy had significant, positive impact on students' learning experiences and learners' behaviors when assessed by peers and instructors and some impact on

**Table 9.1** Cronbach's alpha's reliability

|  | Number of items | Cronbach's alpha |
|---|---|---|
| Learning experience/outcomes | 7 | .943 |
| Student behaviors | 6 | .918 |
| Relation to faculty/students | 7 | .950 |
| Effectiveness of RTTP | 6 | .966 |
| Kind of class/mode of delivery | 6 | .834 |

faculty perceptions of certain learning outcomes. The model of relationship-driven teaching informed questions about relation of students to faculty and vice versa and the kind of class/mode of delivery in which students and faculty encountered or utilized the pedagogy. We also explored the effect of the pedagogy—both on students who took more than one RTTP class and on faculty who used the pedagogy for more than one year. Both students and faculty report that they transferred skills and methods acquired in a Reacting class into non-Reacting classes and beyond. We also wanted to gauge whether the effectiveness of the pedagogy depended on a particular classroom environment/modality of delivery, institutional support, or availability of peer mentors.

The faculty and student surveys permitted us to assess the self-perceptions of faculty and students and, thereby, examine a central question, as yet, unaddressed in the scholarship on RTTP: what is the underlying glue that holds a RTTP classroom together and makes it such a successful environment for both the students and the instructor? The results were compelling and suggestive of the impact of the pedagogy on both students' perceptions of their learning and faculty teaching practice as well as powerful in confirming the principles of relationship-driven teaching and social cohesion in learning environments.

## RESULTS

### *Student Survey: Demographics and Experience with RTTP*

The student survey attempted to measure to what extent the pedagogy influences students' study habits, appreciation of an academic discipline, and their greater sense of autonomy as learners. Results were supplied by 113 self-reported female respondents (70.2%; $n = 161$) and 48 male

**Table 9.2**   Demographic profile of student respondents

|  | Demographic profile | n (%) |
|---|---|---|
| Gender (n = 161) | Male | 48 (29.8) |
|  | Female | 113 (70.2) |
| Age (n = 161) | 17–18 years | 11 (6.8) |
|  | 19–20 years | 70 (43.5) |
|  | 21–23 years | 42 (26.1) |
|  | 24–25 years | 7 (4.3) |
|  | 25+ years | 31 (19.3) |
| Academic status (n = 148) | 1st year | 13 (8.8) |
|  | 2nd year | 45 (30.4) |
|  | 3rd year | 34 (23) |
|  | 4th year | 27 (18.2) |
|  | 5th year | 17 (11.5) |
|  | 6th year | 12 (8.1) |
| Ethnicity (n = 161) | American Indian/Alaska native | 1 (0.6) |
|  | Asian | 5 (3.1) |
|  | Black/African American | 6 (3.7) |
|  | Native Hawaiian/Pacific islander | 2 (1.2) |
|  | White | 130 (80.7) |
|  | Other | 17 (10.6) |

respondents (29.8%). They were asked about their age, academic status, and ethnicity (see Table 9.2).

Concerning age, respondents ranged from traditional college-age students to non-traditional; the largest group of the respondents were in the 19–20 age range, but there was an unexpectedly high number of respondents in the 25+ age range. Most of our student respondents experienced Reacting in the second or third year of their undergraduate experience. The demographic profile of our student respondents did not permit a reliable comparison of RTTP's impacts upon various ethnic groups due to the overrepresentation of white-identifying students.

We also asked about their experience with the Reacting pedagogy. Interesting data emerged from these questions. According to the survey, the majority, 107 respondents (66.5%; n = 161), had experienced one RTTP course. The second largest group of respondents, 31 respondents (19.3%), had experienced RTTP in two courses (Table 9.3). Our respondents reported that they had experienced the pedagogy in a wide variety of classes, from first-year experience courses to upper-division courses in their

**Table 9.3** The number of RTTP courses experienced

| | n | % |
|---|---|---|
| 1 RTTP course | 107 | 66.5 |
| 2 RTTP courses | 31 | 19.3 |
| 3 RTTP courses | 9 | 4 |
| 4 RTTP courses | 4 | 2.5 |
| 5 RTTP courses | 4 | 2.5 |
| More than 5 courses | 6 | 3.7 |

major, suggesting that the faculty have found a variety of curricular "homes" for the pedagogy.

We posed questions on the mode of delivery (e.g., face-to-face, hybrid, online) of students' Reacting classes and virtually all of our respondents encountered it in a face-to-face class. In all of our $t$-test comparisons for students, the kind of class/mode of delivery was statistically insignificant; we believe this is due to the homogeneity of classroom environments in which student respondents experienced the pedagogy. Of the student respondents, only one individual (.006%; $n = 161$) indicated some interaction with RTTP in an online environment, replying to the question, "If you have experienced RTTP in an online class, please comment on that experience," by stating, "The experience was good, could have used more computer experience."

### Faculty Survey: Demographics and Experience with RTTP

The faculty survey attempted to measure faculty perception of student learning, student behaviors, and relation between faculty and students. We were also hoping to gain insight into how RTTP implementation, its successes and challenges, might affect faculty members' approach to learning and instruction beyond their RTTP-based classes and how they perceive improvements in student performance when compared to other classes. Results were supplied by 63 female respondents (64.3%; $n = 98$) and 35 male respondents (35.7%). They were asked about their age, academic status, ethnicity, teaching experience, academic institution, and experience with RTTP (Table 9.4). As with our student respondents, the vast majority of our faculty respondents self-identify as White which reflects the overall profile of faculty across the US. (National Center for Education Statistics 2013; Smith 2015).

**Table 9.4** Demographic profile of faculty respondents

|  | Demographic profile | n (%) |
|---|---|---|
| Gender (n = 98) | Male | 35 (35.7) |
|  | Female | 63 (64.3) |
| Age (n = 98) | 25–34 years | 7 (7.1) |
|  | 35–44 years | 23 (23.5) |
|  | 45–54 years | 35 (35.7) |
|  | 55–64 years | 27 (27.6) |
|  | 65–74 years | 6 (6.1) |
| Academic status (n = 98) | Master's degree | 10 (10.2) |
|  | Doctoral degree | 85 (86.7) |
|  | Professional degree | 1 (1) |
|  | ABD | 2 (2) |
| Ethnicity (n = 97) | American Indian/Alaska native | – |
|  | Asian | 1 (1) |
|  | Black/African American | 1 (1) |
|  | Native Hawaiian/Pacific islander | – |
|  | White | 92 (94.8) |
|  | Other | 3 (3.1) |
| Years teaching (n = 70) | <1 year | – |
|  | 1–5 years | 6 (8.6) |
|  | 6–10 years | 5 (7.1) |
|  | 11–20 years | 29 (41.4) |
|  | >20 years | 30 (42.9) |
| Home institution (n = 70) | Community college | 2 (2.9) |
|  | 4-year residential college | 42 (60) |
|  | Research 1 university | 15 (21.4) |
|  | Other | 11 (15.7)[a] |

[a]Other: 1 respondent for each of the following: "A comprehensive university," "A public college in Canada," "A regional public university," "A regional public university, 20,000+ students," "Comprehensive regional state univ., mostly commuter," "Master's comprehensive," "Public university but not R1," "R 2," "Regional campus of a Research 1 University," "Regional comprehensive public university," and "university"

All of our respondents were currently employed in/retired from the higher education sector with 70 respondents (71.4%) currently tenured/ tenure-track and 28 respondents (28.6%) non-tenured/tenure-track. Concerning their experience with the pedagogy, a majority (43 respondents, 43.9%) indicated they had used RTTP between one and five years; 33 respondents (33.7%) indicated they had used RTTP for more than five years; 22 respondents (22.4%) had used RTTP less than one year. In summary, a very large percentage of the faculty who answered our survey are older, tenured, have been teaching for many years and have used the pedagogy multiple times.

We also asked faculty if their home institution supported their use of RTTP pedagogy; 61 participants (88.4%; $n = 69$) responded "Yes" and 8 (11.6%) responded "No." Institutional support ranged from "My upper administration knows about and supports my use of RTTP" to "My dean knows about and supports my use of RTTP" to "My departmental colleagues know about and support my use of RTTP" to "Support includes financial support (e.g., travel, preceptors, materials etc.)."

### Survey Findings

The survey findings illuminate students' and instructors' perceptions of RTTP and suggest the pedagogy's ability to inspire deeper learning, foster social cohesion among students, and encourage relationship-driven teaching. Given the high-impact nature of RTTP, we asked questions about the effectiveness of RTTP to measure simultaneously both the social cohesion and relationship-driven aspects of the pedagogy. The results suggest that neither social cohesion theory nor relationship-driven teaching alone accounts for the success of the pedagogy. Rather, the pedagogy functions as a hybrid of both models and reinforces the growing body of scholarship on active learning in higher education.

We ran a $t$-test comparison of students and instructors on the impact of Reacting for all five of our categories (Table 9.5). In three of the categories, we noted statistical significance between the groups' perceptions, namely, Student behaviors ($p = .000$), Relation to faculty/students ($p = .000$), and Effectiveness of RTTP ($p = .000$). Intriguingly, on Student behaviors and Effectiveness of RTTP, faculty ($M = 5.81$, $SD = 0.91$; $M = 6.55$, $SD = 0.56$) perceived a greater impact of the pedagogy than did students ($M = 5.28$, $SD = 1.36$; $M = 6.10$, $SD = 1.33$). We were somewhat surprised to see that students perceived the impact of RTTP on Relation to faculty ($M = 5.79$, $SD = 1.36$) was greater than the faculty perception of RTTP's impact on Relation to students ($M = 5.17$, $SD = 1.08$).

**Table 9.5** The impact of RTTP: Comparing students and faculty (*t*-test)

|  | Students (n = 160) | | Faculty (n = 97) | | t | p |
|---|---|---|---|---|---|---|
|  | M | SD | M | SD | | |
| Learning experience/outcomes | 5.56 | 1.46 | 5.65 | 0.81 | −.646 | .519 |
| Student behaviors | 5.28 | 1.36 | 5.81 | 0.91 | −3.722 | .000 |
| Relation to faculty/students | 5.79 | 1.36 | 5.17 | 1.08 | 3.791 | .000 |
| Effectiveness of RTTP | 6.10 | 1.33 | 6.55 | 0.56 | −3.553 | .000 |
| Kind of class/mode of delivery | 4.52 | 1.07 | 4.49 | 0.62 | .262 | .794 |

### *Learning Experience/Outcomes*

The results reported in Tables 9.6 and 9.7 on students' perception of their learning are remarkable. We evaluated students' responses per those who replied "Yes" against those who replied "No" when asked if RTTP affected how they learned and if they learned course content more deeply in an RTTP class. We compared these two groups' responses across five categories composed of 32 individual questions and found that the results were statistically significant in all categories, except "Kind of class/Mode of delivery."

Our student respondents reported that RTTP significantly affected their learning and helped them learn course content more deeply.

Looking at the data from the student respondents provides additional insight into how students defined "learning course content more deeply." For example, 72 respondents (63.7%) obtained "a better understanding of research methodology" in RTTP course(s), while 81 respondents (71.7%) "read and researched beyond the material assigned" in RTTP course(s). Even more impressive are the 90 respondents (79.6%) who either agreed or strongly agreed that they "actively used the information from assignments" and the 91 respondents (80.5%) who either agreed or strongly agreed that they understood "concepts and ideas more deeply than in non-RTTP classes." Most striking of all are the 94 students (83.2%) who either agreed or strongly agreed that they "read assigned material with greater attention to detail" and the 100 students (88.5%) who believed they "engaged in critical thinking more in RTTP course(s)." These are impressive numbers, revealing that our student respondents had a very high level of confidence that the pedagogy helps them learn.

**Table 9.6** The impact of RTTP for students: RTTP affected my learning (*t*-test)[a]

| | Yes (n = 104) | | No (n = 56) | | t | p |
|---|---|---|---|---|---|---|
| | M | SD | M | SD | | |
| Learning experience | 6.21 | 0.69 | 4.31 | 1.70 | 7.885 | .000 |
| Student behaviors | 5.81 | 0.82 | 4.27 | 1.57 | 6.831 | .000 |
| Relation to faculty | 6.32 | 0.76 | 4.82 | 1.68 | 6.282 | .000 |
| Effectiveness of RTTP | 6.55 | 0.53 | 5.13 | 1.89 | 4.833 | .000 |
| Kind of class/mode of delivery | 4.68 | 0.81 | 4.20 | 1.44 | 1.969 | .054 |

[a]In this table, we sorted students according to a "Yes" or "No" response to our question: "Has the RTTP pedagogy affected how you learn?" 104 students replied "Yes" and 56 replied "No." We compared these two groups' responses across five categories composed of 32 individual questions

**Table 9.7** The impact of RTTP for students: I learned the course content more deeply (*t*-test)[a]

| | Yes (n = 113) | | No (n = 47) | | t | p |
|---|---|---|---|---|---|---|
| | M | SD | M | SD | | |
| Learning experience | 6.14 | 0.76 | 4.06 | 1.72 | 7.745 | .000 |
| Student behaviors | 5.77 | 0.84 | 4.08 | 1.60 | 6.862 | .000 |
| Relation to faculty | 6.21 | 0.88 | 4.76 | 1.75 | 5.333 | .000 |
| Effectiveness of RTTP | 6.52 | 0.56 | 4.90 | 2.00 | 4.742 | .000 |
| Kind of class/mode of delivery | 4.64 | 0.82 | 4.19 | 1.56 | 1.609 | .116 |

[a]In this table, we sorted students according to a "Yes" or "No" response to our question: "Do you feel you learned the course content more deeply when you experienced RTTP in our course(s)?" 113 students replied "Yes" and 47 replied "No." We compared these two groups' responses across five categories composed of 32 individual questions

We also asked faculty if Reacting affected how they teach (Table 9.8). We evaluated their responses per those who replied "Yes" to this question against those who replied "No." Virtually all of our faculty respondents reported that Reacting has affected how they teach (90.7%; *n* = 88). We compared those two groups and found that the results were statistically significant in three of our five categories: "Student behaviors" (*p* = .000), "Relation to students" (*p* = .006), and "Effectiveness of RTTP" (*p* = .000).

We were astonished to find that for our faculty respondents, the category of "Learning outcomes" was not statistically significant (*p* = .144). This could be due to the overwhelming number of respondents who replied "Yes" (90.7%, *n* = 88) against those who replied "No" (9.3%, *n* = 9). Among "No"

**Table 9.8** The impact of RTTP for faculty: RTTP affects how I teach ($t$-test)[a]

|  | Yes (n = 88) | | No (n = 9) | | t | p |
|---|---|---|---|---|---|---|
|  | M | SD | M | SD | | |
| Learning outcomes | 5.73 | 0.73 | 5.00 | 1.24 | 1.632 | .144 |
| Student behaviors | 5.91 | 0.84 | 4.75 | 1.00 | 3.688 | .000 |
| Relation to students | 5.26 | 1.03 | 4.10 | 1.30 | 2.823 | .006 |
| Effectiveness of RTTP | 6.63 | 0.50 | 5.90 | 0.64 | 3.614 | .000 |
| Kind of class/mode of delivery | 4.53 | 0.63 | 4.00 | 0.20 | 1.875 | .064 |

[a]In this table, we sorted faculty according to a "Yes" or "No" response to our question: "Has the RTTP pedagogy affected how you teach?" 88 faculty replied "Yes" and 9 replied "No." We compared these two groups' responses across 5 categories composed of 31 individual questions

respondents, even 55.6% ($n = 5$) still agreed or strongly agreed that "Students engage in critical thinking more in my RTTP classes." Also, 50% of "No" respondents ($n = 4$) agreed or strongly agreed that "Students seem to read assigned material with greater attention to detail." The 9 faculty who responded "No" to "Has the RTTP pedagogy affected how you teach?" confound us. They agreed that two student learning outcomes saw marked improvement and yet did not believe RTTP affected their instructional approach. This finding suggests that students saw improvement from the pedagogy, while faculty believed their teaching practice went un-impacted. Perhaps a greater sample size of like-minded faculty could have offered greater details on this seemingly contradictory perception.

Responses to particular questions on learning outcomes, however, were striking. For example, among the faculty who answered "Yes," 54 respondents (62.1%) either agreed or strongly agreed that students read assigned material with greater attention to detail; 60 respondents (69%) agreed or strongly agreed that retention of content was greater in RTTP classes and, impressively, 71 respondents (81.6%) believed that their Reacting students engaged in critical thinking. These results echo those reported by students: 94 (83.2%) either agreed or strongly agreed that they read with greater attention to detail and 100 (88.5%) either agreed or strongly agreed that they engaged in critical thinking more in RTTP course(s). Moreover, at least half of our faculty respondents agreed or strongly agreed with every statement posed about learning outcomes, except the statement on RTTP improving student understanding of research methodology (32.2%).

**Table 9.9**   The impact of RTTP for faculty: Is content-coverage a problem (*t*-test)

| | Yes (n = 30) | | No (n = 67) | | t | p |
|---|---|---|---|---|---|---|
| | M | SD | M | SD | | |
| Learning outcomes | 5.39 | 0.81 | 5.78 | 0.78 | −2.185 | .031 |
| Student behaviors | 5.36 | 0.89 | 6.02 | 0.85 | −3.405 | .001 |
| Relation to students | 4.70 | 0.98 | 5.37 | 1.07 | −2.866 | .005 |
| Effectiveness of RTTP | 6.43 | 0.61 | 6.63 | 0.50 | −1.584 | .120 |
| Kind of class/mode of delivery | 4.35 | 0.54 | 4.57 | 0.65 | −1.525 | .131 |

### *Content Coverage*

Faculty who do not use Reacting often express concerns about content coverage. To investigate this concern, we specifically asked Reacting faculty if that was a problem (Table 9.9). Of our faculty respondents, 67 of them (69.1%; *n* = 97) answered "No." This is comparable to students' perceptions of their deep learning of course content in classes that use the pedagogy; 113 students (70.6%; *n* = 160) replied "Yes" when asked "Do you feel you learned the course content more deeply when you experienced RTTP in your course/s?" Once again, answers to the questions on modality of classroom delivery did not reveal any statistically significant difference between instructors who did not perceive a problem with content coverage in Reacting classes and those who did.

Somewhat surprising, however, is the fact that the questions on the effectiveness of Reacting did not produce a statistically significant difference between the two groups, but individual questions about student retention of material and their use of content did yield interesting results. Among instructors who did not believe content coverage was a problem, many of them (41 respondents, 60%; *n* = 67) either agreed or strongly agreed that student retention of content in Reacting classes was greater than in non-Reacting classes, while 56 respondents (82.3%; *n* = 68) either agreed or strongly agreed that their Reacting students actively used the information from their assignments within the class.

Moreover, the open-ended responses provided by those who replied that content coverage was not a problem are illuminating. One wrote, "You can't cover everything. If you try, students will forget everything. I'd rather cover a few things well and have students retain what they learned." According to another respondent:

In most of my teaching, the focus is on skill development rather than mastery of a particular set of facts, but in any case, RTTP students master the content in more effective ways—e.g. students playing Darwin get a better sense of the importance of competing accounts of the scientific method than in a traditional philosophy of science class.

Another said, "I don't think coverage should be a high priority, especially in history classes, where learning to be a better investigator and interpreter of the past, especially through using primary sources, is my main goal." Another respondent offered this powerful comment:

Complete coverage of any topic in my field within the timeframe of one semester is a losing battle and really not a useful strategy for [students] in the long run. The goal in my classes is quality versus quantity…I'm not focused on developing knowledge of a body of works but instead developing habits of mind: asking questions, weighing information, recognizing logical arguments, making aesthetic choices, explaining positions.

### Student Behaviors and Interaction with Faculty

We asked both students and faculty six questions regarding student behaviors and found statistically significant differences in all of our comparison groups on this issue. This was also true for the $t$-test comparison between students and faculty on the impact of RTTP (Table 9.5). Looking to the individual survey questions on student behaviors, we found impressive and relevant data that did not emerge from the $t$-tests comparing student respondents who replied "yes" or "no" to the question: "Has the RTTP pedagogy affected how you learn?" (see Table 9.6, Student behaviors). Among our survey respondents, 104 (65%) responded "Yes." Among these, our data show either agreement or strong agreement with these statements: "Peers exhibit more empathy toward other points of view" (59.6%; $n = 62$), "Peers absenteeism is less frequent" (68.3%; $n = 71$), "Peers meet outside of class more often" (74%; $n = 77$), and "Peers seem to know one another better" (85.6%; $n = 89$). A majority of respondents also indicated a heightened degree of empathy both for each other (54.8%; $n = 57$ either agreed or strongly agreed) and for other points of view in a Reacting classroom (59.6%; $n = 62$ either agreed or strongly agreed), although the impact here was not as great.

Faculty responses about student behaviors are even more striking than the student responses. Of our faculty respondents, 63 (72.4%) either agreed or strongly agreed that student absenteeism is less than in non-Reacting classes (compared to 55.2% of student respondents); 65 faculty respondents (74.7%) either agreed or strongly agreed that students met outside of class more often; and 80 faculty respondents (92%) either agreed or strongly agreed that their students seemed to know one another better. Not only do faculty perceive that their students know one another better, 68 of them (78.2%) report that they know their students better in a Reacting versus a non-Reacting class and 45 of them (52.3%) report that, after the course ends, they stay in touch with their Reacting students longer than with their non-Reacting students.

We also asked students seven questions about their relation to their faculty and again found statistically significant differences in all of our comparison groups on this issue. (see Table 9.5; Relation to faculty). Again, responses to the Likert-type questions were enlightening. A majority of students either agreed or strongly agreed with these statements: "I stay in touch with faculty longer after the course ends" (72.1%; $n = 75$), "I know my faculty member/s better" (84.6%; $n = 88$), "I feel my faculty care about my learning" (90.4%; $n = 94$), and "I trust my faculty member as someone who cares about my intellectual development" (91.3%; $n = 95$). Something powerful happens in a Reacting classroom that helps bridge the divide between students and faculty and promotes understanding between the two groups.

Even more remarkable are the 83 student respondents (79.8%) who reported a better understanding of a "faculty member's role as a researcher and scholar" and the 97 respondents (93.3%) who appreciated their "faculty member as teacher." We know of no other high-impact practice that reports such an awareness by students of faculty as teachers, researchers, and scholars (Carpenter et al. 2017; Kuh 2008). These results suggest that student empathy extends beyond their peers to their instructors.

These results reinforce our belief that social cohesion in a Reacting class is an important component. It helps bring students together into a collaborative—albeit liminal—learning environment that promotes performance and success. Students tend to get to know each other better and trust each other to do their part in class because the role-playing does not allow them to remain in their established "cliques." They report that they stay in touch longer with their peers, a by-product that could benefit them later in non-Reacting classes. Our results, like those of Webb and Engar (2016), show that students have more empathy for each other and for differing points of view since their role in the Reacting game often requires that they espouse an argument that is diametrically opposed to their own view.

When students report that in Reacting classes they have a better understanding of a faculty member's role as a researcher and scholar and that they appreciate their faculty member as teacher, they are reflecting some empathy for their instructor. This empathy of students for their faculty member—although it is not highlighted in the literature on relationship-driven teaching—seems in fact to be an unexpected fuel that helps drive that kind of teaching in a Reacting class and prompts us to slightly re-frame our view of such teaching. Similarly, there is an exceptionally high degree of engagement between students and faculty in a Reacting class. As noted above, Beaty-O'Ferrall et al. (2010) argue that relationship-driven teaching is rooted in the desire to focus on the whole student and her experiences in order to promote, among other things, engagement with learning. This kind of engagement, as our data demonstrates, is a key component in Reacting classes.

In contrast to the unexpectedly high awareness among students for their instructors' roles, faculty did not perceive that their Reacting students understood their roles more than their non-Reacting students did. For example, only 25 respondents (28.7%) either agreed or strongly agreed that their students understood their role as a researcher and scholar better, while 34 respondents (39.1%) felt that students understood their role as a teacher better.

### *Impact of Taking More than One RTTP Class*

A comparison of students who had taken one course that included a Reacting game with those who had taken more than one Reacting course revealed significant results across four of our five categories. Only "Kind of class/Mode of delivery" did not yield statistically significant results for these students (see Table 9.10).

The results in the categories "Learning experience" (i.e., students' perceptions of a positive and deep learning experience) and "Relation to faculty" (i.e., their perception of a good and solid working relationship with faculty in class and beyond) were notable. Student respondents relayed that they believed the impact of RTTP was meaningful when experienced in one course and that the frequency of the experience (i.e., taking more than one RTTP course) amplified its positive impact. Indeed, they reported high

**Table 9.10**  The impact of RTTP for students: The number of RTTP courses taken ($t$-test)

|  | 1 course | | More than 1 course | | t | p |
|---|---|---|---|---|---|---|
|  | M | SD | M | SD | | |
| Learning experience | 5.29 | 1.59 | 6.07 | 0.99 | −3.744 | .000 |
| Student behaviors | 5.11 | 1.48 | 5.61 | 0.99 | −2.536 | .012 |
| Relation to faculty | 5.55 | 1.45 | 6.27 | 1.03 | −3.593 | .000 |
| Effectiveness of RTTP | 5.92 | 1.47 | 6.40 | 0.97 | −2.272 | .025 |
| Kind of class/mode of delivery | 4.55 | 1.16 | 4.48 | 0.90 | .337 | .737 |

levels of satisfaction with their own learning, with their peers' behaviors (including attendance and attentiveness in class), with their relation to faculty, and with the effectiveness of RTTP in helping them learn. We conclude, based on these findings, that repeated experiences and exposures to the pedagogy may well lead to deeper learning and help students make sense of their learning experiences as well as construct more meaningful relationships with faculty.

### Translating Skills and Methods from RTTP Classes to Non-RTTP Classes

Student responses to open-ended questions on the effectiveness of RTTP and faculty responses to open-ended questions about the impact of RTTP on their teaching were striking. They suggest that both students and faculty transferred skills and methods from a Reacting environment to a non-Reacting setting. One student said, "I was/am much more involved in the classes I take now (after RTTP)." Another student highlighted the spark RTTP ignited in her learning:

> I've developed a near-religious passion for game based learning of all kinds. I am far more inclined to use games and experiential learning in other classes, and in my own life. If I'm having trouble mastering a concept, I'll resort to puppet shows, free writes, and other things to put myself in the shoes of people experiencing whatever I'm learning about . . . [and] I can better see the effects of those historical events in my current life.

Other students affirmed the lasting effects of Reacting: "It led me to pay close attention to the small and seemingly insignificant details in a text and completely destroyed my fear of speaking in front of others"; "It made me a more open person in classes"; "It's helped me to become more open minded"; "Post RTTP it was easier to put myself out there, actively ask questions, and seek help"; and finally, "RTTP challenged me to take control of my learning: the more I researched and the more I knew, the more prepared I was to participate." It appears that students are taking skills acquired in Reacting classes into their other course work or their lives outside of class.

Faculty responses to the open-ended question on whether RTTP has affected their teaching suggest that they too tend to borrow techniques and strategies for promoting engagement and deeper learning from Reacting and use them in instruction in their non-Reacting classes. One faculty member said, "I am much more conscious of the value of giving students more control and choice in the classroom, even outside of Reacting." Another reported that the pedagogy has "motivated me to try to find new ways to foster discussion in a classroom," and another said, "I see teaching completely immersively now and seek to make even my non-RTTP classes as engaging and urgent as RTTP does." On the receptiveness to instructional innovation, one respondent confirmed: "It's taught me to a) trust my students more; b) take more risks (both in form and content) in the classroom." She went on to affirm the benefits of RTTP for her research agenda, stating that the use of RTTP taught her to "think about scholarship differently." Concerning general faculty perceptions of students, one faculty member confessed that because of RTTP, "I don't prejudge students anymore." Just as students seem to be translating learning skills and behaviors from Reacting to other environments, instructors seem to be doing exactly the same thing. Indeed, this is one of the significant ways that Reacting seems to have affected how instructors teach.

In these responses, we see both the impact of RTTP on instructors' teaching philosophies and a powerful collective testimony for the value of relationship-driven teaching. Instructors' responses reveal a confidence that the pedagogy has a positive impact on student behaviors, improves their relation to students, and is an effective strategy, or as one respondent put it: RTTP instructors become "more concerned with how students learn and how [they] demonstrate what [they] are learning." Faculty also report that they perceive RTTP to be an effective pedagogy (Table 9.11).

**Table 9.11**   The effectiveness of RTTP pedagogy

| Items | n | % |
|---|---|---|
| RTTP is an effective tool for promoting active learning | 93 | 97.9 |
| RTTP is an effective tool to create a student-centered classroom | 88 | 93.6 |
| RTTP is an effective tool for moving beyond the standard lecture-based class | 91 | 95.8 |
| RTTP is an effective tool for empowering students to take ownership of their learning | 85 | 89.5 |
| RTTP is an effective tool for promoting student engagement with course material | 87 | 91.6 |

## *Length of Instructional Experience*

Our findings indicate that from early-career instructors (1–10 years) to mid-career instructors (11–20 years) to experienced instructors (>20 years), RTTP offers a deeply impactful approach across the five categories measured in this study. Faculty report that the pedagogy was effective regardless of years of teaching experience. We looked at faculty who had used the pedagogy for less than a year against those who had used it from one to five years and those who had used it for more than five years (see Table 9.12).

In the ANOVA analysis, three groups were compared: 22 (22.4%; $n = 98$) respondents replied they had been teaching with RTTP less than one year, compared to 43 (43.8%) respondents teaching with RTTP from one to five years, compared to 33 (33.6%) respondents teaching with RTTP for more than five years. Given the statistically significant results within three categories (Student behaviors, Effectiveness of RTTP, and, surprisingly, Kind of class/Mode of delivery), we conclude that perceived impacts of RTTP increase through prolonged and sustained use of the pedagogy.

As with students who have experienced RTTP more than once, faculty, at any stage of their teaching career, who have used the pedagogy repeatedly, find that its impact on their teaching and perceptions of their students' learning increases over time. With increased use, faculty exhibit an amplified comfortability in using the pedagogy in any number of instructional settings (Table 9.12, Kind of class/Mode of delivery; $p = .002$).

**Table 9.12**  One-way analysis of variance of the impacts of RTTP by years of RTTP pedagogy use[a]

|  | Source | df | SS | MS | F | p |
|---|---|---|---|---|---|---|
| Learning outcomes | Between groups | 2 | 3.247 | 1.623 | 2.524 | .086 |
|  | Within groups | 93 | 59.809 | .643 |  |  |
|  | Total | 95 | 63.056 |  |  |  |
| Student behaviors | Between groups | 2 | 10.973 | 5.486 | 7.560 | .001 |
|  | Within groups | 92 | 66.767 | .726 |  |  |
|  | Total | 94 | 77.740 |  |  |  |
| Relation to students | Between groups | 2 | 6.384 | 3.192 | 2.839 | .064 |
|  | Within groups | 91 | 102.310 | 1.124 |  |  |
|  | Total | 93 | 108.694 |  |  |  |
| Effectiveness of RTTP | Between groups | 2 | 3.781 | 1.890 | 6.759 | .002 |
|  | Within groups | 90 | 25.173 | .280 |  |  |
|  | Total | 92 | 28.953 |  |  |  |
| Kind of class/mode of delivery | Between groups | 2 | 4.507 | 2.254 | 6.583 | .002 |
|  | Within groups | 82 | 28.073 | .342 |  |  |
|  | Total | 84 | 32.580 |  |  |  |

[a]The three groups compared here include faculty teaching with RTTP for <1 year, from 1 to 5 years, and for >5 years

## *Other Factors: Kind of Class/Mode of Delivery, Institutional Support and Peer Mentors*

For all of our $t$-test comparisons, perceived differences in Kind of class (e.g., first-year experience; "gen ed"; Science, Technology, Engineering, and Mathematics (STEM);, Study Abroad, etc.) or Mode of delivery (e.g., face-to-face, hybrid, or online) were not statistically significant. How this relates to the effectiveness of the pedagogy across several kinds of classes is unclear since our student respondents had experienced the pedagogy in such a variety of courses, from large lectures to small seminars. Similarly, the significance of the mode of delivery is unknown since the number of respondents who had used Reacting in anything other than a face-to-face class was very small. Again, only one student (.006%; $n = 161$) indicated some experience with RTTP in an online environment.

A key component of the pedagogy, as conceived by Mark Carnes, is the use of preceptors or peer mentors to facilitate the game. We wanted to know how many Reacting faculty members had access to this particular resource and what impact a peer mentor might have on the effectiveness of RTTP for both students and faculty. In our survey, 81 student respondents (51.3%;

$n = 158$) reported that their Reacting course did not have a preceptor or peer mentor. For these students, the absence of a peer mentor did not diminish their satisfaction with the pedagogy or their perception of their learning in the course—regardless of the type of course that included a Reacting game. The results for faculty were similar. Of our 98 faculty respondents, only 38 of them report having some kind of peer mentor in their Reacting class. As with the student respondents, the lack of an embedded preceptor or peer mentor did not diminish instructors' perception of Reacting's impact on student learning outcomes in that course, student behaviors, or their relation to students and the overall effectiveness of RTTP. A $t$-test was performed on the impacts of RTTP by a preceptor/peer mentor use and no statistically significant findings emerged.

Again, although most of our faculty respondents—61 respondents (88.4%; $n = 69$)—reported that their institution supported their use of Reacting, 58 of them (93.5%; $n = 62$) indicated they would continue to use RTTP without institutional support. Given the time faculty must invest to become skilled gamemasters, this willingness to use Reacting without institutional support suggests that the pedagogy may increase professional engagement and job satisfaction across faculty ranks and institution types contrary to current national trends on these aspects of instructors' work (Inside Higher Education 2015).

In summary, the kind of class (e.g., first-year experience, "gen ed," STEM, Study Abroad, etc.) or the delivery modality (e.g., face-to-face, hybrid, or online) was not statistically significant for any of our $t$-test comparisons. In addition, the degree of institutional support or the absence of peer mentors did not affect most faculty in deciding whether to use Reacting games in their classes.

## CONCLUSIONS

Student and faculty respondents alike found RTTP to be a powerful learning and teaching strategy that impacts students' behaviors, fosters relationships among students, promotes continuing dialogue between faculty and students, and improves learning. We posit that RTTP humanizes instruction and helps close the gap between teachers and students. Throughout our study, students report that Reacting has changed how they approach learning, and many faculty affirm that it has fundamentally changed how they teach.

For students and faculty who experienced or used the Reacting pedagogy, the Kind of class/Mode of delivery was not statistically significant across the survey data, except for the ANOVA comparison on number of years teaching. Reacting is not a pedagogy dependent on a particular kind of class, particular kind of environment, or particular mode of delivery. It does not require special technology or special classroom furniture; it requires only a dedicated instructor determined to give her students an active and engaging opportunity for deeper learning. Our respondents report experiencing/using it in all kinds of classes—from first-year experience courses, to Honors classes, to upper-level classes required in the major. It is a remarkably flexible and effective pedagogy when innovating with attention to high-impact practices.[1]

For students, Reacting provides a unique environment for engaging with course content and for connecting more closely with their peers and faculty; our data indicate that the more often a student experiences Reacting, the more potent the results in these areas. For faculty too, Reacting provides the same opportunities for engaging students with course content and for constructing a more relationship-driven teaching environment. In addition, faculty reported that the pedagogy changed the way they teach beyond the Reacting classroom. According to our data, the length of a faculty member's teaching experience does not constrain the transformative impacts of RTTP. The pedagogy works equally well with brand new faculty and those who have been teaching for many years. Most of our instructor respondents were older and tenured and had been teaching for more than 20 years. As noted above, instructors report that adopting the pedagogy positively affects their teaching, helps them teach content more effectively, and assists their students to learn content more deeply. Given the responses about both teaching from our respondents, RTTP may be a potent antidote to faculty fatigue and burn-out (Lackritz 2004; Malesic 2016).

One concern that faculty often express when thinking about flipping their classroom or embedding more active learning strategies into their course is that they may have to sacrifice content. This concern leaves them fearful that students may not successfully master information and that their performance evaluations may suffer (Hodges 2006). The results from this

---

[1] Faculty were asked to identify "Three high impact practices RTTP supports most effectively," 72 (29.5%; $n = 244$) selected collaborative learning; 59 (24.2%) selected writing intensive courses; and, 58 respondents (23.8%) selected first-year experience course.

survey suggest that for RTTP faculty there is not a significant trade-off between active learning strategies and content; Reacting faculty report in high numbers that the pedagogy is an effective tool for active learning and that content coverage is not a problem.

Our data on student behaviors and relation to faculty support the notion that social cohesion and relationship-driven teaching serve as crucial elements of the pedagogy. Students know their peers in different contexts and come to know them better; in short, the pedagogy literally pulls students out of their normal, outside-of-class "cliques" and forces them into new circles, new "cliques," of allies and working partners by assigning them roles to play. As Webb and Engar demonstrated in their 2016 article, the mere act of crossing boundaries leads to higher levels of coherence within a group, and as Friedkin (2004) argued, social cohesion is an experience grounded within group membership and the sharing of a common space, both of which may lead to greater investments in the academic environment and greater success.

Thus, we contend that the role-playing within the Reacting pedagogy promotes social cohesion within the class and that this cohesion holds a RTTP class together and distinguishes it as an effective, high-impact learning space. In addition, our survey results support Rogers' and Renard's (1999) conceptualization of relationship-driven teaching. RTTP reflects the motivational learning environments resultant of relationship-driven teaching—environments that require teachers to more fully understand their students' educational and emotional needs, providing opportunities for deeper learning, support, and student success. We assert that a Reacting classroom is a unique setting for the relationship-driven teaching model to thrive shaping the RTTP classroom into a highly effective, significant learning environment for students and teaching space for instructors.

Though this study is conclusive in certain categories of impact for students' and faculty self-perceptions, additional research on RTTP is necessary. The authors welcome individuals interested in participating in a continuation of the data collection begun in this study to be in touch with either Hagood or Norman.

**Acknowledgement** The authors thank Dr. Colleen M. Kuusinen, Assistant Director for the Scholarship for Teaching and Learning at the University of Georgia for her early assistance in crafting the most seamless expression of the survey instruments found in the Appendix. Her suggested revisions and willingness to review our work were crucial to the development of this project.

APPENDIX

## Student Survey

| Category | Sub category (questions) | Response type |
|---|---|---|
| Demographic information | Gender | Categorical |
| | Age | |
| | Current status as a student | |
| | Current student/graduate from at UGA | |
| | Ethnicity | |
| Experience learning with RTTP | In how many courses have you experienced the RTTP approach to teaching and learning? | Categorical |
| | In what kinds of classes have you experienced RTTP pedagogy? Click all that apply | Multiple response |
| | Was a preceptor/peer mentor used in your RTTP class (es)? | Categorical |
| | Please describe what kind of preceptors/peer mentors you experienced in your RTTP course(s). Please click all that apply | Multiple response |
| | Briefly describe the kinds of course(s) in which you have most commonly experienced RTTP--for example, early American History courses | Open-ended |
| | Which **published** RTTP games have you played in your course(s)? Please click all that apply | Multiple response |
| | Which RTTP games **in development** have you played in your course(s)? Please click all that apply | |
| | Which RTTP **Science, Technology, Engineering, and Mathematics (STEM) games** have you played in your course(s)? Please click all that apply | |
| | Has RTTP inspired research ideas for you? | Categorical |
| | If yes, please explain how RTTP inspired new research ideas | Open-ended |
| | Has the RTTP pedagogy affected how you learn? | Categorical |
| | If yes, please explain how RTTP affected how you learn | Open-ended |
| | Do you feel you learned the course content more deeply when you experienced RTTP in your course(s)? | Categorical |
| | If yes, please explain how you learned the content more deeply when RTTP was used in your course(s) | Open-ended |

(*continued*)

| Category | Sub category (questions) | Response type |
|---|---|---|
| Learning experience (7) | I understand concepts and ideas more deeply than in non-RTTP classes | 7-Likert type |
| | I obtained a better understanding of research methodology in my RTTP course(s) | |
| | I engaged in critical thinking more in my RTTP course(s) | |
| | I read assigned material with greater attention to detail in my RTTP course(s) | |
| | I actively used the information from assignments in my RTTP course(s) | |
| | I read and researched beyond the material assigned in my RTTP course(s) | |
| | I feel my arguments are evidence-based in my RTTP course(s) | |
| Student behaviors (6) | Peers' absenteeism is less frequent | |
| | Peers seem to know one another better | |
| | Peers meet outside of class more often | |
| | Peers exhibit more empathy towards each other | |
| | Peers exhibit more empathy towards other points of view | |
| | Peers stay in touch with each other even after the course has ended | |
| Relation to faculty (7) | I know my faculty member(s) better | |
| | I stay in touch with faculty longer after the course ends | |
| | I feel my faculty care about my learning | |
| | I better understand my faculty member's role as a researcher and scholar | |
| | I appreciate my faculty member as teacher | |
| | I trust my faculty member as someone who cares about my intellectual development | |
| | I believe my faculty member cares for me as a person | |
| Effectiveness of RTTP (6) | RTTP is an effective tool for promoting active learning | |
| | RTTP is an effective tool to use in a flipped classroom | |
| | RTTP is an effective tool to create a student-centered classroom | |
| | RTTP is an effective tool for moving beyond the standard lecture-based class | |
| | RTTP is an effective tool for empowering students to take ownership of their learning | |
| | RTTP is an effective tool for promoting student engagement with course material | |

(continued)

| Category | Sub category (questions) | Response type |
|---|---|---|
| Kind of class/mode of delivery (6) | RTTP works well in First Year Experience course or First-Year Odyssey seminar<br>RTTP works well in a STEM (Science, Technology, Engineering, Mathematics) class<br>RTTP works well in a study abroad program<br>RTTP works well in a foreign language class<br>RTTP works well in a hybrid class (meeting face-to-face and online)<br>RTTP works well in an online class | |
| Comments on mode of delivery | If you have experienced RTTP in a first-year experience course or First-Year Odyssey seminar, please comment on that experience<br>If you have experienced RTTP in a STEM (Science, Technology, Engineering, Mathematics) class, please comment on that experience<br>If you have experienced RTTP in a study abroad program, please comment on that experience<br>If you have experienced RTTP in a foreign language class, please comment on that experience<br>If you have experienced RTTP in a hybrid class (meeting face-to-face and online), please comment on that experience<br>If you have experienced RTTP in an online class, please comment on that experience | Open-ended |
| Overall | If you have additional comments concerning your experience with RTTP, please include those below | |

## Faculty Survey

| Category | Sub category (questions) | Response type |
|---|---|---|
| Demographic information | Gender<br>Age<br>Highest level of graduate education<br>Ethnicity<br>Currently employed in higher education/ retired from higher education employment<br>Currently tenured or on the tenure track<br>Current official title/rank; Official title/ rank at the time of the retirement | Categorical/multiple response |

(*continued*)

| Category | Sub category (questions) | Response type |
|----------|--------------------------|---------------|
| | How long have you been teaching in higher education? | |
| | What kind of institution are you currently employed at or retired from? | |
| | Does your institution support your use of the Reacting to the Past (RTTP) pedagogy? | |
| | How does your institution support RTTP pedagogy? Click all that apply | |
| | Would you continue to use RTTP if you had no institutional support for the pedagogy? | |
| Experience teaching RTTP | How long have you used the RTTP pedagogy in your teaching? | Categorical |
| | In what kinds of classes have you used RTTP pedagogy? Click all that apply | Multiple response |
| | Do you use a preceptor/peer mentor in your RTTP classes? | Categorical |
| | Please describe what kind of preceptors/ peer mentors you use in your RTTP classes. Please click all that apply | Multiple response |
| | Briefly describe the kinds of courses in which you have most commonly used RTTP pedagogy--for example, early American History courses | Open-ended |
| | Which **published** RTTP games have you used in your course(s)? Please click all that apply | Multiple response |
| | Which RTTP games **in development** have you used in your course(s)? Please click all that apply | |
| | Which RTTP **Science, Technology, Engineering, and Mathematics (STEM)** games have you used in your course(s)? Please click all that apply | |
| | Has RTTP pedagogy inspired research for you? | Categorical |
| | If yes, please explain | Open-ended |
| | Has the RTTP pedagogy affected how you teach? | Categorical |
| | Please explain why you answered yes or no | Open-ended |
| | Is content-coverage a problem when you use the RTTP pedagogy in your class? | Categorical |
| | Please explain why you answered yes or no | Open-ended |

*(continued)*

| Category | Sub category (questions) | Response type |
|---|---|---|
| Learning outcomes (7) | Student retention of content is greater than in non-RTTP classes | 7-Likert type |
| | Students have a better understanding of research methodology in my RTTP classes | |
| | Students engage in critical thinking more in my RTTP classes | |
| | Students seem to read assigned material with greater attention to detail | |
| | Students actively use the information from their assignments within the class | |
| | Students read and research beyond the material assigned for class | |
| | Students' arguments are evidence-based | |
| Student behaviors (6) | Student absenteeism is less | |
| | Students seem to know one another better | |
| | Students meet outside of class more often | |
| | Students exhibit more empathy towards each other | |
| | Students exhibit more empathy towards other points of view | |
| | Students stay in touch with each other even after the course has ended | |
| Relation to students (6) | I know my students better | |
| | I stay in touch with students longer after the course ends | |
| | I feel that my students understand my role as a research and scholar better | |
| | I feel that my students understand my role as a teacher better | |
| | I feel that my students know me as a person better | |
| | I feel that my students trust me more | |
| Effectiveness of RTTP (6) | RTTP is an effective tool for promoting active learning | |
| | RTTP is an effective tool to use in a flipped classroom | |
| | RTTP is an effective tool to create a student-centered classroom | |
| | RTTP is an effective tool for moving beyond the standard lecture-based class | |
| | RTTP is an effective tool for empowering students to take ownership of their learning | |
| | RTTP is an effective tool for promoting student engagement with course material | |

(continued)

| Category | Sub category (questions) | Response type |
|---|---|---|
| Kind of class/mode of delivery (6) | RTTP works well in First Year Experience course or First-Year Odyssey seminar RTTP works well in a STEM course RTTP works well in a study abroad program RTTP works well in a foreign language class RTTP works well in a hybrid class RTTP works well in an online class | |
| Comments on mode of delivery | If you have used RTTP in a first-year experience class, please comment on that experience If you have used RTTP in a STEM class, please comment on that experience If you have used RTTP in a study abroad program, please comment on that experience If you have used RTTP in a foreign language class, please comment on that experience If you have used RTTP in a hybrid class, please comment on that experience If you have used RTTP in an online class, please comment on that experience | Open-ended |
| Overall | If you have additional comments concerning your experience with RTTP, please include those below | |
| Engagement with RTTP faculty development activities | Are you currently a faculty member at The University of Georgia (UGA) or have you retired from UGA? Click all that apply (attending UGA RTTP conferences) Please click all that apply (attending Regional RTTP conferences) Is your institution a member of the RTTP Consortium? Are you a member of any RTTP committees? Have you written a RTTP game? Please answer "yes" if your game appears anywhere on the BLORG at Level 2 or above | Categorical/multiple response/open-ended |

*(continued)*

| Category | Sub category (questions) | Response type |
|---|---|---|
| | Briefly explain why you decided to write a RTTP game Is your RTTP game connected to your own area of expertise/research? If yes, briefly explain how your RTTP game connects to your area of expertise/research and whether it opened new avenues of research for you If no, briefly explain how you tackled the challenge of writing a game outside of your own area of expertise/research | |

## REFERENCES

Association of American Colleges & Universities. (2007). *College learning for the new global century: A report from the national leadership council for liberal education & America's promise.* Washington, DC: Association of American Colleges & Universities.

Beaty-O'Ferrall, M. E., Green, A., & Hanna, F. (2010). Classroom management strategies for difficult students: Promoting change through relationships. *Middle School Journal, 41*(4), 4–11.

Bishop, C. F., Caston, M. I., & King, C. A. (2014). Learner-centered environments: Creating effective strategies based on student attitudes and faculty reflection. *Journal of the Scholarship of Teaching and Learning, 14*(3), 46–63.

Burney, J. M., Powers, R. G., & Carnes, M. C. (2010). *Reacting to the past: A new approach to student engagement and to enhancing general education. Teagle foundation white paper report.* New York: Barnard College.

Carnes, M. C. (2004). Being there: The liminal classroom. *Chronicle Review.* Retrieved from http://www.chronicle.com/article/The-Liminal-Classroom/9659

Carnes, M. C. (2014). *Minds on fire: How role-immersion games transform college.* Cambridge, MA: Harvard University Press.

Carpenter, R., Morin, C., Sweet, C., & Blythe, H. (2017). Editorial: The role of faculty development in teaching and learning through high-impact educational practices. *The Journal of Faculty Development, 31*(1), 7–12.

Chickering, A., & Gamson, Z. (1987). Seven principles for good practice in undergraduate education. *AAHE Bulletin, 39*(1), 3–7.

Cook, K. S., Cheshire, C., Rice, E. R. W., & Nakagawa, S. (2013). Social exchange theory. In J. Delamater (Ed.), *Handbook of social psychology* (pp. 61–88). New York: Springer.

Fenty, J. (1997). Knowing your students better: A key to involving first-year students. *Center for Research on Learning and Teaching Occasional Papers, 9,* 1–7.

Friedkin, N. E. (2004). Social cohesion. *Annual Review of Sociology, 30,* 409–425.

Hodges, L. C. (2006). Preparing faculty for pedagogical change: Helping faculty deal with fear. In S. Chadwick-Blossey & D. R. Robertson (Eds.), *To improve the academy, resources for faculty, instructional, and organizational development.* Bolton: Anker Publishing.

Inside Higher Education. (2015). *Going through the motions? The 2015 survey of faculty workplace engagement.* Retrieved from https://www.insidehighered.com/news/survey/going-through-motions-2015-survey-faculty-workplace-engagement

Kuh, G. D. (2008). *Excerpt from high-impact educational practices: What they are, who has access to them, and why they matter.* Washington, DC: Association of American Colleges and Universities.

Kuh, G. D., & Hu, S. (2001). The effects of student-faculty interaction in the 1990s. *Review of Higher Education, 24*(3), 309–332.

Kuh, G. D., O'Donnell, K., & Reed, S. (2013). *Ensuring quality and taking high-impact practices to scale.* Washington, DC: Association of American Colleges and Universities.

Lackritz, J. (2004). Exploring burnout among university faculty: Incidence, performance, and demographic issues. *Teaching and Teacher Education, 20*(7), 713–730.

Lamport, M. A. (1993). Student-faculty informal interaction and the effect on college student outcomes: A review of the literature. *Adolescence, 28,* 971–990.

Malesic, J. (2016). The 40-year-old burnout. *Chronicle of Higher Education.* Retrieved from http://www.chronicle.com/article/The-40-Year-Old-Burnout/237979

National Center for Education Statistics. (2013). *Race/ethnicity of college faculty.* Retrieved from https://nces.ed.gov/fastfacts/display.asp?id=61

Proctor, N. W. (2011). *Reacting to the Past game designer's handbook.* New York: Barnard College.

Rogers, S., & Renard, L. (1999). Relationship-driven teaching. *Educational Leadership, 57,* 34–37.

Slater, L. (2004). Relationship-driven teaching cultivates collaboration and inclusion. *Kappa Delta Pi Record, 40*(2), 58–59.

Smith, D. G. (2015). *Diversity's promise for higher education: Making it work.* Baltimore: Johns Hopkins University Press.

Stroessner, S. J., Beckerman, L. S., & Whittaker, A. (2009). All the world's a stage? Consequences of a role-playing pedagogy on psychological factors and writing and rhetorical skill in college undergraduates. *Journal of Educational Psychology, 101*(3), 605.

Swaner, L., & Brownell, J. (2008). *Outcomes of high-impact practices for underserved students: A review of the literature.* Washington, DC: Association of American Colleges and Universities.

Vygotsky, L. S., Cole, M., Stein, S., & Sekula, A. (1978). *Mind in society: The development of higher mental process.* Cambridge, MA: Harvard University Press.

Webb, J., & Engar, A. (2016). Exploring classroom community: A social network study of Reacting to the Past. *Teaching and Learning Inquiry, 4*(1), 1–17.

# CHAPTER 10

# How to Perform Educational Research in Reacting to the Past Settings: A Primer for the Scholarship of Teaching and Learning

*Colleen M. Kuusinen and C. Edward Watson*

As chronicled in Chap. 1 and throughout this book, Reacting to the Past (RTTP) is deeply rooted in what we know about how people learn. Certainly, all good pedagogical practice begins with that foundation; however, it is important that an evidence base emerges that is built upon research once a pedagogy is in practice in the field. This book serves to contribute to that base in meaningful ways, and we are hopeful that you, as a reader of this book, will feel inspired to both adopt RTTP in your course settings and to investigate the effectiveness of your practices as you teach using this method. To assist you with the latter, this closing chapter is provided to help you begin such work. We've approached this chapter with the perspective that readers likely will not have extensive experience with social science or educational research, so it is intended to serve as a primer, a starting point, for those who are beginning a research journey regarding their RTTP

C.M. Kuusinen (✉)
University of Georgia, Athens, GA, USA

C.E. Watson
Association of American Colleges and Universities, Washington, DC, USA

pedagogy and their students. This domain of educational research is often termed the Scholarship of Teaching and Learning (SoTL).

## WHAT IS SoTL?

Put simply, SoTL is studying the effectiveness and impact of your teaching. It is the systematic examination of the dynamic and complex processes of teaching and learning in higher education classrooms conducted by disciplinary teacher-scholars. While many of those who teach practice *scholarly teaching*—teaching that is reflective and informed by research-based best practices—SoTL scholars go one step further: they pose research questions about teaching and learning that they can investigate through well-designed research studies, typically in their own classrooms. As a result of this process of inquiry, data collection, and analysis, SoTL scholars can make data-informed conclusions. By playing the dual role of teacher and researcher, SoTL scholars enrich their understanding of their own teaching, their students, and the nature of teaching and learning within their discipline.

Importantly, the work of a SoTL scholar is not finished once the study has been conducted, the data analyzed, and conclusions drawn. Nor is their work complete when they apply those conclusions to make changes to their subsequent teaching or to design further SoTL research questions and studies. SoTL scholars take the next step to share those findings publicly and make them available for peer review and commentary. The notion of SoTL has its roots in Ernst Boyer's foundational text, *Scholarship Reconsidered: Priorities of the Professoriate*, which argues that teaching, research, and service are all scholarly endeavors that should be more equally valued and pursued with similar levels of inquiry and rigor (1991). Similarly, Lee Shulman, former president of the American Educational Research Association, suggested that the same standards of collaboration and sharing of findings that enriches our disciplinary research can also enrich our teaching; moreover, it can increase the value of teaching in higher education (1993).

SoTL research is conducted in all disciplines and draws from social science research methods; however, disciplinary ways of constructing knowledge are also employed in research by SoTL scholars. The notion of disciplinary styles (Huber and Morreale 2002; McKinney 2013) allows for SoTL scholars to use methods of constructing knowledge within their discipline to investigate teaching and learning in their classrooms. For example, to collect data on the same research question about student engagement in challenging work, scholars in different fields would approach the question differently. Arts and humanities scholars might use content analysis to explore student work, while researchers in psychology might employ survey research methods. Thus, your own disciplinary training can be an asset in conducting SoTL research as long as the method you employ allows you to answer your research question. This chapter will explore a few different common research methods you might employ in RTTP settings.

No matter the research methodology used, by conducting SoTL research, you are part of a critical movement to stimulate scholarly and academic conversation about teaching and learning in higher education, specifically within the disciplines currently and potentially served by RTTP. We hope that you join this movement by creating and sharing the evidence you discover regarding the effectiveness of RTTP.

## WHERE TO BEGIN

If your disciplinary training is not in the social sciences, the most daunting aspect of performing SoTL is likely where to begin. One thing you've probably noted as you've read the chapters in this book is that most of them were written by interdisciplinary teams. In addition to the expert/ instructor from within a specific discipline, s/he is often collaborating with someone who has experience within the social science research field. If you've never engaged in such research, you may want to adopt this model yourself and reach out to a colleague from your institution's school of education or department of psychology to see if they might be willing to collaborate with you. In both of those disciplines, collaboration and joint publications are encouraged, and you'd likely learn a lot by working with someone with such training. Other places to look for a collaborator might be your university's office of assessment, office of institutional research, or teaching and learning center. Many teaching centers' missions include overt support for SoTL. There are likely many opportunities to work with a collaborator, and the first time through a SoTL project, you'll find the experience to be invaluable.

Regardless of whether you are on your own or are working with a group of colleagues, the first step, if you're not already doing so, is to engage in the process we briefly described above as *scholarly teaching*. Another way to think about this is taking steps to ensure that your teaching practice is as strong as it can possibly be. This might include performing a literature review regarding RTTP as well as the learning outcomes you are hoping to impact, attending conferences where RTTP best practices are detailed, chatting with colleagues who have had success with RTTP, attending relevant faculty development workshops on your campus, and journaling about your experiences teaching. All of this reflection and study into how to teach well with RTTP will ensure your practices are as effective as possible. The more your practice is grounded in theory and evidence, the more likely you are to find something of value through your own research.

The next step in the process would be to give some thought to where you anticipate publishing or sharing your research. This is important as it will help you understand the expectations and norms of your final research project. For instance, if your discipline is in English or the Humanities, you are likely very familiar with style and format expectations set forth by the Modern Language Association (MLA). Historians might be most familiar with the *Chicago Manual of Style*. Do you imagine yourself publishing your SoTL research within one of the journals in your field, or do you think you'll consider publishing within a SoTL or education journal? As an example of the latter, the *International Journal of Teaching and Learning in Higher Education* is a multidisciplinary SoTL journal. Rather than allowing a wide range of styles, it, like many other SoTL journals, has standardized around the style expectations of the social sciences and education. These are set forth in the *Publication Manual of the American Psychological Association* (APA). As APA is most closely aligned with education and SoTL, it offers clear guidance regarding the elements and sub-elements of a manuscript and of the things to consider as you plan for your research project.

Chapter 2 of the APA's publication manual provides a list of required manuscript elements, and as you begin your planning, you may want to simply list those headings in a Word file and fill in the blanks as you go. The core elements are Introduction, Method, Results, and Discussion (APA 2010). Your introduction would be largely built upon your findings from your literature review and would conclude with an overt statement of your research hypotheses or questions. The heart of your planning would be determining your methodology, and as a best practice, it's an excellent idea to draft your Method section before you begin your research study. Further, your research questions will provide a rudder for your methodology as all of your methodological choices will flow from those questions.

One way to think about this is *alignment*. Do your research methods align with your research questions? Further, do your data analysis techniques align with your methods? As you write up your results, do they answer your research questions, and are they grounded in the data you collected? In other words, do they all logically match? It is essential that your research questions be well-developed, based upon a gap you've found in the literature, and do indeed articulate something that can be measured and that your method and results follow closely the path charted by your research questions.

## FORMING A RESEARCH QUESTION

Just like disciplinary research, a SoTL research study begins with a research question. This research question should be informed by your own curiosity about teaching and learning in your classroom and with the pedagogy that you employ. From there, you can seek to engage in the literature surrounding your area of interest, narrowing and expanding your question as you read about what other scholars have investigated and what gaps exist in the literature.

Often scholars wonder what kind of research questions one can ask in a SoTL study. A simple but useful framework for two typical types of SoTL questions are "What instructional strategy works for particular [learning] outcomes?" and "What is happening when . . .?" (adapted from Hutchings 2000). While other types of SoTL questions exist (see Hutchings 2000), these two kinds of research questions encompass the vast majority of SoTL work, particularly for those just beginning to engage in SoTL research.

The first type of question is one that seeks to provide evidence about the *effectiveness* of a teaching approach, curriculum, or tool for a particular outcome. To brainstorm this type of question, we typically ask SoTL scholars to think about a particular instructional strategy that they feel strongly "works" or "doesn't work" to teach a particular concept, skill, or idea. Then we ask them what they would need to show their colleagues in order to convince them that everyone—or no one—in their department should adopt this strategy to teach that concept, skill, or idea.

One example of a "What works" question is in Chap. 6 of this book. Gasper-Hulvat and colleagues seek to evaluate the effectiveness of RTTP curriculum on changes in writing engagement in art history. The particular instructional strategy is the RTTP pedagogy, and the learning outcome is critical writing about art history. Similarly, Bernstein and colleagues (Chap. 8) look at the efficacy of the RTTP pedagogy for a different learning outcome: that of competency in cultural differences, teamwork, and public speaking. While these two studies frame the instructional strategy broadly as the RTTP pedagogy and associated curriculum, Bledsoe and colleagues (Chap. 3) focus more narrowly on a particular aspect of the curriculum: the active and bystander roles. They seek to understand if each of those roles is equally effective at improving students' perceived engagement and perceived learning. "What works" questions can focus on broad pedagogies or particular components of a pedagogy or curriculum. Often, new scholars weaken their research questions by asking "Does this work?", but not specifying for what instructional outcome they are aiming. We always have particular goals in mind when teaching, so a best practice is to make those instructional goals explicit and stated within your research question.

The second type of SoTL research question is a "What is happening when...?" question. To brainstorm this type of research question, think about a phenomenon you have observed in your classroom that puzzles, confuses, or even annoys you because you can't quite explain it—or, you think you can explain what is happening, but based off pure conjecture rather than systematically gathered evidence. Once you've thought of that phenomenon, you can design a "What is happening when...?" question that seeks to uncover, illuminate, or make visible what was previously hidden. In Chap. 5, Watson and Moskal ask this type of question: "What issues and challenges are faced by both faculty and students when scaling an RTTP game to large classes?" This study seeks to uncover the obstacles or challenges in scaling RTTP that may not be apparent or visible. In such questions, the environmental factors that impact students and teachers are foregrounded in order to increase our ability to understand the complexities of teaching and learning in higher education classrooms.

Often time, these two types of SoTL research questions work together and complement each other. For example, in addition to the "What is happening when...?" question about scaling up an RTTP pedagogy, Watson and Moskal also seek to assess the efficacy of the game for student learning in the *Modernism vs. Traditionalism: Art in Paris, 1888–89* RTTP game. Combining both types of questions can provide rich data that helps to illuminate the complexities of teaching as well as the contextual and environmental factors that may influence the efficacy of a specific instructional strategy for a particular instructional goal.

## STUDY DESIGNS

After forming your research question(s), the next question to consider is how you will design your study to collect sufficient and appropriate data to answer your research question(s). This would be the Method section mentioned above. At the same time, you must also balance the practical restraints on your time and resources. Your research question(s) determines the appropriateness of methods and sources of data, so keep it close by as you ask yourself the following questions:

- What do I need to collect and from whom to answer my research question?
- From how many participants will I, and can I, collect evidence?
- Do I need a comparison group? How can I ethically create a comparison group?
- When or at what point(s) will I collect that evidence?
- What is the start and end of my study? What constraints on my time and resources must I factor in?
- What ethical issues do I need to consider before designing my study?

Some thoughts on each question are provided below.

*What Do I Need to Collect and from Whom to Answer My Research Question?* This first step asks you to consider what will constitute evidence, or data, that will either (a) provide definitive evidence of the efficacy of your instructional strategy for the outcome intended or (b) provide detailed information about the process or phenomena you are seeking to understand further. Will you collect and analyze student work? Will you survey students? Will you observe students working or faculty teaching?

Your sources of data can be qualitative or quantitative, and they may also contain direct or indirect measures. Common sources of qualitative data in SoTL studies are student assignments, written survey responses, interviews, observations, and/or group discussions. Common sources of quantitative data are exam scores, grades, grading that employs rubrics, or scale responses on surveys. No one method is better than the other; however, one method might be better suited to answering your specific research question. For example, say you are interested in the reasons students have for liking RTTP pedagogy. You have some ideas why they like it based on your literature review, but you're not confident you can list all the possible reasons they might have. In this case, it would be unwise to design a survey question with a list of possible reasons for liking RTTP pedagogy (a quantitative measure); you might miss listing a reason or two that students have and never know it, thus biasing your data. It is much simpler and more direct to ask students in an open-ended question (qualitative measure) to list all the reasons they like RTTP pedagogy. Qualitative measures may lead to the development of quantitative measures. In this example, after asking this open-ended question in a few classes with groups of different students, you will start to see a point where no new reasons are listed that you haven't seen before (this is called data saturation). Then you can feel more confident designing an exhaustive checklist of reasons which you can use in subsequent studies.

Another decision point is whether you can collect *direct or indirect measures* of your outcomes or, ideally, both. *Direct measures* are those artifacts of student work that show concretely students have achieved the outcome. Gasper-Hulvat and colleagues (Chap. 6) use a *direct measure* of critical writing engagement: student essays. This is a direct measure because the essays show and provide evidence that students are critically engaged in the study of art history. In Chap. 3, Bledsoe and colleagues also collect a direct measure of learning from students in the form of an argumentative essay; however, they also collect *indirect measures* of learning. Indirect measures are those from which one can infer that the student likely learned what was intended, but do not provide direct evidence of students doing that task. In this study, the indirect measure was the survey which assessed students' perceived engagement in the task and their perceived learning. Pretty much any time you ask students to self-report how much they've learned, it would be considered an indirect measure. It is often useful to include both direct and indirect measures of your learning outcomes in your SoTL studies to triangulate—or cross-check—your conclusions with multiple sources of data.

*From How Many Participants Will I, and Can I, Collect Evidence?* From whom you need to collect data is also an important question. You might be inclined to say, "Easy—from students!" But from how many students? Do you need evidence from all your students in order to satisfy your research question? Is it feasible to collect the type of data you need from all students? If you have 350 students and you need qualitative data (e.g., a written response) as a direct measure of learning, it may not be possible to analyze 350 written responses within the timeframe you have to conduct, write, and share your study findings. Instead, can you select a *representative sample* of your students from whom you will collect data? A representative sample is subset of a larger group that is similar to the larger group by particular characteristics. For example, if your 350 students are 35% female, 55% seniors, and 80% African-American, you would want to collect data from a subset of students that are equivalent in demographic percentages to the larger group. There might be other salient factors to consider, such as declared major, prior knowledge regarding the topic, or cultural background. Consider the characteristics of your students that make the most sense and may be most likely to impact the results of your study: if your research question pertains to cultural differences among students, it would make sense to use cultural background as a salient factor by which to choose a representative sample.

However, you may be limited by which students are willing or able to participate in your study, but with careful thinking and analysis, this does not need to be a limitation. For example, Bernstein et al. (Chap. 8) identified 381 potential participants, but only some of those volunteered to participate in the study. Appropriately, the authors identify this as a self-selected group because they chose to participate in the RTTP study. A self-selected group may differ in important ways from the total participants; for example, they may be more motivated and enthusiastic which could affect the outcome of interest in the study. Self-selection is common in SoTL research since students must always volunteer to participate in your studies. They can never be forced and their grade cannot in any way be affected by their choice to participate or not in your study. (For more information about ethics in recruitment and study of human subjects, please contact the Institutional Review Board [IRB] at your college or university.) Do not despair if this happens to you: simply acknowledge the limitations of your sample and draw your conclusions from the data, keeping those potential differences in mind. Bernstein et al.'s discussion is an excellent example of how to acknowledge the potential limitations of self-selection yet still draw reasonable conclusions from the data.

*Do I Need a Comparison or Control Group?* The most frequent question we are asked about SoTL designs is how to configure a control group—or group of students who does not receive the instructional strategy under investigation—in order to evaluate the efficacy of a particular instructional strategy. It is true that in such an *experimental design* where students are randomly assigned to the control or intervention group is considered the gold standard of educational research because the researcher can *control* for (or rule out) other factors that might influence results. Thus, experimental designs support causal interpretations of the efficacy of the instructional approach in achieving the intended outcomes.

In experimental designs, the researcher randomly assigns students to participate in either the intervention group (treatment group) or the control group. Important to the validity of these experimental designs is that the control group receives some type of intervention equivalent in duration and quality to that of the treatment group. Why is this important? Imagine that you wanted to test the efficacy of a newly developed RTTP writing task to a game that you've used before. You randomly assign half of your students to do this 1-hour writing task, and the other students answer a questionnaire which takes 15 minutes. When you analyze your results, you see that the students in the treatment group performed better on your outcome measure compared to the control students. However, can you attribute the cause of the better performance to the writing task itself, or could it be that students simply had 45 extra minutes to think through the RTTP material under study? In other words, could engaging in any task related to RTTP for 45 extra minutes cause students to perform better? If your research question pertains to the efficacy of the writing task, then your study design must allow you to infer that the characteristics of the instructional strategy—not the length of time or how well it was implemented—are driving the results you find. In this example, having your control group students do a different writing task or other RTTP activity for 1 hour would allow you to attribute any effects—good or bad—to the writing task you are investigating.

You may be thinking that it would be difficult to randomly assign students to groups or to develop equivalent tasks for your control groups—particularly if you are interested in comparing the efficacy of the RTTP curriculum to some other curriculum. In this case, *quasi-experimental* designs may be more appropriate. In quasi-experimental designs, students are not randomly assigned to one condition (treatment or control). For many who teach more than one section of a course and are interested in two-group designs comparing two sections, quasi-experimental is likely your only option. In most institutions, students must be able to register for the course they desire; therefore, randomization is not possible.[1]

If your research questions center on comparing RTTP curriculum to another similar curriculum, we recommend finding a collaborator to teach the control group. Even if you have multiple sections of the same course, it is generally not a good idea to try and teach one of your own classes with a different pedagogy. Besides the inordinate amount of work this would

---

[1] Randomization in study design occurs at the participant level to control for participant characteristics. While you can randomly choose one section as the treatment and one as the control, in research it is only when *participants* are randomly assigned to the groups that true experimental design is achieved.

create for you, you must be able to provide evidence that you implemented the alternative pedagogy with the same quality you would the RTTP pedagogy and can expect that students would make similar learning gains in the alternative pedagogy (for ethical reasons). Other researchers have tackled this challenge by creating a *matched control group* comprised of students they do not teach. Rather than teach your classes any differently, you collaborate with another professor teaching the same content with a different pedagogy to similar students. In this case, you need to demonstrate that the professor that has a similar expertise with her or his pedagogy that you have with RTTP and also that the other professor's students are similar to yours in terms of baseline knowledge, age, GPA, or other salient factors. While this may seem daunting, remember that your sample (i.e., treatment and control groups) can be a subset of students from each class that match in terms of the salient factors you've identified. Bernstein and colleagues (Chap. 8) did this when they selected a matched control group for their sample of students. Identifying high school GPA and ACT scores as relevant factors, these authors selected students with similar GPA and ACT scores to their students. Creating a matched control group requires a lot of planning and collaboration before implementing your project, but can be an effective way to implement quasi-experimental designs.

If you are not able to create matched control groups, you can still have a control group that differs in some significant ways from your treatment group. If your sample is large enough (a good rule of thumb is at least 30 per group) and you are collecting quantitative data, you can statistically control for the differences between your two groups when running your analyses. If your sample is not large enough or you are not using quantitative data, you can simply document the differences between the groups in your Method section, interpret your findings considering these differences, and mention this as a limitation of the study in the Discussion section.

Finally, also remember that you may be able to use experimental design within your own classroom if you have a large enough group of students. In the previous example about investigating the efficacy of a newly developed writing task, the researcher can randomly assign students to do the new writing task or a similar control task. In other words, rather than think of investigating the RTTP curriculum as a whole, you can also consider isolating components of the RTTP curriculum that you would like to know more about.

While there is value to having a study design with two or more groups, there is also great value in one-group designs, for example, studies conducted in just one of your classes with all of your students (or a selected sample). If you are new to SoTL research, this may be a good place to start in order to develop your confidence and familiarity with SoTL methods and analyses. One-group designs are not necessarily simpler than two-group designs. You may be able to collect rich qualitative data, focusing your efforts on getting to know that group of students more deeply than you have ever gotten to know a group of students before! This is a great benefit of SoTL research; getting to see and understand your students in new ways and thus, understanding your teaching and the processes of teaching and learning with greater depth and precision.

*When or at What Point(s) Will I Collect That Evidence?* This question asks you to consider the timeframe of your study. More than a question about how much time do I have to complete this study (though that is certainly an important consideration), this question asks you to consider when you are most likely, and able, to collect reliable and valid data in regard to your research question. If your research question is assessing the long-term retention of material taught in an RTTP course, then your study design will need to specify what exactly long-term means (3 weeks? 6 months? 2 years?) and how you will keep track of participants over time to reduce attrition or participants dropping out of the study over time. If you are interested in students' perceptions after a learning activity in the RTTP curriculum, you must decide whether you will collect meaningful and rich data *aligned with your research question* from students immediately after the learning activity or after a bit of time has passed. In general, as more time passes, we are less able to recall specific details of an event; however, time to reflect also allows students to move past immediate emotions of dislike or enjoyment in order to synthesize and make sense of the experience in light of other learning. As this example demonstrates, you must think carefully through what kind of data you want and at what point students will be most able to produce meaningful and valid data.

If you are interested in a change in student outcomes (e.g., learning, perceptions, or beliefs) because of an RTTP intervention, then you will likely want to design your study as a *pre-post* (time series) design or an *interrupted time series*. Either of these study designs can be applied to one or multiple group designs. Pre-post designs collect data on the desired outcome from participants before an intervention, to establish a baseline of functioning, and after an intervention, to show changes in the outcome of interest. For example, in Chap. 6 Gasper-Hulvat used pre- and post-unit essay. However, if you are interested in another research question—at which point in a process do participants change as a result of a series of intervention (e.g., activities)—then you might want to consider an *interrupted time series design*. In this type of design, data are collected at multiple time points to more accurately pinpoint at what point participants' performance on the outcome of interest begins to change. If Gasper-Hulvat and colleagues wanted to change their study design (and thus research question) to an interrupted time series design, they might have asked students to write essays after the first, third, and fifth classes. When designing an interrupted time series study, be careful not to fatigue your participants by collecting data at too many time points or by using long, complex, or cognitively demanding data collection instruments (e.g., tests, surveys, or questions). If it is important to your study that you collect data from participants at multiple time points, make sure that whatever you are asking participants to do is simple and relatively easily accomplished: perhaps instead of an entire essay, students can write a focused paragraph at each time point.

*What Is the Start and End of My Study? What Constraints on My Time and Resources Must I Factor in?* Finally, a word of practical advice. As you design your study, excitement will grow and so might the study. More wondering questions might emerge, more outcomes that you might assess with students. Remember that one well-done study will lead to further studies. Be sure that for each outcome or question of interest, you can collect reliable and valid data given the constraints on your own time and resources. Do you have a conference at which you would like to present results from your study? Backward plan: How much time is needed to analyze the data? Often time, qualitative data can take longer to analyze than quantitative data, so be sure to account for that in your planning. The next two sections will help you decide which type(s) of data are appropriate and most often collected in SoTL studies and provide resources to help you analyze those data.

*What Ethical Issues Do I Need to Consider Before Designing My Study?* SoTL research falls under the category of human subjects research and, thus, is guided by a number of ethical principles. The Belmont Report (1974) was written to establish these basic ethical principles and guidelines that should assist in resolving the ethical problems that surround the conduct of research with human subjects. The three guiding principles of human subjects research are respect of persons, beneficence, and justice. Respect for person requires that we respect participants' autonomy and protect those with diminished autonomy. Beneficence ensures that we should do no harm and work to maximize benefits and minimize possible harm to subjects for participating in the research study. Justice ensures that non-exploitative procedures are administered fairly and equally among participants, including the fair distribution of costs and benefits to potential research participants.

Each university that receives federal funding for research in the United States is required to have an Institutional Review Board (IRB) that assists faculty, graduate students, and postdocs in adhering to the ethical principles of human subjects research. While not all SoTL studies will need IRB approval to be conducted, it is still a good idea to develop a relationship with your local IRB and submit the proposal for your study to them for review and advice. For more information on ethics in human subjects research in the United States, consult the Office for Human Research Protections (http://www.hhs.gov). Some countries have national IRBs; if your university or organization does not have an IRB, you will have to contact an independent IRB.

## Spotlight on Qualitative and Quantitative Methods

SoTL studies can collect data that is qualitative, quantitative, or both. Qualitative data are typically those that involve written or spoken responses from participants, but can also be notes on observed behaviors among participants. Quantitative data are data that can be reduced to numbers such as scores on validated test measures, GPA, or from surveys in which participants respond on Likert-type scales rating to what extent they endorse a particular statement. Though extensive resources exist to help you develop skill in designing and implementing all types of data collection (e.g., Dillman et al. 2014), we will briefly address two commonly used qualitative and quantitative methods: interviews and surveys.

Interviews are conducted between an interviewer and participant. Typically, in SoTL studies the instructor is also the interviewer, but it is possible to have another person who knows the study purpose, interview participants. In general, interviews are conducted at times that are convenient for the participant, and can be conducted in-person, over the phone, or over videoconferencing software.

Before interviewing, decide if you are going to use *structured* or *semi-structured* *interviews*. Structured interviews are those in which the researcher develops a set of questions that will be asked to every participant without deviation. Semi-structured interviews are those in which the researcher has a short subset of questions to ask each participant, but based on participant responses may ask additional questions. Neither is considered objectively better than the other; you must decide before you begin which type of interview will give you the data you need and then stick to your interview protocol for each participant. The interview protocol consists of these questions plus an introductory statement that explains the purpose of the interview, how long it will last, and other relevant information to the study. It is highly recommended that you have a qualitative methods expert review your protocol and that you pilot your protocol with participants similar in age to your students.

Another very common data collection tool is a survey or questionnaire. These surveys typically consist of items (questions) that can be either quantitative or qualitative in nature. Quantitative questions typically consist of a question or a statement that participants respond to on a scale of one to five or one to seven. These are called Likert-type responses scales and are generally used to measure participants' beliefs or perceptions.

Though it may seem simple, it is difficult to write good survey questions. For that reason, we recommend that you seek out already designed and *validated* survey measures. Validated surveys are those that have been designed and tested by experts to ensure that they are both reliable and valid. Through your experience with scholarly teaching, you likely came across many studies that used survey measures. Looking through these studies and their methods is a good place to start; be cautioned that not all published surveys are valid and reliable. While there are many statistical measures of reliability, the most commonly reported is Cronbach's alpha. In general, a Cronbach's alpha score of 0.80 or greater has good to strong reliability; 0.70–0.79 is acceptable reliability. If the study does not report the reliability of the survey measure that was used, then we do not recommend using that measure, though you may try and contact the author for reliability statistics.

A great way to locate preexisting survey instruments is the Test Collection Database provided freely online by the Educational Testing Service (ETS 2017). It offers an online repository of tests and surveys that have been published in the scholarly literature. The database will provide you with a citation to where the instrument is located in the literature. You'll then need to locate that article to find the instrument itself, but at that point, you now have a draft of an instrument that might be suitable for your study; however, you may find that you'll need to customize it for your context. Schult and colleagues in Chap. 4 did this by adapting Barry's and Finney's College Self-Efficacy Survey. There, they removed questions that did not relate to their study's context. In addition, search the literature for the specific concepts or ideas that you are investigating. You may need to get creative with the terms you use to search. A search for "engagement" will bring up an innumerable number of studies. Try and think more narrowly: Are you interested in *cognitive engagement* rather than enjoyment? Or, are you really interested in student perception of the *utility* of the course to their future career goals? Consulting with a colleague in education or psychology can help you come up with search terms and respected journals that will help you narrow your search for validated survey measures.

If you do decide you need to develop survey items, we recommend consulting with experts in psychology, educational psychology, or a survey research center on campus for in-depth information on how to design valid and reliable surveys. While there is too much to detail here, there are a few important points to remember. First, use simple rather than technical language that makes sense to your participants. Second, ask more than one question to assess things like "perception of the RTTP activity." Using a set of questions to assess one idea (also known as a "construct") provides more accurate responses from participants. Third, do not make your surveys too long or you risk participants skipping questions or not finishing the survey. You should state on the first page of the survey (along with IRB required information) how long it will take to complete the survey. Finally, pilot your survey with many different people and ask for feedback on the questions as well as the design of the entire survey (e.g., visual appeal and clarity). Have everyone who test runs your survey answer every question and time themselves to get an accurate estimate of how long it will take for your students to complete the survey.

A common qualitative approach particularly useful for those with training in the arts and humanities is content analysis. Content analysis is used to interpret meaning from textual data, typically student-written work. Scholars who are interested in student-thinking or development of critical thinking may find this methodology particularly useful. Through systematic condensing of textual data through coding and interpretation, SoTL scholars make valid inferences. The following section on qualitative data analysis will explain basic approaches to content analysis, though you may find specific resources helpful if you plan to use this methodology (e.g., Hsieh and Shannon 2005; Neuendorf 2002).

Lastly, you do not need to choose either qualitative methods or quantitative methods of data collection. You can do both; this approach is called mixed-methods. In surveys, you can ask your students open-ended questions to collect written responses in addition to numeric responses (see Dillman et al. 2014, for advice on how to maximize student responses to open-ended survey questions). In interviews, you can, for example, ask participants to rank items in terms of importance and then ask them to describe how and why they made those decisions. This would allow you to collect quite rich data across all your participants and in-depth information for each one. Mixed-methods studies are wonderful ways to experiment with different ways to collect data and the affordances and constraints of each.

## DATA ANALYSIS

Once data collection has ended, the next step is to begin the process of data analysis. If you're new to statistical or qualitative analysis and aren't already working with a researcher as a collaborator, you may want to find someone to assist you with this targeted task. As an alternative to the list of possible collaborators listed earlier, you may be able to engage a graduate student from an appropriate field to help you with the analysis. Some larger universities have consulting centers that focus specifically on statistical assistance as well. Beyond a collaborator, a great, free resource for more expansive guidance regarding data analysis than what is provided here is the online *Research Methods Knowledge Base*. This web resource is a comprehensive textbook that addresses many aspects of the research process, including data analysis (Trochim 2006).

Since it has likely been a few weeks (or months!) since you last revisited your research questions, a good place to start your analysis is by reviewing those questions and confirming that the data you have collected will likely provide you with answers to those questions. With this confirmed, you can now dive into the task. The domain of qualitative and quantitative analysis is quite expansive, so we won't attempt to detail the entirety of that world here; however, we have selected a few simple analysis techniques that flow from the study designs described above. Of course, your research questions will dictate your methodology and the associated data analysis, but below are key quantitative and qualitative data analysis techniques you will likely employ.

*Participant Statistics*  As a baseline, whether you have performed a primarily quantitative or qualitative study, you will want to provide a description of those who participated in your study, and this description will likely include a range of demographic information. As examples, how many males and females participated in your study; how many freshman, sophomores, juniors, and seniors; and/or how many undergraduates vs. graduates? Did you collect information regarding ethnicity? Did you collect age information? If so, you should report these breakdowns as well. If you have groups, how many students are in each and what are their respective demographic breakdowns? Reporting this information is essential as it enables readers to better understand the population under consideration and to determine if your findings can reasonably be generalized to the population of students with which they typically work. These are normally easy to report as they don't require in depth analysis; rather, it's primarily a summation of the data regarding the sample or groups in your study. In addition, in two-study designs, you can report on any differences between the control and treatment group that might influence the results you find. Another reason you will want to collect demographic information is that it gives you groups to compare and explore. Are females performing better than males in a given RTTP setting? Knowing your demographics will help you explore such questions. After you've described your study's participants, you will then move into quantitative or qualitative analysis (or both if you've performed a mixed-methods study).

*Quantitative Data Analysis*  The typical starting point for quantitative analysis is to provide descriptive statistics for the data collected. Reporting number of responses, means, and standard deviations are likely the key stats you'll provide. If you are using a survey methodology, as noted earlier, your survey instrument should have included multiple questions to measure each construct. You may have a group of questions (maybe five to eight) that together equate to, say, "student perception of RTTP." You wouldn't report the results of the individual questions; rather, you would find an average for that set of questions for each individual respondent and then report that overall average as the descriptive statistic for "student perception of RTTP." This single, averaged variable is also the one on which you would perform further data analysis, not the individual questions that comprise that construct. As this suggests, there's typically a bit of work you must do to "clean up" your data set before you can really get into the assignment of data analysis.

For a subset of survey questions like the "student perception of RTTP" example above, there is also a process for determining how reliable those questions are collectively at measuring the construct in question. In a statistical software package, such as SPSS, you can determine the aforementioned Cronbach's alpha for a given subset of questions. This is a measure of internal consistency, which is a measure of reliability. Again, a Cronbach's alpha of 0.7 is typically deemed acceptable; however, the closer you get to 1.0, the better the reliability of your set of questions. If you find that your alpha is below 0.7, you may want to perform an item analysis to see if there is a specific question in your subset of questions that is lowering your alpha. If that is the case, then it would be acceptable to drop that question at this point in the analysis to raise the overall reliability of your subset of construct questions. This is another reason why it is good to have several questions that are collectively measuring a single construct. It provides you with flexibility, post-data collection, to improve the quality of your findings. Cronbach's alphas for all of your constructs should be reported, even if you are using a survey developed and validated by other researchers (as is recommended).

Depending on your research question(s), another descriptive statistic you may want to explore and report is correlation. Correlation simply looks to determine to what extent two variables are related. As an example, might stage in college (freshman, sophomore, junior senior) correlate with student satisfaction with RTTP? To consider this, you would want to determine the Pearson product-moment correlation coefficient, also known as Pearson's $r$. Like most quantitative analysis steps, this can be performed quickly with software like SPSS. Pearson's $r$ can be between the values of $-1$ and $+1$, and an $r$ of 0 indicates there is no correlation at all. As a rule of thumb, you might conclude that there is a medium strength of association if your $r$ is between $-0.5$ and $-0.3$ or $0.3$ and $0.5$. If your $r$ is below $-0.5$ or above $0.5$, you're starting to see a pretty strong correlation. The closer it is to $-1$ or $1$, the stronger the correlation. Seeing is a good way to describe correlation strength. If you perform a scatterplot of your two variables, a strong correlation will result if your data points clustering along a linear or non-linear line.

There is one important caveat to note regarding what correlation is and what it is not. One of the most well-known sayings from the statistical world is that "correlation is not causation." Take care as you make sense of your high correlation findings to not jump to the conclusion that one variable is causing the change in the other. Correlation just shows a strength of relationship. There are a number of correlations that logically have no real relationship, and many of these were chronicled in the entertaining *Spurious Correlations* (Vigen 2015). For example, that book reports that there is a very strong correlation between worldwide non-commercial space launches and the number of sociology doctorates awarded. The lesson here is to take care as you determine and report what your correlations actually mean.

Up to this point, all the statistics and analysis techniques we've discussed would be classified as descriptive statistics. Another type is known as inferential statistics. As the name suggests, these analysis techniques enable you to make inferences about populations from a sample rather than simply describe the data that you have in front of you. Common inferential statistical methods include t-test, analysis of variance (ANOVA), and regression. Like correlation analysis, all are easy to perform with tools such as SPSS; however, the more challenging task is often knowing when to use these. Typically, your research questions provide you with the clues you need to make that decision. For instance, if you have two groups of students, such as males and females or your 11:00 a.m. class and your 2:00 p.m. class, and you want to see if their scores on a test or survey are statistically significantly different, you would use a t-test. If you have three or more groups (e.g., freshman, sophomore, junior, senior, or three sections of the same class), you would perform the ANOVA test. With ANOVA, if you do find a significant difference, you would then perform a post hoc test (an option in SPSS) to determine which groups have differences. It could be, for instance, that only your seniors have outperformed the other class rank groups. The post hoc test will tell you specifically which group(s) is not like the other.

For both t-tests and ANOVA, the threshold for determining statistical significance is typically set at 0.05. There is a column in SPSS results tables that is labeled "Sig." for "significance;" you have found a significant statistical difference if the number in that column is smaller than 0.05. If you wanted to take your analysis to the next level and see if one variable predicts another, such as does number of hours of RTTP exposure predict performance in a class, you would then move to linear regression.

*Qualitative Data Analysis* Any kind of research that produces findings not arrived at by means of statistical procedures or other means of quantification would be considered qualitative research (Strauss and Corbin 1990). If you are using content analysis, dealing with student responses to open-ended survey prompts or performing in-depth interviews or focus groups, you are working within the qualitative domain, and a very different set of analysis techniques are required. There are a number of qualitative research genres, such as content analysis, ethnography, phenomenology, and socio-communication studies, and each of these has their own norms and processes; however, what we provide here is a generic qualitative analysis model that might serve as a solid starting point for anyone beginning their engagement with qualitative analysis. The following six steps or phases comprise this generalized approach:

1. Organizing the data,
2. Familiarizing yourself with the data,
3. Generating categories and themes,
4. Coding the data,
5. Interpreting, and
6. Searching for alternative understandings (Rossman and Rallis 2003).

Note that in each phase, reducing the amount of information (i.e., data condensation) is one of the core goals of your work. Also, note that these aren't necessarily discrete activities. In truth, you'll find that analysis is an ongoing activity as you work through these steps. You may find yourself reorganizing things as you go through the coding process, or you may develop new themes as you develop a richer understanding through the interpreting process; however, these are activities that do have a generalized order to them.

*Organizing the data.* The purpose of this stage is to get a handle of the scope of the data you've collected and to organize things in a way where you can easily find your way around in your data set. Software, such as Excel, NVivo, and Atlas.ti, can assist with that work, but if you're dealing with student papers, you may find that file folders and labels work best.

*Familiarizing yourself with the data.* The notion here is that you spend a significant amount of time reading, re-reading, and reviewing the data so that you know it intimately. This is sometimes referred to as "living with the data" or "allowing the data to incubate." As you move to generating themes, having this deep, rich familiarity with your data set will be essential. Take notes as you go along about things that strike you as interesting or seem to be repeated across your participants.

*Generating categories and themes.* At this point, you are now trying to develop some sort of order to the data, and it could be that the categories emerge organically from your participants' own words, but sometimes you'll find yourself creating almost meta-categories that bridge what multiple participants have shared. Your note-taking can aid you in developing these categories. Both of these approaches evoke what is termed grounded theory (Glaser and Strauss 1967); however, your literature review prior to beginning data collection may also provide guidance to your development of themes. If you generate your categories and themes before reviewing your data set, this is termed *a priori* theme development. Regarding strategies, you may find that using Post-it Notes, magic markers, and index cards are helpful to this process. As you might imagine, there is a lot of revision that takes place as you determine categories and themes.

*Coding the data.* The coding process flows from the themes you've created and serves to facilitative interpretation and analysis. You will note where in your data the various themes appear. One of the goals here is to determine which themes emerge most often, which are the strongest in your data, and which are most relevant to your research question(s); however, there is a mechanical qualitative approach where you might simply count how many times each theme appears; those raw numbers can tell you a lot.

*Interpreting.* This is the process of meaning-making during qualitative analysis. Some refer to this as figuring out the story the data are telling. As a result, it's not specifically rule-bound and embraces the notion of providing thick, rich descriptions, and narratives that result from the data. As you go through the interpreting process, you may want to ask yourself "What is going on here?", "What is the essence of the phenomenon I'm studying?", and "What is the story these data tell?" Most likely, you'll find yourself oscillating between what you theoretically understand about the themes you're exploring, what your participants tell you, and what common sense might suggest. Incorporating all three into a meaningful whole is the purpose of qualitative research.

*Searching for alternative understandings.* Qualitative research also embraces the search for alternative interpretations. Rather than dismissing such opportunities, try to determine if there are other plausible options, if your argument is strong enough to withstand these other viewpoints, if your argument is well supported by your data, and if your argument is credible in light of these alternatives. You may find it useful to share your findings with colleagues not familiar with your study but familiar with the topic and get their feedback. In short, embrace the opportunity to find alternatives and to make meaning of them, and document your attempts to do so in your Method section.

In addition to this generic model for qualitative analysis, there are additional practices you should employ. Most certainly, a team approach is preferred. Having more than one reader of the data contributing his/her perspectives on themes, codes, and interpretations is essential. You'll be surprised by the interpretations your colleagues generate beyond your own, and it's important that these ideas be captured by your process. It is also important that you attempt to articulate and recognize the biases and pre-conceptions you bring forward to your qualitative project and check them periodically to see if they are influencing your viewpoints. If you are a strong believer in RTTP pedagogy and are confident in your teaching practice, recognize that bias as you progress through your analysis. It will be a challenge to be unprejudiced and open-minded, but it is a key characteristic of an exemplary qualitative researcher.

As a final thought on qualitative research, it may be that your data set is student work (papers, projects, performances, etc.) rather than information that results from interviews, open-ended survey question, or focus-groups. In those cases, scoring student work is typically performed using rubrics. As a result, this type of qualitative data set can be "transformed" into quanti-tative information, and descriptive and inferential statistical approaches can be used to describe and analyze the data. A best practice for using rubrics to examine student work in this way is to have two or more reviewers score each student artifact of learning. Ideally, before the work of scoring begins, you would have a "norming" session where the reviewers examine student work, compare their answers, and reach mutual understanding about what each category on the rubric means and what examples of it look like. It's important that those scoring have a common view of how to use the rubric, and these comparisons and discussions will help to ensure reliability as the process unfolds. After scoring has occurred, you should then look at *interrater reliability* to further guarantee fairness and accuracy. A simple way to assess interrater reliability is percent agreement, though more advanced statistical methods of interrater reliability exist. One of the advantages of having three reviewers is that if one is way off the mark, as determined by the statistical interrater reliability analysis, you can drop his/her scores and retain the other two.

## WRITING YOUR MANUSCRIPT

As mentioned in the "Where to Begin" section above, it is important to decide early in your process where you hope to publish your study, as elements of your development will be influenced by the norms and publication expectations of that disciplinary domain. As you begin to write your manuscript in earnest, those manuscript expectations should again be front and center. Your disciplinary journals certainly have guidelines; however, if you imagine submitting to an education journal or a multi-disciplinary teaching and learning journal, such as the *International Journal of Teaching and Learning in Higher Education*, the *Journal of Excellence in College Teaching*, or the *International Journal for the Scholarship of Teaching and Learning*, those all require adherence to the *Publication Manual of the American Psychological Association* (APA), 6th Edition. APA's style expectations may be new to you, so we encourage you to pick up a copy of APA's publication manual and review Chap. 2. It provides clear guidance regarding what comprises each section and subsection of an APA formatted manuscript. In many ways, that chapter can serve as a checklist regarding what you should address in each section and subsection.

In addition to overall manuscript formatting, you'll want to make sure your tables and your references are formatted based on APA expectations. Many multi-disciplinary journals make their first suitability pass based on appropriate formatting and adherence to APA. If your tables utilize boxed cells and your references are all MLA formatted, you are likely to receive a rejection within a few days of submission.

The last piece of advice we have in regard to your manuscript revisits the notion of *alignment* mentioned above. Your literature review should conclude with research questions that logically flow from that narrative. Your methodology and research design should logically be crafted to respond to those research questions, and your results should specifically address those research questions. Further, your discussion should flow directly from those results. Manuscript misalignment is the error we see most often by those who are new to SoTL research. As an example, if you haven't discussed gender differences in your literature review, and your research questions don't ruminate on the topic, then you shouldn't include the results of a t-test comparing males and females in your manuscript. Of course, you could go back and see if the literature has explored this topic already, incorporate what you discover through that literature review, and then revise your research questions to evoke gender differences. That would indeed then bring your manuscript into alignment. If you follow the appropriate style expectations for the journal you are pursuing and align your manuscript from introduction through discussion, your manuscript will make it earnestly into the peer review process.

## SHARING YOUR WORK

Publishing your work is the main goal for many SoTL researchers, and as this chapter has pointed out, you should have target journal(s) in mind early in the research process. However, publication is not the only way in which to share your work. Presenting of work at conferences is an excellent way to share your SoTL work and connect with potential future collaborators. There are several RTTP specific conferences occurring throughout the year. The University of Georgia offers a RTTP Winter Conference every year in January and Barnard College hosts a RTTP Faculty Institute every summer. In addition, there are many conferences dedicated to higher education teaching which would gladly welcome presentations on game-based pedagogy. In such conferences, you would need to think critically about how to present your study and findings as relevant to educators in a variety of disciplines and to those who have never considered game-based pedagogy. Some widely-known conferences include the Conference on Higher Education Pedagogy (CHEP), the International Society for Exploring Teaching and Learning's (ISETL) Annual Conference, the Lilly National Conference on College & University Teaching, the International Society for the Scholarship of Teaching and Learning Conferences, and many more.

You may also consider asking your department, college, or teaching and learning center if you can give a talk about your work. While you may have to do more explaining about what SoTL is and how RTTP works, you'll find that this is a great method to build a community of teacher scholars in your own community and build excitement and value around SoTL and RTTP.

## CLOSING THOUGHTS

As a RTTP practitioner, you know from first-hand experience that RTTP is highly rewarding for you and your students. The Scholarship of Teaching and Learning provides the structure by which this experience can be formalized and shared with a community of scholars who value rigor and a strong evidence base for best teaching practices. In doing so, the impact of your practice can extend beyond your classroom to other RTTP practitioners, to those interested but hesitant to begin Reacting, to administrators, and even more broadly to the higher education community. Through systematically planning for, documenting, and sharing your teaching insights and questions, your teaching practice becomes an equal scholarly endeavor to your disciplinary research, pursued with similar levels of inquiry and rigor, thus increasing the value of teaching in the higher education community (Boyer 1991; Shulman 1993). We hope that this chapter provides you with the needed tools to begin, to continue, or to enhance your skills conducting research on teaching and learning in your RTTP classroom.

## REFERENCES

American Psychological Association (APA). (2010). *Publication manual of the American Psychological Association* (6th ed.). Washington, DC: American Psychological Association.

Boyer, E. (1991). *Scholarship reconsidered: Priorities of the professoriate.* Princeton: Carnegie Foundation for the Advancement of Teaching.

Dillman, D. A., Smyth, J. D., & Christian, L. M. (2014). *Internet, phone, mail, and mixed-mode surveys: The tailored design method* (4th ed.). Hoboken: Wiley.

Educational Testing Service (ETS). (2017). *Test collection at ETS.* Retrieved from http://www.ets.org/test_link/find_tests

Glaser, B. G., & Strauss, A. (1967). *The discovery of grounded theory: Strategies for qualitative research.* Mill Valley: Sociology Press.

Hsieh, H. F., & Shannon, S. E. (2005). Three approaches to qualitative content analysis. *Qualitative Health Research, 15*(9), 1277–1288.

Huber, M. T., Morreale, S. P., & Carnegie Foundation for the Advancement of Teaching, & American Association for Higher Education (Eds.). (2002). *Disciplinary styles in the scholarship of teaching and learning: Exploring common ground.* Washington, DC: American Association for Higher Education.

Hutchings, P. (2000). *Opening lines: Approaches to the scholarship of reaching and learning.* Menlo Park: The Carnegie Foundation for the Advancement of Teaching.

McKinney, K. (Ed.). (2013). *The scholarship of teaching and learning in and across the disciplines.* Bloomington: Indiana University Press.

Neuendorf, K. A. (2002). *The content analysis guidebook.* Thousand Oaks: Sage.

Rossman, G. B., & Rallis, S. F. (2003). *Learning in the field: An introduction to qualitative research.* Thousand Oaks: Sage.

Shulman, L. S. (1993). Teaching as community property: Putting an end to pedagogical solitude. *Change: The Magazine of Higher Learning, 25*(6), 6–7.

Strauss, A., & Corbin, J. (1990). *Basics of qualitative research: Grounded theory procedures and techniques.* Newbury Park: Sage.

Trochim, W. M. K. (2006). *Research methods knowledge base.* Ithaca: Web Center for Social Research Methods. Retrieved from http://www.socialresearchmethods. net/kb/

Vigen, T. (2015). *Spurious correlations.* New York: Hachette Books.

# INDEX

Note: Page number followed by 'n' refers to notes.

© The Author(s) 2018                                                                221
C.E. Watson, T.C. Hagood (eds.), *Playing to Learn with Reacting to
the Past*, DOI 10.1007/978-3-319-61747-3